Doña Teresa Confronts
the Spanish Inquisition

Page of testimony written by Doña Teresa.

(Archivo General de la Nación, Mexico City, Ramo Inquisition, vol. 596, exp. 1, folio 84.)

Doña Teresa Confronts the Spanish Inquisition

A Seventeenth-Century New Mexican Drama

Frances Levine

For Kathy an adventure in history to read —

UNIVERSITY OF OKLAHOMA PRESS : NORMAN

Also by Frances Levine

Our Prayers Are in This Place: Pecos Pueblo Identity over the Centuries
(Albuquerque, 1999)

(co-editor) *Battles and Massacres on the Southwestern Frontier: Historical and Archaeological Perspectives* (Norman, Okla., 2014)

Publication of this book is possible through the generosity of Edith Kinney Gaylord.

Library of Congress Cataloging-in-Publication Data
Names: Levine, Frances.
Title: Doña Teresa confronts the Spanish Inquisition : a seventeenth-century New Mexican drama / Frances Levine.
Description: Norman : University of Oklahoma Press, 2016. | Includes bibliographical references and index.
Identifiers: LCCN 2015045757 | ISBN 978-0-8061-5336-0 (hardcover : alkaline paper)
Subjects: LCSH: Aguilera y Roche, Teresa de, approximately 1622– | Aguilera y Roche, Teresa de, approximately 1622—Trials, litigation, etc. | Governors' spouses—New Mexico—Biography. | Dissenters—New Mexico—Biography. | Inquisition—New Mexico—Santa Fe. | Crypto-Jews—New Mexico—Santa Fe—History—17th century. | Political culture—New Mexico—Santa Fe—History—17th century. | Santa Fe (N.M.)—Social conditions—17th century. | Santa Fe (N.M.)—Church history. | Spain—Colonies—Church history.
Classification: LCC F799.A35 L48 2016 | DDC 978.9/02092—dc23
LC record available at http://lccn.loc.gov/2015045757

The paper in this book meets the guidelines for permanence and durability of the Committee on Production Guidelines for Book Longevity of the Council on Library Resources, Inc. ∞

1 2 3 4 5 6 7 8 9 10

In memory and friendship

Gerald T. T. González

(1943–2011)

Discord was pleased to happen upon Jealousy,
the more so when she learnt what was afoot, for
it could serve her own ends very suitably.

Orlando Furioso, 1533
Ludovico Ariosto

Contents

Illustrations

Preface and Acknowledgments

I HAVE LIVED IN SANTA FE, NEW MEXICO, for more than thirty years, and for more than a decade I served as director of the New Mexico History Museum. The most important entity in the museum's collection is the Palace of the Governors. When I began working there in 2002, I researched stories of several governors whose terms of service embraced the span of New Mexico history. France Scholes had long ago reported on the discord that surrounded several of the Spanish-colonial governors who served in the late sixteenth and early seventeenth century. Governor López de Mendizábal was among the governors who had enraged the Franciscans, leading to church-state conflicts that characterized the first eighty years of the Spanish settlement. His term was among the most rancorous in New Mexico history, but there was little published in English about the equally tumultuous life that his wife endured in New Mexico.

This book began as a casual conversation and later correspondence with Gerald González in the summer of 2010. We were invited speakers at a lecture series, Southwest Seminars, in Santa Fe. Both of us were speaking on topics in colonial history. Gerald had been researching his own genealogy as a descendant of crypto-Jews who had fled Spain and then Portugal in the fifteenth and sixteenth centuries, eventually settling in New Mexico with other early colonizing families. Gerald had also been part of the research team that assisted Stanley Hordes with his expansive research project on the conversos and crypto-Jews of Mexico and New Mexico. Both had researched the kinship and social connections among families in Mexico and New Mexico who had been accused of secret Jewish practices. They concluded that in the isolated social milieu of northern New Mexico, conversos and crypto-Jews found a home that was far enough from colonial authorities that they could keep some centuries-old traditions and oral histories alive. Gerald had painstakingly reconstructed the genealogies of Doña Teresa Aguilera y Roche and her husband, Bernardo López de Mendizábal, governor of New Mexico from 1659 to 1662, when both were arrested by local officials in a sweep that captured a small group of people accused of secretly practicing Jewish rituals.

As the director of the Palace of the Governors museum from 2002 to 2014, I often thought about the events that took place in that building over the past four centuries. I was interested in the artifacts and stories that we might use in exhibitions and programs to contextualize the life of its residents. I asked Gerald to help me generate a list of artifacts similar to those that the governor and his wife possessed when they were arrested in Santa Fe, to help us in planning the restoration of the rooms at the palace. My research focused on the wives of several of the governors. I wondered what their life was like, especially as I had come to know several of the wives of recent governors. Gerald and I spoke often about Doña Teresa, and we finally decided that our discussions ought to culminate in an article. That soon became two articles and several public presentations during Santa Fe's quadricentennial year in 2009–10, and then we began planning a book on this fascinating woman. In the early winter of 2011, Gerald began to feel ill, and when he was diagnosed with a terminal illness he knew the end would come too soon to finish the book. He continued, as long as he was able, to send me e-mails with ideas and research notes. When he died on All Saints' Day, November 1, 2011, I happened to be in Mexico. His photo and our last e-mail became part of an All Souls' Day (November 2) altar in memory of loved ones who had been so important in my life. Carey González, Gerald's wife, packed up his notes, microfilm, and reader, and gave them to me with the message to follow up on the story. And so I have continued to write this. Gerald's voice is here in several places, and when I disagree with his interpretation I have noted it, keeping alive in some small way our many conversations and our mutual respect for our different conclusions.

The record of Doña Teresa's trial and her exquisitely detailed defense have been transcribed, translated, and annotated by the Cíbola Project, a group of philologists working at the University of California, Berkeley, on the linguistic analysis of key documents of New Mexico's colonial history. The pioneering work of Jerry Craddock and his students, the Cíbola Project scholars, has delved deeply into the proceedings and of Doña Teresa's patterns of speech and writing. The Cíbola Project transcription and translations of the voluminous trial transcript also allowed me to understand more fully the story of her life in the palace and became my window into domestic life in the colonial capital. Their detailed analysis of her speech and writing illuminated the dramatic quality of Doña Teresa's testimony. The transcripts of the many witnesses offered a view of family life in the palace that was more intimate than I ever imagined, and permitted me to look behind the usually closed doors of elites living on the far northern frontier of the Spanish colonial empire. The project's carefully annotated trial record and translations of the documents are used here wherever I have quoted from the trial record.

Cynthia Baughman, formerly editor of *El Palacio*, the journal of the Museum of New Mexico system, encouraged me to take this story to a wider audience. I appreciate the work that she and Natalie Baca, graphic designer for my articles in *El Palacio*, did in choosing illustrations that brought Doña Teresa's story to life with engravings, paintings, and artifacts selected by Josef Díaz, curator of Spanish colonial and Mexican period art. Josef has a wonderful eye for colonial material culture, and he was able to review the list of items in the arrest records and select examples appropriate to the time and place. Kate Nelson, writer, editor, muse, and friend, was always supportive in urging me to keep on writing and laughing even when administrative tasks seemed to dominate my every waking hour. Shelley Thompson, director of Marketing and Research for the New Mexico Department of Cultural Affairs and publisher of *El Palacio*, has always been generous with her support and friendship, and encouraged me always to write for *El Palacio*.

Anna Merlan, my daughter and an accomplished writer and reporter, taught me how to curb distractions and write in shorter bursts, increasing productivity. My son, Steve Merlan, read each published piece and rewarded me with his music and his gentle warmth. Tom Merlan, my husband, is a scholar of New Mexico history who has deftly edited several drafts, helped to translate several documents, and been a source of the support that makes my research and writing possible. I am grateful for his comforting presence.

I wrote early drafts of several chapters while on a retreat in India in 2013. I am indebted to the Guru Ram Das Ashram, Sarab Singh, Gurminder Singh Khalsa, and Mr. and Mrs. N. N. Singh for making my stay so comfortable and surrounding me with so much love, humor, and good cheer. Thank you to Dr. Inderjit Kaur Khalsa, the Bhai Sahib, for taking me into her family and the world of Sikh culture.

I was fortunate to travel to many of the places where Doña Teresa lived so many centuries ago. In Bilbao and the País Vasco, Spain, I learned much about the history of New Mexico from that land of so many of our ancestors. I made many friends, to whom I say Agur. I visited the beautiful city of Cartagena, Colombia, with my husband in the spring of 2014. It was there that Doña Teresa met her husband, and where her father was arrested by the Spanish Crown as well. In Mexico City, where I have been fortunate to develop deep friendships, I have benefited from the study of collections at the wonderful Franz Mayer Museum and enjoyed good friendship with director Héctor Rivero Borrell Miranda. Likewise, Rodrigo Rivero-Lake has opened his home and collection to me, answering many questions about conversos, crypto-Jews, and colonial iconography. Carmen Gaitán Rojo, director of the Museo Nacional de San Carlos, was the first person to show me the materials that might support the Palace of the Governors' exhibition on Mexican conversos in such an engaging way. Felipe, Ana, and Andrés Siegel were my teachers about so many Spanish colonial art forms, I hardly know how to recognize their expertise appropriately. Muchísimas gracias to Dr. Alicia Gojman Goldberg and her husband, Isaac Backal, for sharing with me so generously their wealth of knowledge and vast collection of Mexican Inquisition artifacts and documents. Thank you to my dear cousin Patricia Gamboa for opening your arms to a long-lost family member.

Tom Ireland edited the appendices and helped me to scale down the mass of materials that the Cíbola Project has provided. Thanks to Ron Duncan Hart, Cordelia Snow, Enrique Lamadrid, and Jerry Gurulé and two anonymous reviewers who provided important edits catching many errors. Those that remain I must own.

Michael Kamins and Jessica Habjan adapted Teresa's story to a fine *Colores!* production for New Mexico PBS. I am so pleased with the drama and authenticity they brought to that work and the friendship that grew during many hours in the editing booth on that and many other film projects we did together.

June-el Piper prepared the manuscript, deftly correcting my habit of inserting commas and line breaks whenever my fingers paused on the keys. Kathleen Kelly and Bethany Mowry of the University of Oklahoma Press shepherded this book through the acquisition review process, while Emily J. Schuster and Katrin Flechsig guided me skillfully through the editing and publication steps. The talented Gerry Krieg prepared the lovely map illustrating the geographical setting of this dramatic story.

To friends, family, and colleagues who often heard me use the writing and publication process as an excuse for not taking time for them, I hope holding the book in your hands is proof that I was not avoiding you. Thanks to Anne Marie Thurmond, Mary Birkenmeier, Karen Goering, and the other members of the leadership team of the Missouri History Museum, who kept the museum running so smoothly that I could make the publication deadline . . . almost. I am grateful to Chris Gordon, director of Library and Collections, for his interest in this topic and for taking time to read the manuscript so carefully.

The study that follows is an attempt to understand the social milieu of Santa Fe and to explore the charges surrounding the accusations against Governor López de Mendizábal and Doña Teresa. I am inspired by Doña Teresa's courage to clear her name, the strength of her convictions, and the brave actions that she took, so many of which are apparent in the words that she committed to paper more than three and a half centuries ago. You have not been forgotten.

Doña Teresa Confronts
the Spanish Inquisition

Introduction

I, Licenciado Don Juan de Ortega Montañés, prosecutor for this Holy Office[,] declare that this lady, not fearing God, and at grave peril to her conscience, neglecting the obligations of a true, faithful, and Catholic Christian, and forsaking that faith, has followed and does follow the ceremonies of the superseded law of Moses, carefully putting on clean clothes on Fridays, first washing her feet, and not attending mass on the days of obligation, even in fine weather and with the church very near her residence, wherefore suspicion has arisen against the aforesaid . . . , committing so dreadful a crime against what the holy faith of the Gospel teaches . . . by the evidence I present with due solemnity so that her criminal behavior may be stopped and punished, and so that the aforesaid may forswear the blind error in which she lives and others may be chastened by her example.

So begin the proceedings of the Holy Office of the Inquisition in Mexico City against Doña Teresa Aguilera y Roche and her husband, New Mexico governor Bernardo López de Mendizábal, on charges of secretly practicing Judaism and ignoring their Christian obligations. Their crimes were detailed in indictments against each of them. He stood accused of more than thirty counts of practicing Judaism, and she faced forty-one. The governor had already been found guilty by a civil tribunal at the end of his term of office that brought other charges against him for malfeasance in office. Of those charges, he was found guilty of more than half and was prohibited from holding public office for eight years. The Inquisition charges in many ways were more serious—both he and his wife faced sanctions that could damage their family for generations to come and even bring death upon them if they could not prove their innocence. López de Mendizábal in fact died in the Inquisition prison in Mexico City before the case was resolved, but Doña Teresa fought on for almost two years before they were vindicated. Their story captures a time in New Mexico history when the long arm of the Spanish Inquisition reached to the remote colony and spread fearful accusations.

Prelude to the Case

Summer, especially those without the cooling monsoon rains, can be long and hot in New Mexico. The sun sears your skin, and the dirt beneath your feet can scorch right through the soles of your shoes. For centuries it has been the time of year when native peoples dance and pray devoutly for rain, and when farmers and ranchers of other cultures do the same, following their own traditions. It is not a time of year for wasted effort or frivolous undertakings. So it must have been tense and yet transfixing during the summer of 1662, when Santa Fe's fragile Spanish settlement was sundered by the arrest of the governor, his wife, and several of his supporters by officials of the Holy Office of the Inquisition. It was not simply a difference of opinion on religious matters that led to their arrest. It was a power struggle between civil and ecclesiastical leaders over the control of the colony. Their differences arose, in part, over the appropriation and control of native peoples' land and labor, and the place of holy obligations amid the practical concerns of supporting the colony. Many Spanish officials and colonists still held grandiose expectations of riches that might be hidden in the parched landscape of this frontier. For much of the seventeenth century the balance of power between governors and clerics was tenuous even in the best of times. During the term of Governor Bernardo López de Mendizábal (1659–62), the conflicts between church and state reached an unprecedented level of acrimony and swept through Santa Fe.

Santa Fe was the only official colonial settlement, or villa, in northern New Spain, and even there the population was small. Only about one hundred or so Spanish-speaking people—government officials, soldiers, settlers, and clergy—were living there in some forty houses, the *casas reales*, and the church *convento*. Factions were intimate and feuds threatening. Some two-hundred native people then living in Santa Fe and serving in the churches, households, and governor's residence must have been aware of the gathering storm, as well.[1] It must have been obvious that this fragile outpost could fail. In the summer of 1662 intrigues that had been building for at least two years reached a frenzy in the colonial capital, the far northern frontier outpost of New Spain.

The governor and his wife, Teresa Aguilera y Roche, were among a small group of citizens arrested by local officials of the Holy Office of the Inquisition on charges of practicing Jewish rituals in secret; they had been accused by the Santa Fe clergy and their neighbors, as well as by their household staff. The first to be arrested were four of the governor's closest advisors, all of them military officials: Captain Nicolás de Aguilar, Sergeant Major Diego Romero, Sergeant Major Francisco Gómez Robledo, and Captain Cristóbal de Anaya Almazán. Each accusation was no small matter. It could become a matter of life or death for the accused. Not even the governor or Doña Teresa would be spared if they were found guilty.[2]

As Don Bernardo and Doña Teresa had traveled up the Camino Real four years earlier on their northbound journey to the governor's new post, they never could have imaged that they would be returning in 1662, he in shackles and both under heavy guard. Standing before the Inquisition tribunal in Mexico City was not likely something that Doña Teresa or the governor expected when they arrived in New Mexico to take up life in the casas reales, which they referred to as their palace. Much of the drama that would unfold took place within the private quarters of the governor's household in the Palace of the Governors, the same building that still defines the north side of the Santa Fe plaza. It is also likely that Inquisition officials never expected to be challenged by a woman as determined to clear her name as Doña Teresa. She was the only woman from New Mexico ever tried by the Inquisition in Mexico City for the crime of being *judaizante*, or secretly practicing Judaism. Her defense, documented in a series of handwritten briefs that she prepared for the court, are a remarkable historical resource for the details that they provide about social customs and daily life in seventeenth-century New Mexico. They are even more extraordinary in being written by a woman with formal education and experience in a world largely unknown to most New Mexicans of that era.

New Mexico's colonial history lasted for more than 280 years. The colony was part of Spain longer than it was part of Mexico, and longer even than it has been a state of the United States. Spanish colonial history and recognition of Spanish ancestry are still important to many Hispanic New Mexicans. The possibility of *converso* and crypto-Jewish identity among those who came to New Mexico in the seventeenth century is a topic that holds a special fascination. Conversos were those people who gave up Judaism and converted to Catholicism. Crypto-Jews, in contrast, were those who outwardly assumed a Catholic identity while continuing to practice Judaism in secret.

New Mexico became the far northern frontier of Spain's New World colonies in the late sixteenth and early seventeenth centuries, just as the power of the Inquisition was exerting its orthodoxy in the far corners of the Spanish empire. Distance from central authority made the remote colony of New Mexico a suspicious place where authorities thought Jews might be practicing their religion in secret. But were Doña Teresa and her husband truly conversos or crypto-Jews? Or were these charges simply part of a larger practice by factions in the church or political spheres that used the Inquisition to silence opposition? I argue here that the latter was the case with Doña Teresa. Historian Marc Simmons concluded his study of witchcraft in the Pueblo and Hispanic communities of the Southwest, noting, "A folk society, such as that on the Rio Grande, was strongly conformist and suspicious of any member whose deviant behavior suggested association with the black arts."[3] The same adherence to conformity and the fraught relations between church and state appear to have played a role in the accusations leveled against Governor López de Mendizábal and Doña Teresa. Their trial record is replete with accusations of heresy, immorality, greed, witchcraft, and finally, in a kind of crescendo, charges of being judaizante.

In the subsequent chapters, I also examine the impact that church-state conflicts had on the Pueblo Indians in New Mexico, and the ways in which that added further to the deterioration of Governor López de Mendizábal's administration. López de Mendizábal was, in surprising ways, a progressive voice for the freedom of native people, allowing them to practice their faith and to assert some level of sovereignty over their lands and labors. Several authors have pointed out the hypocrisy among the friars and the seventeenth-century governors, each of whom argued that they represented the best governance and protection for native peoples. The antagonism and disagreements between church and state officials ensnared Pueblo villagers in an irresolvable and intractable situation. Ramón Gutiérrez aptly characterizes the confusion and tension created by the governor's permissive attitude toward traditional Pueblo dances and his criticism of the friars' exploitation of Pueblo labor at the same that he himself was extracting trade goods from the same villages. Moreover, underlying this tension was the question of whether New Mexico was to be ruled by a theocracy with power descending through the word of God or was to be governed by a secular authority administered through a political bureaucracy. Carroll Riley proposes that if Governor López de Mendizábal's more permissive policies had been implemented, they might have forestalled the Pueblo Revolt of 1680 by permitting Pueblo Indians to practice native rituals and use traditional means in response to the deteriorating climatic and health conditions in New Mexico.[4] The accusation that the governor, Doña Teresa, and their cohorts engaged in converso or crypto-Jewish practices added to an already volatile social milieu of competing authority and orthodoxy.

Constructing Identity, Situation, and Context

Who are you? Or more politely, one might ask, What is your name? Where do you come from? Who are your people? Are you related to so-and-so? These are questions we hear often, and how we answer them reflects the endless process of defining and asserting our identity. In northern New Mexico, the answers reflect a long process of negotiating history, community, religion, and *mitote*, or the gossip that neighbors might say about who you are and who your people were.

The complexity of Sephardic identity is visible in the terms that throughout history have been applied to people of Jewish descent in Spain. Sepharad is the Hebrew name for Spain. Sephardim were the people who created Jewish life in medieval Spain. It refers to a near-mythical place in Spain from the tenth to the end of the twelfth century that was in many ways a second Jerusalem. The term conveys the community identity of Jewish people whose central role in Spain added to a rich multicultural society. The terms *conversos*, *crypto-Jews*, *marranos*, and *anusim* relate to events set in motion by repression and forced conversion in the fourteenth century and then the expulsion of Jews from Spain in the fifteenth century. *Conversos* meant those who accepted conversion to Catholicism to avoid expulsion. *Crypto-Jews* were those who continued to practice Judaism in secret rather than give up their traditions and religion. *Marranos* or "swine" was a term that the Spanish applied to Jews as an insult, deriving from Jewish food prohibitions. *Anusim*, the forced ones, is a more modern term used by practicing Jews to refer to those forced to embrace Christianity. These terms carry the weight of a history of oppression and also resistance. They are still used in tracing the history of those who practiced their faith in secret and those who were forced to convert or flee. Sepharad may no longer exist as a geographical place, but it is a powerful ingredient of identity for descendants of its mournful history.

It is not likely that any of the witnesses who testified at the trials of the governor and Doña Teresa knew exactly what Jewish religious practice entailed. But the reports they offered of rumored activities in the governor's household show a heightened level of suspicion for what they, and the inquisitors, attributed to possible Jewish origins. The details of the couple's arrest and the records of their trials vividly depict the social history of Santa Fe in its early years as a Spanish possession in North America. The historical period is not well known to the general reader, and this book tells the story of colonial Santa Fe from the perspective of a woman who lived a life of prestige and yet was not immune from suspicion and persecution. Doña Teresa's life in New Mexico will be surprising to many readers for its contemporary themes—conflicts between the authority of church leaders and politicians, the weight of evidence versus hearsay in legal proceedings, and the predicament that the governor's unrestrained appetites created for his wife. Their arrest and the accusations leveled against them are set within a much longer history of Jews in Spain and the social controls exerted by the Inquisition even in the most remote corners of Spain's New World empire.

The Expulsion of Jews and Muslims: 1492 Here and There

The very words "Spanish Inquisition" evoke powerful images of robed and hooded zealots seeking to rid the Iberian peninsula of Jewish and Muslim infidels. But the reach of the Spanish Inquisition was also felt on the far shores of the Spanish empire. Jewish people had lived in Spain for more than fifteen hundred years when they were expelled by the new and powerful Catholic Kings. The Jewish diaspora from Spain unfolded from the marriage of Ferdinand of Aragon and Isabella of Castile. Their union in 1469 began the process of unifying Spain's powerful kingdoms, setting in motion a series of events that first seemed to protect Jewish people who were part of the Spanish court, but ultimately brought about the end of Sepharad.

It seems unfathomable that such drastic measures followed centuries in which Christians, Muslims, and Jews built a culture known for its blending of these three religious traditions. Why destroy the web of social relations and intercultural accomplishments? Why attack the centers of learning that had taken root throughout the peninsula since medieval times? In Córdoba, Sevilla, and Granada, *mudéjar* works of art and architecture showed the skill of artisans steeped in styles that mixed Muslim and Christian symbols. *Mozarab* philosophers—Christians who lived under Muslim, and Muslims who lived under Christian rule in medieval Spain—navigated the fluid social milieu of both religions, contemplating the wonders of the universe in treatises on mathematics and science. Jewish doctors and philosophers wrote tomes on health and the human condition. Many authors have captured that golden age of Spain, a time when Christians, Jews, and Muslims produced glorious cities with ornately embellished palaces, set in Eden-like gardens of trees, fruit, and flowers, where learning was revered and shared on every subject imaginable.[5] The tomb of Ferdinand and Isabella in the cathedral of Granada carries inscriptions in Latin, Castilian, Hebrew, and Arabic, even now recalling the legacy of these diverse heritages. The text of that inscription, however, proclaims their legacy as "destroyers of the Mohammedan sect and the annihilators of heretical obstinacy," a reference to the Jews.[6] Within this bold inscription is the message that despite the flowering and melding of diverse traditions, Spanish history was not without periods of intense persecution of both Jews and Muslims.

Violence against the Jews grew across Europe following the Black Death in the mid-fourteenth century as Christian zealots blamed Jews for the plague. This rage flared in Sevilla in the summer of 1391, thence spreading to the kingdoms of Castile and Aragon. In the fifteenth century as the Christian monarchs reached across the peninsula to consolidate the Spanish kingdoms, Muslims and Jews were forced to convert, flee, or hide their faith and pretend to practice Christianity. Perhaps as many as one hundred thousand Jews converted to Catholicism. Local ordinances written in communities across Spain restricted important positions and property ownership to those with genealogical purity of blood, or *limpieza de sangre*; that is, free from the stain of Jewish or Muslim ancestry. Jane Gerber, in her history of the Jews in Spain, concludes that the restrictions made it utterly impossible for conversos to assimilate into the new social order of a unified Spain.

King Ferdinand sought the pope's complicity to enforce the ideals of purity, and in 1481, Pope Sixtus IV established the Holy Office of the Inquisition.[7] The Inquisition in Spain was an institution with complicated political and social motives. It was established to punish those whose political views deviated from local norms or power bases as much as to ensure the orthodox practices of all Christians. Following the unification of Spain and the expansion of the Spanish colonial empire, religious and civil authorities each used the Holy Office for their own ends.

The world changed forever in 1492, a year of enormous significance that saw the emergence of Spanish empire and changed the fate of Muslims and Jews then living in Spain. It would take almost another century for the full impact of three events of that year to be felt globally. The momentous events are captured by the Spanish historian Bartolomé de Las Casas in an account published in his 1542 edition of a log kept by Cristóbal Colón, whom we celebrate as Christopher Columbus.[8] Columbus addresses his log and his flattery to Queen Isabella and King Ferdinand.

> On January 2 in the year 1492, when your Highnesses had concluded their war with the Moors who reigned in Europe, I saw your Highnesses' banners victoriously raised on the towers of the Alhambra, the citadel of that city, and the Moorish king come out of the city gates and kiss the hands of your Highnesses and the prince, My Lord. And later in that same month, on the grounds of information I had given your royal Highnesses concerning the lands of India and a prince who is called the Great Khan . . . and of his and his ancestors' frequent and vain applications to Rome for men learned in the holy faith who should instruct them in it, your Highnesses decided to send me, Christopher Columbus, to see these parts of India and the princes and peoples of those lands and consider the best means for their conversion. For, by the neglect of the Popes to send instructors, many nations had fallen to idolatry and adopted doctrines of perdition, and your Highnesses as Catholic princes and devoted propagators of the holy Christian faith have always been enemies of the sect of Mahomet and of all idolatries and heresies. . . . Your Highnesses ordained that I should not go eastward by land in the usual manner but by the western way which no one about whom we have positive information has ever followed. Therefore having expelled all the Jews from your dominions in that same month of January, your Highnesses commanded me to go with an adequate fleet to those parts of India.[9]

Columbus's journal entry refers to the Spanish siege of Granada that in March 1492 brought more than seven hundred years of warfare between Christian and Muslim rulers to an end. In the same month, a writ of expulsion called the Alhambra Decree, penned on behalf of the new Christian kingdom, banished Jews from Spain. And finally, Columbus refers to his own *capitulaciones*, or orders, signed on April 17 in the Santa Fe military camp near Granada, that directed him to undertake the expedition that would lead to the discovery of the peoples and places of the "New World." This arc of history connects Santa Fe, Spain, to Santa Fe, New Mexico, in a series of actions and responses that stemmed from these three seminal events.

The Alhambra Decree spells out in the strongest of terms King Ferdinand and Queen Isabella's determination to rid Spain of those whose beliefs challenged Catholicism.[10] The decree justifies expulsion as a last resort since neither sequestering the Jews in ghettos, nor banishing them from Andalusia, had been sufficient to keep them from "persisting in their evil ways." It concludes by ordering Jews to leave Spain by the end of July 1492 and never return. The writ, prepared in the careful hand of a fifteenth-century scribe, first reflects on the many restrictions that Ferdinand and Isabella had tried to impose on the Jewish community in Andalusia, and then concludes chillingly:

> Therefore, with the advice and opinions of the eminent clergy and nobility and knights of our Kingdoms, and of other persons of learning and knowledge of our Council, after much deliberation, it is agreed and resolved that all Jews and Jewesses be ordered to leave our kingdoms, and that they never be allowed to return. And further we order in this edict that all Jews and Jewesses of whatever age who live and reside in our Kingdoms and domains, whether or not they were born there and for whatever reason they may have come to be there, leave with their sons and daughters, their Jewish servants and relatives, old and young, of whatever age, by the end of July of this year. And they dare not return to our lands or to any part of them, either to live or in transit or in another other manner whatsoever. Jews who do not comply with this edict and are found in our Kingdoms and domains, or who trespass on them in any way, shall be put to death and all their belongings shall be confiscated by the royal Treasury. And they shall be punished without trial, judgment, or statement.[11]

The response from Jewish leaders in Spain was equally powerful. Two rabbis, Isaac Abravanel and Abraham Seneor, writing as representatives of the Jewish community, chastised the monarchs and predicted that one day Spain would regret an expulsion that marked the end of an age of learning and the beginning of a decline. Abravanel wrote, "The unrighteous decree you proclaim today will be your downfall. And this year, which you imagine to be the year of Spain's greatest glory, will become of Spain's greatest shame."[12]

And yet with so firm an eviction, there was little choice. Jews began a diaspora that also fueled the Spanish and later Portuguese exploration of the world, led first by Christopher Columbus. Columbus himself may have been fleeing from the long arm of the Inquisition, or he may have been a converso. It is unlikely that the question will ever be answered definitively. Columbus is something of an enigma, and many authors have pointed out his obscure and contradictory ancestry: an Italian who wrote in Castilian, Catalan, and Portuguese—surely the language of seamen—but why didn't he write in Italian?[13] Among his sailors were at least a half-dozen conversos.

Far off in what would become New Mexico, there was not yet a Spanish presence on the Rio Grande, nor knowledge of that other place that would also come to be known as Santa Fe.

CHAPTER ONE

Becoming New Mexico

SPANISH EXPLORERS ENTERED THE HOMELANDS of Pueblo Indian communities along the Rio Grande in the mid-sixteenth century. They noted the existence of a wide-ranging trade network and the many different languages spoken, but they may have failed to grasp the social complexity of a landscape the explorers would later claim as the most remote Spanish New World colony. Lacking the fabled treasures of Mexico and Peru, New Mexico was settled largely as a missionary field. But this ecclesiastical status did not protect the Pueblo people or Spanish settlers from conflicts of jurisdiction between church and civil authorities. This chapter traces the seminal events from 1540 to 1680; that is, from the beginning of the Spanish exploration of New Mexico to the Pueblo Revolt that exiled Spanish settlers, clergy, soldiers, and governing officials in the late seventeenth century. Spanish colonial history, and in particular, the construction of ethnicity and identity in this far northern frontier outpost, deeply marked modern New Mexico. Identity, genealogy, and a sense of lost ancestry are still profoundly relevant to many New Mexicans.

The Great American Southwest Takes Form

As King Ferdinand and Queen Isabella began their reformation of the Iberian Peninsula in the mid- and late fifteenth century, on the other side of the world from Granada, Pueblo Indian communities were dealing with their own internal changes. As in Spain, changes begun in earlier times would have far-reaching repercussions. The late thirteenth century saw massive shifts in the regional settlement pattern throughout the arid lands of the American Southwest. The move began with a coalescence into fewer, larger settlements along the major river valleys. Previously unoccupied areas now had villages. These new settlements—the Hopi mesas of northern Arizona, the slopes of the Chuska and Zuni mountains of west-central New Mexico, the Middle and Upper Rio Grande drainage, the edge of the eastern plains at Pecos, and the village complexes in the Salinas and Galisteo basins of central New Mexico—were occupied when the Spanish explorers arrived in 1539.[1] By then, the Pueblo peoples who had produced the distinctive Mimbres pottery of southwestern New Mexico and those people who had built architectural wonders had left Chaco Canyon and villages along the lower Colorado drainage. Navajo and Apache Athapaskan speakers had arrived and their nomadic ranges bounded the Pueblo heartland.

What accounted for these shifts has puzzled generations of archaeologists. Was it a climate shift or environmental factors that brought so many people to make such a substantial shift in lifestyle? Was it the spread of a new regional religion, or a social change, that was manifest in new designs on pottery and murals, and in new underground religious houses called *kivas*? Or were people brought together into larger villages because of a technological evolution and more-efficient farming practices that could support larger communities? Did the abundance of rainfall in the eastern Pueblo region between the late thirteenth century and the mid-fifteenth century coincide with the change in farming practices? Could the much larger villages, some as large as two thousand rooms in the Rio Chama drainage, have become desirable, as Pueblo villagers fortified themselves against one another or to defend themselves from the newly arrived semi-nomadic Navajo and Apache people? It was a likely a combination of factors that led Pueblo villagers to respond to specific variables in each location. The important point for Spanish-sponsored *entradas*, or exploratory expeditions, into the region in the mid- and late sixteenth century is that the area was already a complex mix of cultures and language groups who were highly skilled at living in this arid landscape. In this land of little rain, Pueblo, Navajo, and Apache people had worked out a modus vivendi that sometimes embraced peace and other times was forged in warfare. By shifting their settlement patterns and using a range of trade practices and social partnerships, the native populations of the Southwest balanced their often precarious world.

From Myth to History

There is a surprisingly direct connection between first contact made by Columbus in Hispaniola in 1492, and the first colony built in New Mexico just over a century later. The Spanish entradas began in the Caribbean and progressed first to Florida, then to the Yucatan and Central Mexico. From their eventual bases in the Valley of Mexico and the northern Chihuahuan desert, Spanish explorers ranged northward to the Pueblo heartland along the Rio Grande. In a kind of conquest genealogy, Columbus's expedition led to several explorations of the circum-Caribbean and the Florida and Mexico coasts, including Juan Ponce de León's explorations of Florida in 1513 and Cortéz's conquest of Mexico starting in 1519. Cortez's expedition spurred other explorations of the Gulf Coast of Florida and the lower Mississippi River.[2] From there the link to New Mexico picks up directly as described by Álvar Núñez Cabeza de Vaca in his *Relación*.[3] He was one of four survivors of the ill-fated Pánfilo de Narváez expedition that was shipwrecked along the Gulf Coast in 1527. Cabeza de Vaca produced one of the most remarkable documents of first contact, based on the survivors' eight-year odyssey from the Gulf Coast, then across Texas, and ultimately to the Mexican frontier settlement of Culiacán. His account of the native settlements far to the north of the territory then occupied by Spaniards—though not as far as the Pueblo Indian villages—began the chain of events that led to the exploration of the Rio Grande. Myth was also a powerful motivator in successive explorations, as Spanish explorers set about to find waterways they hoped would lead them to lands rich beyond their dreams in spices, textiles, and magic elixirs that perpetuated youthful vigor—and in some cases, to the seduction of women of mythically endowed proportions.[4]

The first Spanish expedition to make contact with Pueblo people was that of Fray Marcos de Niza, whose 1539 exploratory expedition was guided by another of the Narváez expedition survivors. Esteban, often referred to as "Estebanico," was a black man of Moroccan descent and enslaved to another of the Narváez expedition's survivors, Andrés Dorantes. Following their return to Culiacán, Dorantes sold Esteban to the first viceroy of New Spain, Antonio de Mendoza, who sent Esteban as a guide for Fray Marcos. Esteban's survival was due in part to his abilities as a healer, or at least he is so portrayed in the account of Cabeza de Vaca. Whether or not Esteban knew the route from the frontier of Mexico to the edge of the Pueblo heartland, he led the expedition into imminent danger. Esteban's considerable luck and powerful presence ran out at Zuni. Fray Marcos sent Esteban ahead into the Zuni village known as Kiakima, where he was killed.[5] How close Fray Marcos came to the Zuni villages is still a matter of conjecture. He described to

Viceroy Mendoza a kind of shimmering mirage, seven glorious cities that conveyed the hope of another medieval myth of golden cities founded long before by Portuguese bishops. In Fray Marcos's account these cities became known as Cíbola. On the basis of the word of Fray Marcos, a man of the cloth and a witness to previous discoveries of great wealth in Mexico and Peru, Mendoza awarded the right of exploration to Francisco Vázquez de Coronado for what would turn out to be an immense area of southwestern North America.[6] By the time Coronado's expedition reached Zuni in July 1540, Fray Marcos was in disgrace. Coronado reported to the viceroy "that he had not told the truth in a single thing he said."[7]

Coronado spent two years (1540–42) among the Pueblo Indians. He did not discover the riches dreamed of by his investors.[8] However, the vast knowledge recorded by the expedition's chroniclers about native peoples of the region and speculation about the likely routes followed by the expedition continue to fascinate scholars.[9] Coronado named his elusive earthly paradise Quivira, but it too vanished before him like a mirage. The scale of his retinue—some two thousand, eight hundred members leading thousands of horses and assorted livestock—forever changed the landscape and native communities of the Southwest. But there was no immediate push for Spanish settlement into the Rio Grande corridor. It would be another two generations before an authorized Spanish expedition went north. Even with the hardships that Coronado's chroniclers reported, and the trials he suffered for his efforts, the myth of a Cíbola or a Quivira persisted, and interest in the far north was never completely extinguished.

For the next forty years after Coronado's expedition, rich silver strikes in New Spain and growing commercial opportunities on the frontier, as well as warfare with northern Mexican tribes, kept Spanish attention focused south of the Rio Grande pueblos. On the expanding northern Mexico frontier, however, the stories of native people living in pueblos, weaving cotton cloth, and farming, as told in Cabeza de Vaca's account, continued to stimulate interest in what lay even farther north.[10] The mining center at Santa Bárbara on the Río Florido in the modern state of Chihuahua was the far northern frontier of New Spain and the fountainhead for the next wave of late sixteenth-century explorations. Fray Agustín Rodríguez ministered to bands of nomadic Conchos Indians in this region, hearing their stories of the tribes and villages still farther north. After the Law of the Indies of 1573 was decreed, which required official sanction for the settlement of new lands,

Fray Agustín pleaded his case to Viceroy Mendoza for a missionary expedition. He would be the perfect man for the pacification and conversion of native peoples he might encounter, he asserted. The viceroy approved, and to protect the friar and his small religious party, Captain Francisco Sánchez Chamuscado was authorized to lead the military escort. In all, the party numbered three friars, nine soldiers, nineteen native bearers and servants, six hundred head of livestock, and some ninety horses.[11] It was far smaller than the Coronado expedition and had a clear goal of ministering to the peoples it might encounter.[12] For the soldiers, however, at least part of their incentive to join the expedition came from information they had read in Cabeza de Vaca's narrative. Leaving Santa Bárbara in June 1581, the group reached the confluence of the Río Conchos and Rio Grande, where they encountered not just a convergence of great waters, but also a mingling of several nomadic tribes and village-dwelling groups. Proceeding up the Rio Grande, the expedition's scribes recorded the ruined and occupied villages they encountered, creating an ongoing debate among generations of historians and archaeologists who have attempted to correlate the more than sixty names of villages and peoples with abandoned sites and modern Pueblo communities.[13] On August 21, 1581, about thirty miles south of Socorro, the group took possession of the province they named San Felipe del Nuevo México at an occupied village where they were received by a large gathering of people.

In September, Fray Juan de Santa María, determined to return to Santa Bárbara to seek additional support, left the expedition at the Galisteo Basin, east of the Rio Grande corridor. He was never heard from again. The other two friars—Fray Agustín and Francisco López—with their Mexican Indian servants remained in New Mexico among the Pueblo people at Puaray near present-day Bernalillo. Captain Chamuscado used his small force to explore widely before returning to Mexico, but he too died before he reached Santa Bárbara. The survivors of the Chamuscado-Rodríguez expedition stirred the Spanish interest in the pacification of these northern pueblos, estimated to have more than 130 thousand people. Viceroy Mendoza heard the accounts of expedition members Hernando Gallegos, Pedro de Bustamante, and Hernando Barrado in Mexico City on May 15, 1582.[14] They noted substantial silver lodes and reported on the architecture, industries, and lifeways of the Pueblo people. They recalled fields of cotton, corn, beans, and "calabashes," and the flocks of turkeys kept by the villagers of the north, and their encounter with the remarkable buffalo. They spoke of the *rancherías* of the nomadic tribes they had met on the Staked Plains (Llano Estacado) east of the Rio Grande. The viceroy supported their appeal for a venture to save the two friars left behind and to convert natives from the "devil's" grip in this next phase of expanding New Spain's far northern frontier. Gallegos, as a "discoverer" of New Mexico, petitioned King Felipe II to allow him to pacify the region at his own expense, but his bid was not successful.[15]

The next expedition to New Mexico was a dramatic combination of rescue mission and flight of an accused murderer. Antonio de Espejo, a wealthy cattle rancher from Celaya, near Guanajuato, Mexico, had barely cleared his name in the case of a mortal assault on one of his vaqueros, when he assumed responsibility for a small contingent of soldiers and a friar to rescue the friars left behind in Puaray, New Mexico.[16] Espejo's party of one friar, fourteen soldiers, and 115 horses and mules left Mexico in November 1582 on a ten-month-long mission. Fray Bernardino Beltrán had joined the endeavor to give it the legal color of a missionary expedition. They received conflicting accounts concerning the survival of Fray Agustín and Fray Francisco. But once they reached the Tiwa villages, they learned that the friars had been murdered. Espejo and Beltrán were then free to explore the region more widely. Espejo and Diego Pérez de Luján wrote accounts of the expedition.[17] On their return to Mexico, their descriptions of the Pueblo people as clothed and sedentary, and of the rich potential of the land, with prospects for mines and *encomiendas*, gave the viceroy the confirmation he needed to seek permission from the king to mount a colonizing expedition. The king's *cédula*, or decree, of April 1583, authorizing the viceroy to choose a leader for the settlement of what they hoped would be another Mexico received no shortage of responses. Gallegos, Espejo, and others stepped forward with their proposals, but it was more than fifteen years until an authorized expedition was mounted.

The discovery of rich silver lodes near Zacatecas, Mexico, propelled colonial expansion north out of the Valley of Mexico, extending colonial institutions into this northern frontier. This wealth sustained the northern frontier until the late 1580s and 1590s when the mines began to dwindle, and social conditions frayed along with the economic depression. At about the same time, the Inquisition expanded its reach, exerting a powerful surge in Mexico by ordering the arrest of several hundred people between 1589 and 1596 for the crime of being judaizantes. Some half-dozen trials of faith (*autos de fe*) and burnings were held in 1590–1603.[18] The rapid expansion of the frontier coupled with increasing conflicts with native peoples made for volatile conditions. Luis de Carvajal, then governor of the newly founded settlements in Nuevo León, was arrested for his conduct of Indian pacification and extensive slave-trading in the north. Although he was freed of the slaving charge, his foes then prodded the Inquisition to investigate his reported heresy. Matters were made worse by the flagrant Jewish practices of his namesake nephew, who also lived in Nuevo León, and memories of charges leveled against the family in Portugal nearly a century earlier. Carvajal was then arrested and tried by the Inquisition in 1589, where testimony ranged from accolades for his Christian piety to whispered suspicions of Jewish ancestry. The inquisitors sentenced him to public penance in Mexico City followed by six years of exile from New Spain. His dramatic auto de fe and penance took place on February 24, 1590, but he was never exiled. Instead, he languished in an Inquisition prison for almost a year until he died there in February 1591.[19] The circumstances of Carvajal's legal and Inquisition trials may have been at least one catalyst in a series of events that would lead his lieutenant governor, Gaspar Castaño de Sosa, to undertake a hastily conceived, and thoroughly illegal, colonization of New Mexico, for which he too would pay with his life.

At the end of July 1590, as the frenzy of the recent autos de fe surely must have been felt in Nuevo León, Gaspar Castaño de Sosa organized a caravan of settlers to move en masse to the Pueblo region. Though warned by the viceroy, via his emissary Captain Juan Morlete, not to leave without proper authorization, Castaño's party made a hasty departure, not even bringing a priest along. Why they took such a risk is a fascinating bit of historiography. In the earliest sources to discuss the expedition, historians generally take Castaño at his word—that the Nuevo Léon mines were insufficient to support the population.[20] And while that was certainly true, a larger social dynamic was also in play. Almost all the settlers of Nuevo León had been recruited by Governor Carvajal in 1580 from Portugal, under special circumstances that allowed them to enter Mexico without proof of their *limpieza de sangre*, purity of blood. No doubt many were conversos, or new Christians, but perhaps some were also crypto-Jews who used the isolation of the frontier to continue their secret practices. Did Castaño leave Mexico to protect those colonists from the Inquisition? If that was the case, it was a vain hope. Officials pursued Castaño's colony to New Mexico. He was arrested in March 1591 near Santo Domingo Pueblo on the middle Rio Grande, by the same emissary of the viceroy, Captain Juan Morlete, who had warned him not to attempt to move the colony.[21] Captain Morlete's instructions, issued by Viceroy Luis de Velasco in October 1590, empowered Morlete to free any Indians who had been enslaved by Castaño, and to set a good example with kindness, mercy, and justice so that the natives would know that the Spanish settlers and priests desired to protect their well-being and convert them.[22] Castaño did not receive the same treatment. He was escorted from New Mexico in shackles and his entire colony placed under arrest. Castaño's appeal to the viceroy, written one year from the time he had led the colony northward, pleaded his case, noting that as a person with some authority he was "invariably the object of hate and envy." In his plea, Castaño includes no reference to Christ or the Trinity, but only invokes the intercession of God, which suggested to Stanley Hordes that Castaño or some in his party had some converso or crypto-Jewish affiliation. His words could not save him, and he was found guilty of "invading" lands inhabited by peaceable people. In 1593 he was sentenced to exile in the Philippines for six years of service to the king of Spain, but he died soon after his trial, on board a ship in the Moluccan Islands when the Chinese galley slaves rebelled.[23]

Viceroy Velasco began almost immediately to search for the right person to colonize New Mexico. He sought a man with sufficient family standing and wealth to subsidize the colony, a principled Christian who might attend to the moral teaching and protection of native peoples—not solely to explore for mineral wealth—and a person with some degree of loyalty to the viceroy himself.[24] The successful contender, Juan de Oñate, apparently met all of the requirements and had a genealogy that mirrored the *mestizaje*, or mixing of cultures, and social complexity of Spain's and New Spain's finest families. His father, Cristóval, a Spanish Basque, had arrived in Mexico soon after the conquest and had taken up the pacification and settlement of the silver-mining area near Zacatecas. His mother, Catalina Salazar de la Cadena, was descended from a family with roots in the Jewish diaspora from Spain. Don Juan married Isabel de Tolosa Cortés Moctezuma, who descended from the Spanish conqueror and the Mexica leader. After her early death he took on the role of *adelantado* of New Mexico, an administrative and military title used by those who settled new lands under the authority of the king, and whose heirs would inherit rights and privileges from this conquest. He was also the *primer poblador*, meaning founder or first settler of this "other Mexico."

Oñate took more than two years to assemble the required colonists, livestock, and supplies. The inventories enumerate every animal, nail, and seed that would be needed to establish the colony. Each colonist listed his or her household members and everything they were bringing to the new land. When Oñate formally took possession of the lands along the Rio Grande on April 30, 1598, he left no grain of sand, no sliver of vegetation, and no living or inanimate thing outside of the control of the king of Spain. He claimed all current and future settlements for the most Christian king Don Felipe II and the most holy Trinity, and made vassals of all people within the new domain.[25] There is no question that the oath was meant to preclude the practice of crypto-Judaism and what the Spanish clerics and some governors would come to see as paganism among the native peoples. Some authors have raised the question of what Oñate knew of his own Jewish heritage, and whether Viceroy Velasco knew of the conversos in his own family history. Did Oñate know that the ancestry of his maternal grandmother and his fourth maternal great-grandmother showed that he was descended from a wealthy Jewish family from Burgos, Spain? Did he know that his fourth great-grandmother was the sister of the chief rabbi of Burgos in the fourteenth century? Or had this Jewish family history been lost in the ethnic cleansing of Spain in the fifteenth century, and in the reckoning of Oñate's descent from the illustrious exploits of his father and mother's families in Mexico?[26]

As for the others who ventured to the remote colony of New Mexico, Oñate's closest aides were his trusted nephews Juan de Zaldívar, as second in command, or *maese de campo*, and Vicente de Zaldívar, as sergeant and recruiter. Oñate's contract stipulated he was to assemble two hundred men, fully equipped for the colonizing venture; all of their provisions; and thousands of head of livestock. The six hundred to seven hundred men and women who composed the colonizing party were a mixture of races, ancestry, and origins. Of the 129 soldiers of European ancestry, 70 percent listed Spain or Portugal as their birthplace. Of the forty-eight women listed in the inventories, 60 percent were born in Spain, and five women, or 10 percent, were *criollas*, or women of Spanish ancestry born in the New World.[27] There were native peoples from many parts of Mexico, as well as mulattos who were born of African and native parents. And among this diverse group there were, no doubt, descendants of conversos and crypto-Jews, some of whom had fled Spain for the short-lived protection of communities in Portugal. Several members of Oñate's expedition had already been to New Mexico as

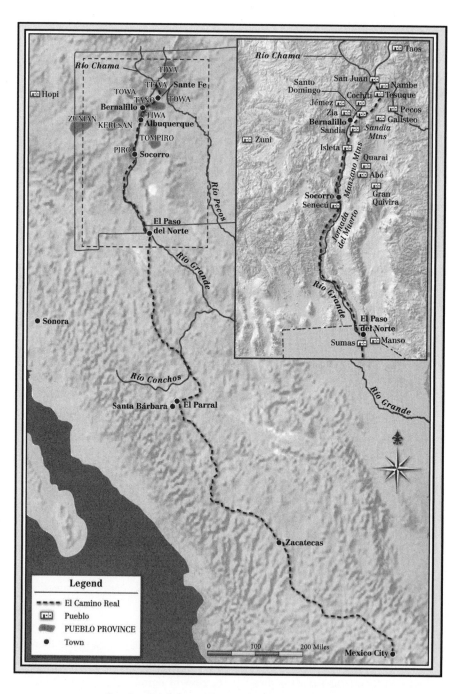

Camino Real from Mexico City to Taos Pueblo.
(Map by Gerry Krieg. Copyright © 2016, University of Oklahoma Press.)

22

members of the failed Castaño de Sosa party. One of them, Juan de Rodrí-guez Nieto, may have been the same man burned in effigy in Mexico in the auto de fe of 1601. Oñate's caravan also included a woman, Doña Inés, who was returning home to the Tano village of San Cristóbal. Doña Inés had been taken from her community by Gaspar Castaño de Sosa, and both he and Oñate may have hoped that she would be their translator and cultural broker, as Malinche had been for Cortés.[28] The colonists inched up the Rio Grande to what would be the start of Spain's northernmost colony at the Tewa pueblo of Ohkay Owingeh.

Colonial Settlers on the Northern Rio Grande

Among Oñate's captains was Gaspar Pérez de Villagrá, whose epic poem *Historia de la Nueva México* captured the dramatic events and heroic deeds of the earliest decade of the colony.[29] While Villagrá dismisses in the main the mixed heritage of the "base, corrupt and untrustworthy" settlers of the Indies, presumed to be the conversos of Mexico, he finds every opportunity to praise the adelantado Oñate, including Oñate's hybrid ancestry in his adulation.[30] History would not judge Oñate so kindly. The enduring images of the colonization of New Mexico are the awful events of warfare that took place in the winter of 1598–99 with Oñate and his nephews on one side and the Pueblo defenders of their mesa-top village at Ácoma on the other. The battle has seared its way into history and oral traditions surviving from the early seventeenth century. Despite the volumes that have been written about the battle of Ácoma, it remains among the most tensely negotiated inter-pretations of history.[31] The intensity of the Pueblo and Spanish meeting has largely overshadowed the exploration of the presence of conversos or crypto-Jews among the settlers, until the past several decades.

Stanley Hordes was among the earliest authors to extend the historiogra-phy of Jews in Mexico to the possibility that Jews were among the *primeros pobladores*, or first settlers, who came to New Mexico with Oñate. Hordes names two men who had been on the ill-fated Castaño de Sosa expedition—Juan de Victoria Carvajal and Juan Rodríguez Nieto.[32] Other families and individuals came from lineages that likewise appear to trace back to converso or crypto-Jewish families in Spain. Cristóbal de Herrera took part in the campaign at Ácoma, but subsequently returned to Zacatecas, where he was denounced twice for reading Judaic teachings, in 1614 and 1626.[33] Bartolomé

Romero is part of an enormous kin network of which only some remained in New Mexico after those first difficult years in the struggling colony.[34] Even the first settlement at the junction of the Rio Grande and Río Chama failed to prosper, and within the first decade the colony was moved to Santa Fe. Hordes traces the ancestry of several families with surnames of Romero, Gómez, and Benadeva for whom he finds connections back to converso or crypto-Jewish trial records in Spain as well as Mexico and other far-flung outposts of the Spanish empire. When Oñate appealed to the colonists in the frontier settlements of Mexico for more recruits to help settle and hold this tenuous New Mexico enterprise from the brink of failure, others of Spanish and Portuguese ancestry, including relatives of Francisco Gómez and the extended Gómez Robledo family who would later be accused in New Mexico of practicing Judaiasm, joined the colony in New Mexico.[35]

A Jewish Legacy on the Frontier

Against the background of recent exploration of the genealogies of New Mexico's earliest settlers, historians have sought to answer the question of how Jewish ideas and practices may have been preserved in the Northern Rio Grande settlements. Modern-day New Mexicans whose predecessors followed the diaspora from Spain to Portugal, and in some cases from Portugal to the Ottoman Empire, have long known, at least anecdotally, that their ancestors were among those who fled Sepharad (the Hebrew word for the Jewish settlements of medieval Spain, explained in the introduction). Family histories ignited the curiosity of some modern New Mexicans, who withstood the possible rejection or ridicule of family and friends to claim their identity by following the rites of Jewish or crypto-Jewish ancestors. It is not a simple matter to be recognized as a crypto-Jewish person, or a descendant of one, in northern New Mexico. Sephardic Jewish heritage there tends to be more complicated than any other hyphenated identity of the postmodern period.

Anthropologist Seth Kunin set out to explore the social complexity inherent in the terms that have been applied to Jewish people of Sephardic descent—*conversos, crypto-Jews, marranos,* and *anusim.* These terms arose in an atmosphere of forced conversion in the fourteenth century and the expulsion of Jews from Spain in the fifteenth century. Kunin briefly traces the pathways of the diaspora that brought Jews to Mexico, and the conditions that may have permitted them to find further refuge in the far reaches of the Northern Rio Grande, even as Inquisition enforcers migrated to the region as well.

Kunin examines the experiences and practices of crypto-Jewish people in modern New Mexico and southern Colorado as they explore publicly their emerging identity over the decade of his fieldwork. He reports on several cases of crypto-Jews gradually understanding their family history, and aspects of what he refers to as "performance" or public display of their Jewish ancestry that then defines their own cultural identity. And yet, for all his contextualization of the nuances of expressing an identity long suppressed, it is still difficult to grasp the essence of what makes for crypto-Jewish identity. And maybe that is the point. Kunin argues that through secrecy, appropriation, and acceptance of a wide range of ritual practices—a complex process of identity formation that he refers to as bricolage—modern crypto-Jewish identity is highly individualized and varied in its public expression by any individiual.[36] In her book *Hidden Heritage*, Janet Jacobs takes the argument of the individual interpretation of Jewish ancestry one step further. Based on interviews she conducted in New Mexico and Texas among those who identified as converso or crypto-Jewish by ancestry, she found that they embraced an expansive definition of themselves as being culturally mixed and in some cases racially diverse as well. They rejected a conventional view of Jewish practice defined by what others saw as Jewish norms.[37]

Photographer Cary Herz spent more than twenty years documenting Hispanic individuals of crypto-Jewish descent who recalled memories of their family traditions in interviews and posed for photos illustrating them. Her photographic subjects revealed their attachment to their crypto-Jewish roots in the interviews she recorded and artifacts that they cherished and that, in some cases, their ancestors had touched.[38] Dreidels, candlesticks, menorahs, and religious medals with Jewish stars as well as Catholic saints were markers of deeply held beliefs. Herz recorded the moments as Hispanic families in New Mexico and Texas celebrated the Sabbath, lighting candles and praying. Moreover, she recorded images and memories of individuals whose journeys of emergence brought them to express an ancestral identity that embraced some aspects of Judaism. The academic debates over myth and memory, reclaimed or authentic identity matter little to those who have found their way to Jewish practice or back to their roots as descendants of conversos or crypto-Jews.

The arguments of researchers and individuals eager to latch on to even slim clues as proof of Sephardic ancestry have their detractors. Chief among those who refuted the persistence of Jewish practices and identity in northern New Mexico has been folklorist Judith Neulander. She has disputed the conclusions largely by discrediting the interview methods used by some researchers, and their failure to consider the historical presence of other religions. She argues that Seventh-day Adventists might have introduced the observance of the Sabbath into New Mexico's rural Hispanic communities in the twentieth century. Reporters Barbara Ferry and Debbie Nathan traveled to northern New Mexico for the *Atlantic Monthly* to find the "truth" between these two perspectives. Predictably, they found neither argument to be wholly "true." Rather, they found that identity trumps history and in some cases defies history.[39] In recent years religious avocation has only become more complicated as members of Hispanic communities embrace new forms of Jewish and Christian Messianic traditions.

Medical science has introduced yet another perspective on the legacy of Jewish ancestry in northern New Mexico and southern Colorado. Researchers have found a marked elevation in the occurrence of a rare skin disease—*pemphigus vulgaris*—that seems to cluster in population groups who anecdotally and genealogically descend from Iberian Jews.[40] In the same region a rare genetic mutation that leads to elevated occurrences of breast cancer has been positively correlated with Iberian Jewish descent.[41]

The following story of the Inquisition's investigation of Doña Teresa Aguilera y Roche, wife of the governor of New Mexico, in the mid-seventeenth century unfolds against this background of historical research and anthropological inquiry. The documents and genealogical evidence point to the existence of Iberian and Mexican settlers with Jewish ancestry in northern New Mexico, including some investigated for this crime by the Holy Office. But whether the weight of evidence shows that the governor and his wife practiced Jewish rituals and maintained a secret life as Jews in the small, closed society of New Mexico remains to be seen.

CHAPTER TWO

Intrigue in the Royal Palace

WHAT DID SHE LOOK LIKE, this alleged heretic who brazenly walked through the casas reales, the Palace of the Governors, laughing over her readings and sipping hot chocolate even on the holiest of days? And why was she putting onion peels on her feet and spending so much time on an ordinary Friday changing the table linens, bathing, and fixing her hair? To her household staff and neighbors there was only one likely explanation for this outrageously strange behavior: she must be a Jew. The staff described her stormy temperament, her bathing and hairdressing, as well as pastimes they found unusual. They recalled in detail when she went to church and when she did not, when she spoke out against local authority and local culture and when she compared Santa Fe unfavorably with other places she had been. During her time in the Inquisition prison in Mexico City, her jailers noted minute details of her clothing and food preferences, carefully tallying the amount she would be charged for the food she ate, the sewing thread she used, and the curious amount of chocolate she consumed. And in her defense, she responded to their accusations by accounting for her actions and reactions and speculating on the motives of her enemies. From the excellent documentation in her Inquisition trial record we know more about Doña Teresa than perhaps any other New Mexico governor's wife at any time in history. The stresses of her life in Santa Fe are vividly told and the desperation of her defense before the inquisitors becomes almost palpable.

Her Physical Presence

Doña Teresa's testimony before the Inquisition in Mexico City contains both her memories of the journey north when the couple first set out for New Mexico, perhaps with some optimism, and when she returned four long years later as a prisoner of the Holy Office. At the time when Doña Teresa

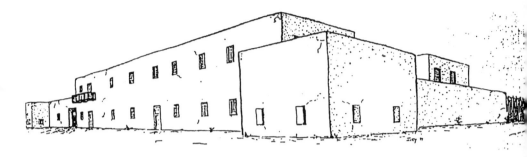

Figure 1. Late seventeenth-century casas reales, or Palace of the
Governors, as conjectured by James Ivey.
(Courtesy of James Ivey.)

first arrived in Santa Fe, she was about thirty-five years old, and her husband
was nearing forty.[1] Four years later when she arrived at the secret Inquisition
prison in Mexico City on April 11, 1663, the warden entered her appearance
in the registry as well as that of her husband. He described her as a "woman
of good build, aquiline visage, and rather fair," perhaps reflecting the Irish
ancestry of her mother. But she described herself as nearly maimed by the
hardships of the journey. She suffered, she claimed, the whole time she was
on the Camino Real—on her arrival in New Mexico and on her return to
Mexico when she entered the prison. She suffered from the harsh environment and described herself as delicate in constitution, distressed by everything. In her own evocative words she recalled that on the journey north,
she did all she could to protect herself from the effects of sun and wind, and
from the "inclemency of the weather and extremes of temperature unbearable even for a bronze statue."[2]

On their journey north they reached El Parral (present-day Parral, Chihuahua) in April 1659 after some four months on the road, having traveled
about 140 miles from Mexico City. Doña Teresa was suffering from a miscarriage that left her even more weakened. During Holy Week she was com-
pelled to hear mass from her bed in El Parral, where she remembered crying
out in pain day and night. She was still gravely ill when the couple took to
the road again. Her accusers would use this failure to attend mass as another
example of her insufficient dedication to Christian duties. On a slip of paper
the arresting officers found among her possessions, she listed her ailments.[3]
Although the list is not among the documents of the trial, throughout the
trial she referred to her many afflictions at different points in her life—a heart

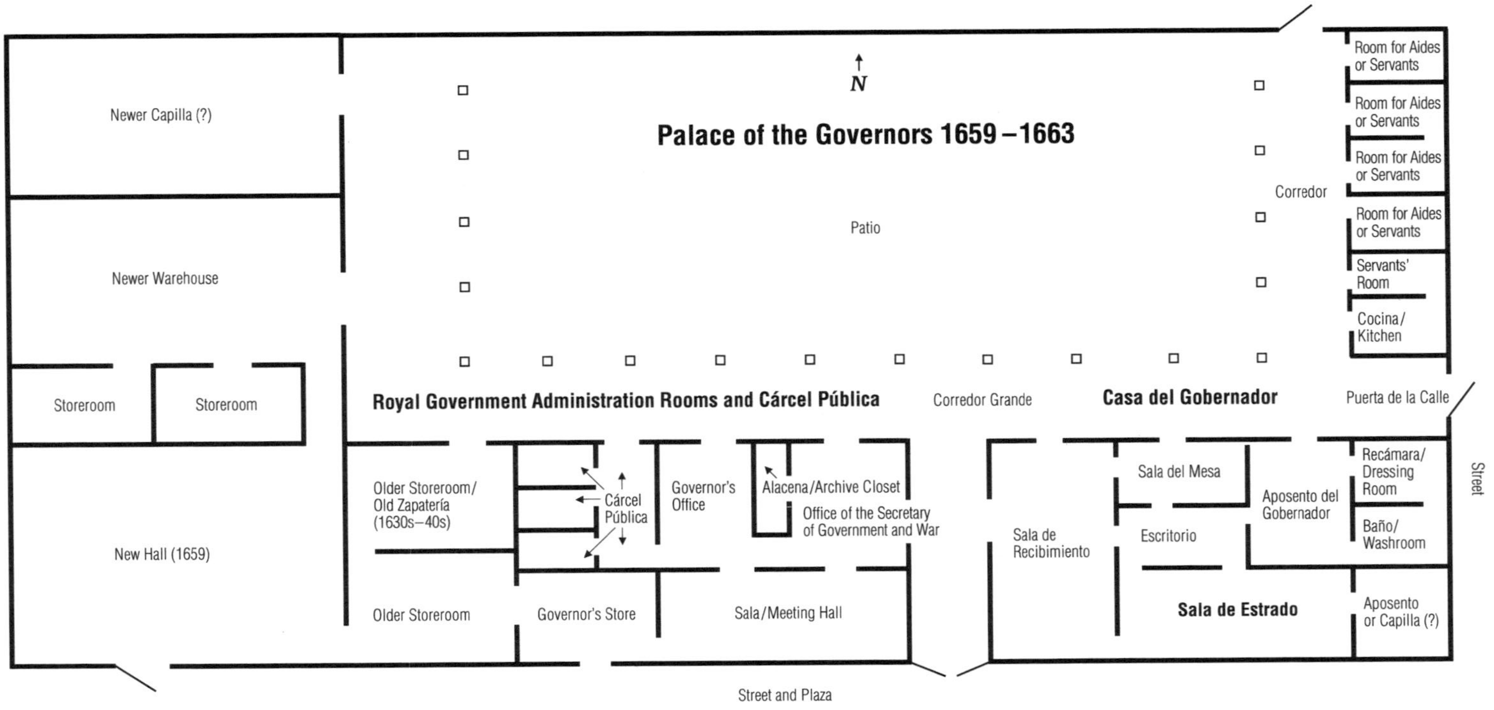

N
Palace of the Governors 1659 – 1663
Newer Capilla (?)
Newer Warehouse
Patio
Corredor
Room for Aides or Servants
Room for Aides or Servants
Room for Aides or Servants
Room for Aides or Servants
Servants' Room
Cocina/ Kitchen
Storeroom
Storeroom
Royal Government Administration Rooms and Cárcel Pública
Corredor Grande
Casa del Gobernador
Puerta de la Calle
Street
New Hall (1659)
Older Storeroom/ Old Zapatería (1630s–40s)
Cárcel Pública
Governor's Office
Alacena/Archive Closet
Office of the Secretary of Government and War
Sala de Recibimiento
Sala del Mesa
Escritorio
Aposento del Gobernador
Recámara/ Dressing Room
Baño/ Washroom
Older Storeroom
Governor's Store
Sala/Meeting Hall
Sala de Estrado
Aposento or Capilla (?)
Street and Plaza

Figure 2. Mid-seventeenth-century casas reales interior plan, as conjectured by José Antonio Esquibel and Robin Gavin.
(Courtesy of José Antonio Esquibel, from *El Palacio* 115, no. 4 [2010], 51.)

ailment as a child, gout and sensitivity to heat and cold, pains in her arms, corns on her feet. She carried with her an assortment of herbs, pastes, and powders including pepper, saffron, rosemary, lavender, snuff and incense, sulfur, green and white unguents of unspecified composition, and, of course, her beloved chocolate. Some of the items were used as food or spices and others surely were medicinal. When she served time in the Inquisition cells, she was charged for medicines that included rosemary, pellets of unsalted fat, oils of sweet almonds and rosemary, and cordials, and for medical procedures that included enemas, bloodletting, and seven visits by a doctor. To sum up her condition, she attributed much of her suffering and ill health to an overall delicate constitution challenged by the conditions of her life in Santa Fe, abuses by household staff, and her husband's ill temper.

Doña Teresa's hair must have been long, in the fashion of the 1650s, as the inventory of her boudoir makes reference to curling irons, ribbons, a large comb, and other accoutrements for her coiffure.[4] Her maids complimented her on the way her hair looked when she took the time to curl it. But they observed that she often did this on a Friday, which the household staff took as evidence of her preparing to greet the Jewish Sabbath. Doña Teresa explained in her defense that she needed at least two days to complete her hairdressing, as it was painful because she suffered from gout in her arms and legs. She elaborated that often she did not curl her hair because of the time it took and because it singed the hair.[5] Then she specified that in summer she bathed and washed her hair every Saturday morning, until the weather became too cold.[6] She related in great detail the timing and duration of her ablutions, making clear that when she deviated from her Saturday bathing schedule it was either for a Christian holiday, or because she needed extra time with her hair preparation. She differentiated between how she prepared her hair for Christmas and other Christian holidays, adding ribbons, roses, and flowers, with the plain way she wore it most of the time. As it became clear that the charges against her included the minute dissection of her personal habits, she told the court that she had been angry with her maids for gossiping about her bathing schedule. She testified that she had discussed the matter with her husband and he had addressed her with endearments, saying, "Go on, my dear, and wash whenever you like, because this is no Inquisition matter for a Christian."[7]

Doña Teresa was attended by a household staff composed of native women and a few people of mixed-race ancestry, some of whom were listed as property on the inventory of possessions. One servant, described as a *mulatilla* by her jailers and more precisely as a *morisquilla* by Doña Teresa, was a women of mixed African and Spanish ancestry named Clara who was about thirty-nine years old at the time of Doña Teresa's arrest. A boy named Diego, a *mulatillo* of about seven or eight years of age, was also listed on the inventory. They both carried papers identifying them as enslaved and they may have served Doña Teresa during her prison term as well.[8] It is not clear if Diego was the child of Clara. The governor testified that a young *mulata* girl was permitted to sleep in his and his wife's quarters at times, but her relationship to Clara and Diego is not discernible from the record.

When she entered prison in Mexico, Doña Teresa claimed to have had four native women as slaves with her on the journey south who were either sold or died on the road from maltreatment. They were named Ana, Catalina, Josefa, and María. In her testimony before the Inquisition, Doña Teresa attributed much of her suffering to the four women, whom she accused of gossiping about her and of inciting much of the intrigue that swirled through the governor's residence in New Mexico. She was correct, and we learn many of the intimate details of life in the royal palace from the testimony of Clara, Ana, Catalina, Josefa, and María before Inquisition officials. Other native women—two identified as Quivira or perhaps Plains Indians named María and Micaela, two Apache women named Isabel and Inés, and a Mexican Indian woman named Cristina—were also part of her Santa Fe household. They too either testified or were accused of being part of creating the hostile atmosphere in the governor's household. In addition to those women, whom she knew by name, there were others she simply identified as a cook, a laundress, or the daughter of a servant, many of whom she came to know because of her husband's indiscretions with several of them.

Ancestry, Education, and Geography Created Her World View

Doña Teresa labeled herself as a native of the Italian city of Alessandria oltre il Po, in the Piedmont region of Italy. Her father, Colonel Don Melchor de Aguilera, had held several important military, administrative, and diplomatic posts in Alessandria and the adjacent fortified town of Monferrato. Her mother, Doña María de Roche, was a native of Ireland. According to her testimony about her ancestry, Doña Teresa's grandfather, Don Juan de Roche, had lost property in war with England, and fearing for his children, he sent them and his wife, also named María, to live in Spain with the Marqués de Santa Cruz.[9] Doña Teresa mentioned her grandfather's apprehension that if he left his children in England they might be raised in the "wicked" sect, presumably Protestantism. His daughter Doña María lived with the Marqués de Santa Cruz until her marriage by proxy was contracted to Don Melchor de Aguilera. The marqués and his daughter, the Marquesa de Bayona, traveled to Genoa with Doña María, where her marriage to Don Melchor was celebrated.[10] Following their marriage, Don Melchor and Doña María moved to Milan, where they began their family life.

Their daughter Teresa was born and baptized in Alessandria in the parish church of Saint Dalmatius in about 1623 or 1624. Her parents lived in the town until she was eight or nine years old, and then they sent her to the convent of San Ulderico (Olderico) in Milan, where her father was posted as the assistant to the colonel-in-chief and captain of the Spanish infantry. She attended convent school for only seven or eight months and then returned to her parents' home because she was suffering from a heart ailment. But, she carefully added, while in Milan she was confirmed in the magnificent cathedral, the Duomo, and was able to recite all the key prayers quite well— Our Father, Ave Maria, Credo, Salve Regina, and the confession in Latin. She told the inquisitors that she knew the prayers in Spanish as well. Ironically, among the books seized from her when she entered the Inquisition prison was a small board-bound book printed in Seville in 1642 entitled *El perfecto Cristiano*, or The Perfect Christian.

The Aguilera family appears to have left Milan in the early 1630s—perhaps around 1634—when Doña Teresa's father took up service in the Basque region serving as governor and captain general of Fuenterrabía, a fortified town on the Río Bidasoa along the French-Spanish border.[11] Doña Teresa recalled leaving Fuenterrabía for Granada when she was twelve or thirteen. The family, including her mother and father and five children, left Spain for the New World in April 1638, when Melchor de Aguilera became governor of Cartagena de Indias in Nueva Granada (present-day Colombia). She remained with her parents some five or six years before she married Bernardo López de Mendizábal and went with him to live in Mexico City.[12]

Cartagena is still one of the most elegant of the colonial capitals established by Spain in the Americas. Located on the coast of Colombia, it was both a magnet and a target for pirates and thieves beginning in the sixteenth century. After the city was attacked by Francis Drake in 1586, the Spanish crown hired Italian military engineer Bautista Antonelli to design the defensive bulwark for the city. Gradually, over the next century, the city was enclosed behind an impressive defensive wall with towers and fortified positions, making it a key port in the trade between Spain and the Americas. By the 1630s, when Melchor de Aguilera went to Cartagena de Indias as governor, about six thousand Spanish settlers were living in the area. Cartagena sheltered a prominent population of Jewish merchants who emigrated there from Portugal. For more than a half-century, between about 1580 and 1635, the merchants actively participated in the sugar, shipping, and contraband trades. Then here, too, the Inquisition exerted its power, driving the Jews away or underground. But the Jewish role in the history of Cartagena has left its mark in place names that survive to this day, such as the stretch of coastline still known as Punta Judío.[13] The impressive fortifications and protective wall that now stands on the hill overlooking both the town and the bay would take more than two centuries to be completed, leaving the settlement largely unprotected in the seventeenth century. Don Melchor had his own political and economic problems that took him back to Spain to stand trial in the early 1640s after he was accused of smuggling gold. As the daughter of the governor, Doña Teresa had the European ancestry and access to fine goods of the intercontinental trade that surely marked her as a sophisticated and privileged young woman when she met and married the brash López de Mendizábal. Her family was not in Cartagena long enough to become more connected with the *mestizo* culture that characterized this and other ports in the Americas.

Doña Teresa testified with great specificity to this distinguished but geographically displaced genealogy during her appearance before the Inquisition, to show that she was descended from true Catholic Christians on both sides of her family, transversely and collaterally. She made her family's connections to highly placed royals and lesser titled nobility clear and discernible. She did her best to recite the genealogy of her parents, as well as her maternal and paternal grandparents, her aunts and uncles, and brothers and sisters, to show that all were good Christians who had never left the Catholic provinces. She concluded emphatically "that she [had] always considered, and seen that others considered, all her parents, grandparents, and relatives to be Catholic Christians, free of any bad blood, without any of them, or this confessor, having been arrested, reconciled, or subjected to public penance or punishment by the Holy Office of the Inquisition."[14] Her ancestry and life experiences show that she came from a world and social class quite different from the majority of Santa Fe's residents in the mid-seventeenth century. And this contrast was, in part, the source of much of what she found unappealing about Santa Fe, and what her accusers found so alien about her.

Her Clothing and Textiles

In several places in the trial docket, Inquisition officials inventory Doña Teresa's possessions. And in each list, the description of the clothes she wore and the fabrics they were made of provide some fascinating details about the lifestyle of this woman of privilege living on the far northern frontier of New Spain. The most vivid description of her clothing comes at the moment of her arrest in the palace. Fray Alonso de Posada, the custodian of New Mexico missions, observed each layer of clothing and each piece of jewelry she donned on the morning of her arrest in the palace on August 27, 1662.

> And with kindness, Doña Teresa de Aguilera was ordered to finish dressing. And she put on a doublet of blue fabric, and beneath that a scarlet damask corset, a blouse of Rouen linen embellished with silk tufts. Then she put on a red petticoat with five tiers of silver tips, and an underskirt of baize or the coarse cloth of this land, bracelets of coral, strings of beads, a thick braid of beads of blue and other colors and false pearls. All of which, along with the shoes she had on, was soiled.[15]

A longer list of clothing appears in the inventory of items taken from her home later that same day, clothing that she had already given to her husband's successor, Governor Diego de Peñalosa, and her possessions were inventoried again when she entered the Inquisition prison. A translation of the inventory of their household goods is found in appendix A. Some items were returned to her while she waited in the Inquisition cells in Santa Fe; others were removed and stored in part as evidence for her trial, and some were sold by officials in New Mexico and Mexico to support her needs while in prison. Local officials also confiscated trade goods—wool and cotton blankets, hides, chocolate, sugar, and other items—taken as partial settlement of accounts that were calculated by Peñalosa to be owed to the crown as a result of López de Mendizábal's residencia, or audit of his term in office.

When Doña Teresa entered prison on August 11, 1663, in Mexico City, her clothing was again described in detail:

> [She was] found to be wearing a bodice of satin plush with a flower pat-

tern in brown, black and white, lined with purple taffeta and with buttons of silver thread, a mantelet of scarlet wool, adorned with silver-tipped ribbons, and lined in blue taffeta with buttons of silver thread, [and] a petticoat of scarlet wool with five sets of silver-tipped ribbons, lined or rather trimmed in yellow damask.[16]

Further, she wore gold earrings; a necklace and bracelets of glass beads, coral, and pearls; and in her pockets were a rosary, a small cross, and a bronze medal that she asked to keep with her in her cell. The governor, too, entered prison wearing clothing made of fine fabrics, including a short plush gabardine jacket and serge, or silk twill, breeches.[17]

The inventories of confiscated items make it clear that Doña Teresa's closets and trunks contained a mix of locally woven utilitarian fabrics used for household items and a surprisingly varied amount of fine imported fabrics used for her clothing. The imported fabrics reflect the late seventeenth-century global trade. Textiles and spices were the coin of the realm, prized trade goods for Spanish, Portuguese, Dutch, and English governors and entrepreneurs. An early seventeenth-century Dutch official characterized the trade, saying that cloth from the Gujarat area of India could be traded for Sumatran pepper and gold, which in turn was exchanged for cotton and coins from East India, where sandalwood and spices could be bartered for different spices as well as gold and silver from the Orient, which then were used to buy other spices and goods from Arabia, and, he concluded, "one thing leads to another."[18]

In detailing what Doña Teresa was wearing, her captors were assessing her wealth and access to a world of finery. Although they did not often detail the patterns on most of her clothing, they usually mentioned their quality and place of origin. Her bodice was a flower-patterned plush satin in brown, black, and white. Her blouse was woven of fine linen from Rouen, France. Her petticoat was likely made with fine-grade wool produced from French or Spanish fleece and trimmed with imported, fine-quality Chinese damask.[19] The scarlet of her petticoat and mantelet as well as the blue taffeta lining of her mantelet indicated that she had access to workshops and the dyes that produced these rich, rare colors. Likely her cape was dyed with cochineal from Mexico, made from the dried carcass of an insect that lives on varieties of *Opuntia* cacti. Cochineal satisfied the world's search in the sixteenth century for the "perfect red,"[20] and wherever the garment was made—whether in Mexico or Europe—the dye to produce the scarlet hue came from the Indies.

The taffeta that lined Doña Teresa's cape might have been made in China or Europe and then dyed with an indigo grown in Mexico or Asia, which produced blues in a variety of hues depending on the technique used for processing the plant. Her understockings came from Toledo and were likely finely woven woolen fabric from workshops in Spain. She owned at least one pair of sea-green silk stockings and a multicolored silk shawl that no doubt were made in China or the Philippines for the Manila galleon trade, which connected far-flung ports in the Spanish empire. She owned several flaxen bonnets and an old blue bonnet of embroidered silk.

The silver threads used to create the buttons and trim of her clothing represented a merging of the Old and New Worlds. The silver probably had come from Mexico, whence it was exported as part of the crown's tribute. Once in Spain, it would have been hammered and cut into strips that were wound around silk or linen cord to produce a filament used for knotted buttons and embroidery thread. Teresa had in her home more than sixteen yards of medium-quality Flemish lace, a trim frequently used for ruffled collars, cuffs, and bodices of women's clothing seen in many seventeenth-century portraits. And in her possession, too, were the red ribbon roses, lace, silken threads, and other ornaments that she used when she took the time to coif her hair. She also owned perfumed soaps, a small crystal perfume bottle trimmed with emeralds and gold, and a belt with thirty-eight equal-sized pieces of gold, one with stones that the guards thought might have been diamonds, and several other pieces of jewelry in various states of repair. (Plate 1 shows a mid-eighteenth-century portrait of a young woman wearing a dress of an embroidered fabric. She stands next to a harpsichord, another marker of her education and social status.)

The gold, gems, silk, damask, lace, and fine woolens of Doña Teresa's wardrobe defined her prestige and status and visibly differentiated her from women in local costume. Her costume seemed to contain only a few items that were produced in New Mexico. Her baize underskirt that she put on under her scarlet petticoat was a locally made fabric. Baize, or *bayeta*, was a lightweight wool flannel. Along with *sabanilla*, another white woolen fabric of various grades, bayeta was produced in New Mexico and was among the *efectos de pais*, or local products that were used internally and occasionally produced for export via the Camino Real. Although she did not seem to wear much of the locally produced fabrics, she did use these fabrics inside the palace living quarters.

The Palace Domestic Quarters: Furniture and Household Objects

On the night before her arrest, Doña Teresa was asleep in an inner hallway of the palace with three of her friends: Doña Ana Robledo, Doña Catalina de Zamora, and Doña Antonia González. The three women were told to leave, and they picked up the mattresses they were sleeping on and left. Ana Robledo and Catalina de Zamora had been in the casas reales before, no doubt, because of their commercial and family ties to the elites of Santa Fe and because of their husbands' service to Mendizábal. Ana Robledo was the wife of Captain Francisco Gómez Robledo, who had been arrested by Fray Alonso de Posada's Inquisition forces on May 2, 1662. He was being held in the Inquisition cells at Santo Domingo Pueblo. And Catalina de Zamora had been there for happier occasions, as when she was married to Diego Pérez Robledo in the palace in April 1641.[21] But this night there was no happy celebration; it was a tense and somber moment. Doña Teresa might have expected that her arrest was imminent and invited her friends to be with her in her hour of need. But could she possibly have been prepared for Inquisition officials to enter her private quarters? The arresting officers—Fray Posada, Sheriff Don Juan Manso, Fray Nicolás de Freitas, and two military representatives, Captain Antonio de Salas and the armorer Joseph Jurado—found a passkey in an outer door and made their way to the women's chamber.

Doña Teresa was one of very few governors' wives to have come to New Mexico at any time in the long colonial period. And she was the only one to have penned an account of her life in the Palace of the Governors. She must have been justly proud of the remodeling that she and the governor had undertaken in the three years they lived in the palace. Artisans from the Tewa and Pecos pueblos had remodeled the crumbling adobe under the direction of Juan Chamiso, a master adobe-mason who was born in Mexico.[22] When work was completed, just a year before the Inquisition descended on the governor's home, the workers had added four rooms as living quarters, a *torreón* or tower and battle-ready parapets, as well as an orchard and a grand courtyard on the palace grounds. Among the eighteen rooms then in the casas reales was a special space where Doña Teresa might have felt especially protected. The *sala de estrado* or *pieza de estrado* was a Moorish tradition imported to Spain and the New World. The area served as a private space, screened or curtained off, where women entertained their friends while relaxing, eating, smoking, or sewing, among other pastimes.[23]

Often the area was a raised platform at the end of the *sala* or living room. The *estrado* was furnished with cherished and comfortable pieces, and was where the señora would have expected to receive male family and close male friends of the family on rare occasions.

We gain a glimpse of the furnishings of Doña Teresa's private spaces from the inventory of her goods as well as descriptions of her behavior offered by the household servants in their testimony. At the moment of her arrest she was seated on a bed in a room on the east end of the palace that may have served as an estrado. Figures 1 and 2 are conjectural reconstructions of the overall elevation and interior rooms of the palace compiled by James Ivey and José Antonio Esquibel, respectively, from descriptions they took from documents dating to the López de Mendizábal trial.[24] They show the estrado positioned east of the receiving room that the governor likely used for official visitors, and west of the *capilla*, or chapel, in the southeast corner of the building. Doña Teresa was surely surprised by the intrusion into her private living quarters. In Fray Alonso's vivid description of her anguished cries for justice, he notes that she turned her face to an image of Our Lady, one of several religious objects she owned. The other religious items in the inventory included "a figure of Christ half a *vara* in size with a canopy of blue linen," "a sash of purple netting for devotion to Our Lady," "a small silver reliquary of Our Lady and San Juan, and other paper reliquaries and two rosaries," and "a book titled *Angeli Custodis*," which was almost certainly a religious tract about guardian angels, as several such works are listed in Italian bibliographies of the seventeenth century. Teresa owned crosses made of silver, jet, and another of manatee hide, a prized trade good of the time. Although her household staff testified that Governor López de Mendizábal and Doña Teresa were not observant Christians, these items and her anguished appeal to the Virgin at the time of her arrest seem to indicate her faith was part of her personal and domestic life, and a source of strength in Santa Fe and in her Inquisition cell. (Plate 2, Our Lady of Sorrows, perhaps captures the anguish that Doña Teresa may have felt watching her possessions being enumerated for sale by the Holy Office.)

In the estrado she had a desk with books and papers that aroused the suspicions of her maids and servants. They testified that she took great care to keep the drawers locked and never let them see what was in them. Doña Josefa de Sandoval, a household servant and witness, testified that Doña Teresa took excessive care to protect the middle drawer, and although this witness often went to open the said desk, she was never allowed to see or open the middle drawer of the said desk; and she tried diligently to see what she had in the said drawer and was never able to see it because of the care they took that no one should open it.[25]

The room in which the guards found Doña Teresa and her companions seems to have retained its Moorish-inspired design and furnishings. The women slept on mattresses and pillows on the floor. Perhaps the "Moorish" carpet noted in the inventory of items and delivered to her in her Inquisition prison cell was originally used on the palace's adobe floor. Also among her possessions was a pillow filled and covered with vicuña wool, to this day an expensive textile traded from Peru. Likely the brass brazier, the small copper coal pan, and the small brass hand-warmer found in the inventory of goods taken from the palace were also used in this room, when she sought the warmth of a cozy place in a climate she found unbearably cold. And maybe the folding screen covered with painted elk hide and the woolen doorway covers on the list of confiscated goods enclosed this private space. The many chests and boxes containing sewing, lacemaking, and knitting materials and supplies were likely kept in the estrado, where she would have spent time doing this delicate handwork. She also owned a small stool and a dressing table with a mirror, another small gilded mirror, a large hair comb, and cosmetics, as well as a brass basin, towels, several lace-trimmed washcloths, and eleven bars of soap. (Plate 3 is an outstanding example of a rare sewing box of a style called *chinoiserie* because of its Oriental design elements. This example also contains carved wooden bobbins for winding threads.)

Doña Teresa and the governor owned several traveling desks and trunks listed on the inventory. Such movable storage items were common in colonial households, as they served both to transport and to store clothing and other household items. In one small writing desk the Inquisition guards found some small pieces of cloth, one-half pound of cinnamon, some powders, and some fastening pins. In another writing desk, made of tortoiseshell, they found a small silver cover for a clay pot, a little cross made of jet, a small coffer sheathed in tanned leather with a reliquary of Our Lady and San Juan, other reliquaries and two rosaries, as well as a pair of gloves trimmed with black lace. The largest of the writing desks, with eleven drawers, contained a patterned gold cylinder, or perhaps a drinking cup or decanter, set into a stone base; some large net coverings, perhaps used over beds or tables; a pair of pliers; some bracelets of silver and others of corral and abalone; some yardage of lace and netting; two "old" bars of chocolate: and three dozen perfumed cakes that might have been soap or a delicacy. (Plate 4 shows a type of seventeenth century traveling desk, an *escritorio*, such as Doña Teresa might have used.)

Among the confiscated kitchen items were a cauldron, a spit, a marble mortar and pestle, a hatchet, several barrels of different sizes, a *mano* and *metate* (a hand stone and grinding slab) from New Mexico used for grinding corn, a copper scoop, a broken silver scoop, a large clay pot, some small gourd cups, and fourteen clay cups made by Apaches, which likely were made of micaceous clay. The arresting officers also seized two small chests for storing salt.

Several different utensils and containers for preparing, serving, and storing chocolate were listed in Doña Teresa's inventory of confiscated possessions. One chest, called a *petaca*, was made of hide, and in it the guards found a quantity of chocolate. More bars of chocolate were found in several other chests and trunks, and a chocolate drinking cup from Michoacán. They also found chocolate stored in a Chinese porcelain container and in a ceramic *chocolatero*, a jar from Puebla, Mexico, made of earthenware with a locking top. This type of pottery was likely majolica, the tin-glazed earthenware found in archaeological sites in New Mexico and recognized as a marker of elite Spanish households. She also owned two platters, five plates, and a cup from Puebla.[26] The guards found a loaf of sugar; a pitcher; a copper pot called a *jarro de chocolate* for heating water or milk for preparing chocolate; a gourd cup; and a small chocolate beater or *molinillo* with a silver base. These last items were kept together in a small chest, which must have been one of her cherished possessions, given her fondness for drinking chocolate. On a wooden tray that the guards said came from China, they found two additional broken coconut cups with silver feet, four hand mills used to make vanilla paste, and some pieces of *achiote*, a spice and coloring agent that is used in place of saffron. The chocolate itself was confiscated by the guards for sale or use by the authorities. (Plate 5 is a majolica ceramic chocolatero with a locking metal top, and plate 6 shows a chocolate cup made of coconut shell with silver handles, probably similar to Doña Teresa's. Plate 7 is a copper pot for making hot chocolate and a Japanese-made porcelain cup.)

The inventory contained what was described as a "locally made" carpet and nine old cushions, which might have been made of the coarse, sturdy woolen fabric called *jerga*, woven throughout the province in a twilled or plaid pattern. Cotton and woolen blankets, or *mantas*, as well as hides and leather garments made in Hispanic and Pueblo villages were valued for trade on the Camino Real and are listed in the wills of colonial New Mexican men and women. Doña Teresa's household inventory contained few hides or blankets, but then she and the governor had turned over to the Inquisition officials a quantity of these trade goods when they were arrested, which might account for their near absence in the household inventory.

The contents of the couple's bedroom, which was probably adjacent to the estrado, reveals much about the more elaborate furnishings and textiles they brought north for use in the palace. Governor López de Mendizábal and Doña Teresa slept on a bed made of a kind of wood that the inventory identifies as *granadillo*, a fragrant red wood.[27] Fray Alonso de Posada described the bed with characteristic attention to detail, mentioning that it had four pillars with the headboard in two parts, five crossboards, and fifty-eight balusters, or spindles, of which thirty-five were small, four were large, and the rest medium-sized. It was all held together, Posada noted, with eight iron screws, nine posts, and eleven boards. By its style, the bed could have been made in Mexico, and the couple undoubtedly brought it with them from there, but it might also have been imported from a number of places on the Spanish trade routes. The inventory noted it was covered with an old bedspread and topped with an old canopy of Chinese silk, as well as white cotton curtains. There were two wool bedsheets, a torn woolen tablecloth,[28] and several different types of covers and blankets. Four silver candlesticks, a silver drinking cup and spoon, and some brass candlesticks were also found in the bedroom. (Plate 8, the painting of *Birth of the Virgin*, shows a style of bed that approximates the bed described here by Posada.)

The kitchen artifacts of the governor and his wife described in the Santa Fe arrest inventory are consistent with archaeological materials recovered from seventeenth-century deposits in excavations in and behind the palace.[29] The Apache ceramics and other locally made pottery show that even the governor's household used utilitarian tableware and cooking pots that came from trade with their indigenous neighbors. Their food was not described in great detail, but the cooks in the palace testified that the governor and Doña Teresa ate meat and bread and drank chocolate even on the holiest of days. The faunal remains recovered from the archaeological excavation behind the palace undertaken between 2002 and 2005 were primarily sheep or goat, some cattle, and a small amount of wild game. In all of the pair's railings against the deficiencies of life in New Mexico, they never complained about the food or lack of it.

When the final inventory of their household was complete, the contents of the private living quarters of Governor López de Mendizábal and Doña Teresa were loaded onto two wagons, in boxes that had been sealed, tied, and labeled "Fisco Real," signifying that the items were now property of the royal treasury. Then they were transported to the *convento* at Santo Domingo Pueblo, where the Inquisition prison cells were located. In what was perhaps a small show of sympathy for Doña Teresa, Fray Alonso removed several personal items to the cell where she was to be held. He took her "sleeping bed" and pillows, and recorded that the bed had two mattresses covered in brown linen, along with two linen sheets and linen pillows with cotton covers. He also placed a striped tablecloth on a table in her cell and brought her a rug and cushions, and several changes of clothing and slippers. He left her the small chest with her chocolate-making utensils, a small comfort in this otherwise grim situation.

Her Pastimes

The maids and other servants often remarked in their testimony that Doña Teresa read books in Latin and Italian—languages unknown to her household staff. Among the books confiscated at the time of her arrest, only one was named in the inventory, the *Angeli Custodis*, mentioned earlier. She told the maids how unfortunate it was that they could not read and that they could not understand the other languages that she read, because she was reading an amusing love story that made her laugh with delight. She reminded the inquisitors that she was born in Italy and that she continued to read in Italian—specifically, the work *Orlando Furioso*[30]—so that she would not forget her native language. It was again Josefa de Sandoval who provided the specific testimony, saying:

> She declares that Doña Teresa de Aguilera had a book in the Italian language with which she used to entertain herself, and sometimes she would laugh, and she would say to this witness, "Look how pretty! I wish you could read and might understand this language." And she said that the said book was about love, but this witness does not know what it contained.[31]

That Doña Teresa was well acquainted with a range of handicrafts seems evident from the variety of tools, fabric, and trim in her possession as listed in the Santa Fe inventory. She had several small boxes and chests filled with materials that seamstresses, embroiderers, and knitters would use—a variety of fine fabrics, ribbons, and lace, as well as pins, needles, thread, silver thimbles, and half-finished items of clothing. She kept many different colors of silk and wool yarn, and the embroidered clothing and household items seem to indicate that she was an accomplished embroiderer, which is consistent with the training that a woman of her station would have received. She owned knitting needles and bobbins for lacemaking. She may have also tried working with *pita*, a thread made of agave fiber and often used in Mexico for fine stitching on leather, hides of which were found among her possessions. She continued to request fabric, thread, and trim for clothing for herself and her maid that she sewed while she was in prison.

She seems also to have liked music and dance, as among her goods were castanets and an old face mask of red taffeta trimmed with silk, but neither she nor the servants provided specific testimony about her or the governor's musical tastes. One of them dipped snuff, or at least they had some amount in their home, along with a small amount of wine. But their greatest indulgence was surely drinking chocolate. Doña Teresa may also have been involved in the sale or trade of chocolate. In the drawers of one of her chests, she had left a written note showing the amount of chocolate and sugar that she had given or sold to several people in Santa Fe. Further, when she entered the Inquisition prison, she had in her possession several notes, perhaps as part of preparation for her defense, showing the names of people with whom she had done business in the trade of cattle, as well as receipts for trade goods, livestock, and for the donation of masses.

Fray Alonso confiscated their coach. He described it as a large coach in bad repair and described the worn condition of the seats; the torn curtains; the missing footboard, pommels, and clamps on the coach box; and the broken wheel rims. It must have been awhile since Doña Teresa had ridden in the coach through the shady groves that bordered the Santa Fe River and the *acequias* that fed cool shade trees throughout the valley.

The Sum of Her Heritage and Her Experiences

Although we do not have the good fortune of possessing a painting or artist's rendering of her, Doña Teresa's own words and those of her jailers best describe her, as well as her condition and reactions to her situation. Shortly after she arrived at the secret Inquisition prison in Mexico City in April 1663, she appealed to be moved to a more comfortable cell. Complaining of being nearly crippled by the length of her imprisonment in New Mexico and the conditions of her journey from New Mexico to Mexico, she feared that she might be permanently disabled and her life threatened if she were not sent to a less humid cell. She asked for better treatment. It is not entirely clear whether it was her characterization or her jailer's, but the notation of her request for a new cell describes her as "a woman raised amid much pomp and luxury."[32] But the description certainly is consistent with her ancestry and status. In many ways the improvements that she made to the Palace of the Governors were consistent with the role of women in homemaking in the seventeenth century. The palace became more than a frontier outpost. It was not simply a government building but a social center and a home. The fine furnishings, expensive fabrics, and tableware were goods she would have been expected to own and display if she had never moved from Cartagena or Mexico City. How could she have known that on Mexico's far northern frontier they made her an object of suspicion and jealousy? Or that her education and ability to read and write in several languages made her the target of outlandish claims? As the widely traveled daughter of the governor of Cartagena, having grown up in privilege in Alessandria, Italy, and Granada, Spain, she was far better educated than most of the men and surely all of the women in New Mexico at the time.

CHAPTER THREE

A Gathering Storm

THE EXTENSIVE INQUISITION dossier on Governor Bernardo López de Mendizábal began before he even crossed the Rio Grande into New Mexico. It contained complaints sent back to the viceroy in Mexico City by Fray Juan Ramírez during the northbound journey he shared with the governor and Doña Teresa in 1658–59. Quickly it became all too clear that the two men were becoming bitter enemies. The records contain further depositions given by servants and civil and church officials detailing actions, reactions, and sins of the governor and his wife. This chapter describes the Inquisition process and another example of a case involving a woman connected to New Mexico's colonial history who came before the tribunal in Spain and Mexico. The discussion of Doña Teresa's case introduces the witnesses whose testimony painted in such lurid detail the intrigues of the governor's household and the scandals that swept through Santa Fe.

The Inquisition

When the term "inquisition" is used in casual conversation, it conveys a vexing trial.[1] During the sixteenth and seventeenth centuries in the Spanish empire and its viceroyalties in the Americas, being subject to the Inquisition could be tantamount to a death sentence. Inquisition proceedings illustrated in paintings and engravings have fostered the idea that the hearings were like spectator sports with a tribunal of judges and a gallery of onlookers. Although such may have been the case in some instances, there were more subtle aspects. The Inquisition, the utmost inquiry, involved the scrutiny of words, deeds, and thoughts by one's close associates—what one historian has characterized as the minute observation of daily routines and surveillance of the mind that pervaded daily life in Spanish towns and colonies.[2] Complaints or reports from *familiares*—lay employees of the Inquisition—or from ordinary citizens could lead to an arrest on suspicion of heresy. Behavior that constituted actionable, or at least reportable, offenses ranged from the mundane to the seditious, from possibly misunderstood words and deeds to truly heinous crimes.

Although the Inquisition was much more active in Spain and Portugal than in the Americas, its activity on the outposts of the Spanish empire was significant. During the period from 1571, when the Holy Office extended its presence to Mexico City in the Viceroyalty of New Spain, to 1700, when the Inquisition lost some of its zeal owing to the Bourbon Reforms, officials in Mexico heard some 1,900 cases. Of these about one-third were for actions that in our own times might be considered inconsequential religious lapses; slightly fewer were for heresy, in which baptized Christians denied tenets of the faith. Impious or imprudent speech and blasphemy could be considered heretical behavior. In more serious cases of heresy the accused was suspected of practicing Judaism, Protestantism, or "Mohammedanism." Reading seditious literature or engaging in practices that were interpreted as magic, sorcery, or eroticism aroused by magic were also actionable crimes. And some charges like sodomy, masturbation, and homosexuality were classified as nefarious sins. Heretics could be tried for treason, in addition to being prosecuted for their sins, in the power-suffused atmosphere of the colonies. Far away from the control of central authorities, cultural and racial mixing in the colonial realm brought about new social norms that often challenged Church tenets, and it was left to the inquisitors to interpret behavior and determine if it was unlawful, sinful, or subversive.[3] In many ways, the Inquisition in the New World colonies served both as the main administrator of social control and the enforcer of religious doctrine.

Proceedings and Actors

When suspects were arrested, their goods and personal belongings were immediately impounded and inventoried. These goods would be used to pay for the expenses of housing and feeding the accused and to pay for the administrative costs of the Inquisition trial. Accused prisoners were allowed a bed, two sheets, a coverlet, and two complete changes of clothing, including undergarments. Once imprisoned, the accused ordinarily would have three audiences before Inquisition officials—but the number of appearances depended on the length of their imprisonment and the resolve of the accused to clear their name. During the first audience, the accused were admonished not to conceal anything they might have said or done that was contrary to the Catholic faith. The accused were promised clemency if a full confession was made, often before being told what the charges were. Then they were required to give a complete account of their life—a *discurso de la vida*—describing their relatives going back two generations. Finally, they were given the first of three formal admonitions to bare their conscience by confessing their crimes. Throughout the length of their imprisonment and trial proceedings they were admonished again and again to tell the truth and to confess their sins and heretical actions.

An Inquisition trial differed from a civil trial in that the inquisitors served as investigators, hearing officers, and judges rendering the final verdict. The Inquisition proceedings generally began with a reading in church of the edict of faith, which urged anyone who might have anything to confess or information concerning others' errors of faith to come forward voluntarily.

The proceedings, which involved many interrogations, admonitions, the presentation of inspections, and reports, were long-drawn-out and cumbersome. A notary, serving as the official scribe for the proceedings, recorded the actions and testimony of official audiences and was responsible for safeguarding all paperwork, including a count of the sheets of paper that might be given to the prisoner. The notary would record the testimony of the accused, as well as that of witnesses, both voluntary and involuntary. The transcripts were not often verbatim but a combination of summaries, characterizations, and sometimes direct quotes.

Several months after the initial audience, the accused would be furnished with a formal accusation including an itemized list of the charges. They were not told, however, whose testimony was the basis for the charges. There was no opportunity to confront the witnesses. After consulting with a lawyer—usually selected by the accused from a list of three provided by the Inquisition—the accused would respond to the charges. Males suspected of practicing Judaism would be required to submit to a physical inspection to determine if they had been circumcised. There could be periodic, unannounced audiences, as well as more formal audiences when the admonitions were again read to the accused.

The accused, spending long intervals waiting to be interviewed by inquisitors, was forced to endure months or years of imprisonment before the final outcome. And perhaps that was the intent—to leave the accused languishing to examine his or her own conscience in the deprivation of a prison cell. The inquisitors would finally consider all of the information and render a sentence either for acquittal, dismissal with no verdict, or punishment. The more dire punishments ranged from exile and confiscation of the accused's estate to public penance or even death. Public penance required the convicted to be formally decked in penitential garments called *sanbenitos* and publicly recant their errors. In addition to wearing *sanbenitos* for a designated period or for life, a lesser sentence might include restrictions and penalties such as being forbidden to wear silk, to put on gold or silver jewelry, to ride on horseback, or to bear arms. Public penance and executions by burning were performed during a rite called the *auto de fe*. Execution, if called for, was carried out by civil, not religious, authorities.

The Inquisition Reaches into New Mexico

At the end of the seventeenth century, when Europeans had been in New Mexico for almost a century, Governor Diego de Vargas described the colony as "remote beyond compare." But as remote as it was from Spain, New Mexico was not beyond the reach of the Spanish Inquisition. The Holy Office of the Inquisition, first brought to the colony in the seventeenth century, was part of the official apparatus of the Catholic Church. Knowing when and how the Holy Office established power over civil authorities is central to an understanding of the troubled times that embroiled New Mexico in the first half of the seventeenth century.

In 1612, during the early years when Governor Pedro de Peralta was directing the construction of the Villa of Santa Fe, Fray Isidro Ordóñez arrived as Father Custodian of the Franciscans. He asserted, rather stridently, that the Church had authority over the settlement and over the governor himself. Peralta's orders for the founding of the Villa of Santa Fe, to the contrary, specified both the layout and form the villa should take and granted Peralta sole jurisdiction over the governance of settlers and native peoples. The tension between the supremacy of the governor over the missionaries and Indian people and the influence of the Church over civil affairs set the tone for the rivalry over power and authority. Ordóñez and a dozen missionaries began their work among the Pueblo Indian communities. They established their headquarters at Santo Domingo Pueblo on the middle Rio Grande, about thirty miles south of the colonial capital of Santa Fe, and from there proceeded to the capital, acting with presumed authority to release soldiers and settlers who desired to leave New Mexico. The split between the governor and the friar widened when Fray Ordóñez suddenly announced that he represented the Holy Office and ordered Peralta's excommunication. Only the intervention of friars who sided with Peralta, and settlers who appeased Ordóñez, convinced the two to attempt a truce. Nonetheless, by the summer of 1613 their conflict had gone so far that the friar had the governor's chair removed from the church, and the governor fortified the casas reales against the priest.

The showdown continued for weeks until Governor Peralta attempted to leave New Mexico to seek refuge or assistance in Mexico City. Ordóñez intercepted him near Isleta Pueblo and returned the governor to Sandia Pueblo, where he was held in shackles to await his fate. Peralta escaped eight months later, in March 1614, and attempted to reestablish his authority in Santa Fe. He failed, and Ordóñez used Peralta for the next year as a symbol and warning to Pueblo Indians and settlers alike by moving the degraded governor from cell to cell in conventos at Santo Domingo, Sandia, and Zia Pueblos.

The arrival of the succeeding governor, Bernardino de Ceballos, in 1614, might have been the end of Peralta's ordeal, but Ordóñez watched as an intimidating presence during the official review of the outgoing governor's term of service, guaranteeing his continued imprisonment. It was not until 1615, in Mexico City, that the Holy Office exposed Fray Ordóñez's fraudulent assertion of power over the governor. Ordóñez then underwent his own trial by the Inquisition, a proceeding that went on for two years. Governor Peralta was ultimately exonerated, but the drama of the Peralta-Ordóñez clash had set the tone for church-state relations and must have been seared into the memories of settlers and Pueblo Indians alike.

Sor María de Jesús de Ágreda, the Blue Nun

Fray Alonso de Benavides arrived in the colony in 1626 as father custodian of the expanding numbers of Catholic clergy and carried with him the official authority of the Holy Office to administer matters of morality, heresy, and orthodoxy. Benavides recorded his impressions of the missions and settlements of New Mexico in a *Memorial* first published in 1630 and revised in 1634.[4] He may have hoped (in vain) to be named bishop of the new territory. In the first edition of his *Memorial*, Fray Alonso reported on the miraculous appearance of the "Blue Nun" among the Jumano peoples living east of New Mexico and on the lower Rio Grande.[5] The story continues to fascinate scholars and the faithful with its mix of mysticism, faith, and pre-Reformation reasoning. María de Jesús de Ágreda, an early seventeenth-century nun in Ágreda, Spain, claimed to have been transported spiritually to New Mexico. But did she really claim to have done such a thing?

Benavides, in his official capacity as investigator for the Holy Office in New Mexico, was asked by the archbishop of Mexico City to look into stories circulating in New Spain about Sor (Sister) María de Jesús, who claimed to have traveled spiritually to the eastern New Mexico plains. She had "bilocated" while in a trance-like state, she said, without physically leaving her convent, to minister to the native peoples and bring them the word of God.[6]

Benavides identified the group as the "Humana" Nation. The name Jumano was applied to several different groups living near the confluence of the Rio Grande and Río Conchos, as well as to nomadic groups on the southern high plains in Texas.[7] Indian peoples identified as Jumanos traveled to the Salinas and Rio Grande Pueblos to trade and petitioned Fray Juan de Salas, serving at Isleta Pueblo in the mid-1620s, for permission to be baptized. Because so few priests were serving the missions of New Mexico, the request was not granted. Then, in 1629, the Jumanos' pleas suddenly took on some urgency with the archbishop's directive to Benavides to investigate the Blue Nun rumors. Benavides first sent Fray Juan de Salas and Fray Diego López to the Jumano villages on the plains several days south and east of Santa Fe. The friars were greeted by a throng of Jumano villagers carrying crosses and asking for baptism. They told of a beautiful young woman dressed in blue, the signature color associated with the Virgin Mary and later in the century worn by the Franciscans, who preached to the native peoples in their own language. Armed with the friars' reports, Benavides conducted a full-scale investigation of the matter, including an interview with the sister herself in Ágreda, Spain, in April 1631.

María Coronel y Arana was born in 1602 into a family of minor nobility and fervent Catholics in Ágreda, a small mountain town in the province of Soria in northeastern Spain. Her father, Francisco Coronel, may have been a distant relative or a direct descendant of a famous fifteenth-century converso.[8] Her mother, Catalina Coronel y Arana, took the family's Catholicism to a new level of devotion when she convinced all the men in the family to join monasteries and then, with her two daughters, founded a convent in the family home. Perhaps the family saw these demonstrations of piety as a means to erase the stain of their converso ancestry. From an early age, and in such a devout atmosphere, young María became something of a mystic and prodigy as an interpreter of the life of the Virgin Mary. Her influence spread so far and wide through her teachings and writings that she later became the confidante of King Felipe IV, a position that may well have earned her the respect of Inquisition officials and protection against denunciation for heresy.[9]

Benavides, after several long days spent interviewing the nun, then about twenty-nine years old, concluded that María de Jesús knew such minute details of the Jumanos and the New Mexico plains that she must be the divine messenger the Indians had described. Inquisitors in Spain continued their own investigations of Sor María until the mid-1650s to determine whether her trances and bilocation were actionable examples of heresy or a true miracle. She was a compelling witness, speaking confidently in her own abbey where the interviews took place.

To this day, the nun's strong advocates seek her canonization, while others remain skeptical about her motives and those of Benavides. Some wonder if she had already read Benavides's *Memorial* before they met, and so was able to repeat words from his own report. Whether or not one accepts the story of her ability to bilocate, the facts of her life are historically significant to this discussion of conversos. Her life story shows that some families whose roots traced back to Jewish ancestors before 1492 became fervent and devout New Christians. Even today, María de Jesús de Ágreda, known as the Venerable, has staunch followers who visit her abbey in Spain and venerate her in New Mexico and West Texas. In many ways Sor María was treated very gently by the inquisitors in Spain, and Benavides may have used her as a vehicle for his own desire to seek more missionaries for the field.

The Growing Discord in New Mexico

The 1620s were a period of missionary expansion in New Mexico with the arrival of more priests from Mexico. Several mission churches were enlarged, and the first generation of Pueblo acolytes served in them. Franciscan custodian Fray Estevan de Perea, who oversaw the expansion of several churches and remained in New Mexico throughout much of the seventeenth century, was himself evidently descended from a converso family on his maternal side, although it does not seem to have hindered his career.[10] Relations between the missionary friars and civil authorities vacillated until the administration of Governor Luis de Rosas (1637–41), whose abuses of power and his physical humiliation and denouncement of the clergy grew to unprecedented proportions.[11] His term in office was beset with wide-ranging charges against him, from enslavement of Pueblo people in the casas reales—manufacturing textiles for export—to his utter disregard for church doctrines and the missionary fathers. He might have been tried by the Holy Office had he not been murdered by a gang of men including a betrayed husband whose wife evidently had an affair with the governor. Stanley Hordes argues that the pro-Rosas faction in Santa Fe was made up of several families of Portuguese and probable converso origins.[12] After the damage done in the Rosas years, the number of priests declined and several mission communities were deteriorating. Apache attacks on Zuni, Pecos, the Salinas Pueblos, and other Pueblo and Navajo communities rendered the colony increasingly on edge.

Governor Bernardo López de Mendizábal arrived in the fractious colony during the summer of 1659 already at odds with the new Franciscan father custodian, Fray Juan Ramírez. They had quarreled even before they left Mexico over their respective offices and expectations of each other. Their fight was on even before their feet hit the dusty soil of the Santa Fe plaza. During the journey, the differences between the two men intensified and the relationship deteriorated badly. At El Parral, Don Bernardo, Doña Teresa, Fray Juan, and a small group of travelers left the main caravan and proceeded ahead to make better time. At Socorro, Don Bernardo excoriated the friar in charge for not welcoming him with appropriate ceremony. The governor took similar offense at the inadequate receptions he received from the friars at Sandia and Santo Domingo. At Santo Domingo, Fray Juan tarried behind, allowing Don Bernardo and Doña Teresa to arrive in Santa Fe first, where he was formally installed as governor of the Province of New Mexico on July 11, 1659. Although it had been customary for the governor and governing cabildo, or administrative council, to give the incoming custodian, in this case Fray Juan, a formal reception, Don Bernardo declined to do so, adding to the growing friction between the civil and religious segments of New Mexico's government.[13]

López de Mendizábal's first major action, taken during the summer of his arrival, set the tone for his administration by alienating both clergy and a significant faction of the colonists: he increased the pay for native people who served as laborers from half a real to a full real per day. He ordered that native people performing work for the Franciscans in the missions were to be paid as well. And he restricted the kinds of services that they could perform to those related to what was necessary for the church or the friars' living quarters. Finally, he restricted the number of livestock the Franciscans could export to pay for church furnishings.[14] Adding insult to these restrictions, López de Mendizábal told the missionary fathers that their church furnishings could be simple mantas (locally made, coarsely woven cotton or wool blankets) laid over crude *jacales*, or adobe and pole huts, and that they did not need elaborate furnishings.

The governor quickly began to build up a stock of goods to ship south to El Parral for sale and personal profit. To facilitate this business, he confiscated two hundred oxen from the settlers to pull wagons he required the native carpenters to build for him. He also pressed native peoples into service to haul salt from the mineral-rich lakes east of the Manzano Mountains to sell in El Parral. He apparently organized an expedition to the plains to capture slaves from the nomadic Navajo and Apache tribes, bringing back seventy captives—contrary to Spanish law. The calculation of exports that he shipped in 1660 is extraordinary, totaling some 1,350 tanned deerskins, 600 pairs of woolen stockings, 300 *fanegas*—or about 480 bushels—of piñon nuts, and enormous quantities of finished clothing items, salt, and buffalo hides. This cargo could only have come from the labor of native peoples and out of the proceeds that some of the *encomenderos* thought was their specific right, further dividing interests in the colony into more and more factions.[15]

When the supply caravan returned to Mexico City in the fall of 1659, Fray Juan Ramírez included a report on López de Mendizábal's activities. Ramírez included testimony of several of the other priests who had been in the governor's entourage on the northbound journey. In testimony recorded beginning in March 1660, they recalled the governor's intemperate remarks. He had challenged the authority of the friars, saying that only he had dominion over spiritual and temporal matters. The friars reported on the rumors that the governor and his wife bathed and changed their clothes on Fridays, that they failed to attend to their Christian duties, and did not attend church. To add to the brewing storm, the governor was accused of indiscretions, abuses, and offenses against women in his own household as well as in the more remote villages. And so it began—an investigation and trial that would last almost four years, not ending until months after the governor's death.[16]

Ramírez sent a second report by special messenger in November 1660 in the wake of López de Mendizábal's inspection of various missions and pueblos. During those visits the governor challenged the jurisdiction of the church and the authority of the priests in their own missions. He upbraided them with his own brand of vicious verbal abuse and then initiated policies that had the effect of increasing the burden on the Franciscans for running the mission farming and stock-raising industries. He allowed the Pueblo villagers to return to practices that had previously been forbidden and suppressed by the Catholic Church. And he supported the Pueblo people in claims and complaints they raised against the missionaries.[17] López de Mendizábal permitted kachina dances to be held openly in the Pueblo villages as well as in Santa Fe, much to the revulsion of the priests. Ramírez and Fray Josef de Espeleta both testified before the Inquisition tribunal in Mexico City in the spring of 1660, offering their observations as well as the affidavits of several other friars on the misdeeds and apparent heresy committed by the governor, and the suspicious behavior of Doña Teresa.[18]

By late 1660, the viceroy had decided to replace López de Mendizábal with a new governor, Diego Dionisio de Peñalosa Briceno y Berdugo.[19] Nearly two years would elapse, however, before the transition of power took place, and in that interregnum Santa Fe would have to contend with a volatile mix of two former governors and a governor-elect in the midst of an ever-expanding Inquisition investigation.

At the end of each governor's term of service in the Spanish colonies, the succeeding governor conducted an official investigation of his predecessor's administration. This assessment, known as the *residencia*, gave local citizens, soldiers, and Indian people the opportunity to make and seek settlement of claims for offenses and debts that the governor had incurred, before he left the colony. The incoming governor often embargoed the possessions of the outgoing governor to ensure a source of goods and funds that might be needed to settle the claims. In the hands of an unscrupulous successor, the residencia became a way of extorting bribes and liberating property for the succeeding governor's own band of appointed officials, political allies, and business partners.

Former governor Don Juan Manso de Contreras, the immediate predecessor of Don Bernardo López de Mendizábal, did not accompany the supply caravan on its return to Mexico City, despite having been appointed as an official for the trip. Don Bernardo waited to start Manso's residencia proceedings until after the caravan had left, using the residencia as an opportunity to extort wealth from Manso.[20] When discussions over a bribe to speedily conclude the residencia broke down, the governor took possession of one hundred mantas, twenty-seven oxen, and eighteen Apache captives that had belonged to Manso. As the residencia dragged on into the spring, Don Bernardo appropriated iron for repairing wagons and for making wagon wheels. He took corn and wheat and additional Apache captives from Manso as well. He placed Manso under guard, alleging he had been told that Manso planned to escape. Inevitably, the residencia proceedings created more factionalism among the colonists, many of whom were loyal to Manso. Others became alienated from Don Bernardo, as he removed some local officials from office to replace them with his own associates. In the end, several colonists helped Manso on at least three occasions by carrying dispatches to the viceroy, and two colonists helped him escape to Mexico City in September of 1660.[21]

López de Mendizábal reassigned some of the encomiendas held by certain colonists. Under the encomienda system, the encomenderos were entitled to receive a designated amount of tribute from the households in an Indian pueblo in exchange for providing for the protection of the pueblo and supporting the Christianization of its inhabitants. Because the encomiendas provided the colonists' families with sustenance as well as material wealth, they were highly sought after.[22] Don Bernardo pursued his own business interests with considerable application. At his store in the palace in Santa Fe, the seat of government, he sold and bartered goods to the colonists, including sugar, chocolate, clothing, and imported textiles. To satisfy the colonists' debts he sometimes confiscated portions of the encomienda receipts. During his tenure as governor he dispatched at least three wagon trains to El Parral and Sonora loaded with goods for sale or exchange. Based on notes found among her possessions, there is some evidence to suggest that Doña Teresa was involved in the sale or trade of livestock and chocolate as well.

On February 1, 1661, following his arrival in Mexico City, Manso obtained a decree from the viceroy that restored his property and that of the colonists who had helped him escape. The decree also transferred jurisdiction over matters involving Manso from López de Mendizábal to newly appointed governor Peñalosa. Peñalosa was directed to return the records of Manso's residencia to Mexico City for review. Adding to the volatility of the situation, Manso was appointed as *alguacil*, or bailiff, of the Inquisition, acting under Fray Alonso de Posada, who replaced Fray Juan Ramírez as the Franciscan custodian and the commissary of the Inquisition in New Mexico.[23]

The Posada Investigations

Fray Alonso de Posada left Mexico City in early February 1661 and arrived in Santa Fe in late May. He was no stranger to the colony, having served in the Hopi mission at Awatovi from 1653 to 1655 in the far western part of what was then considered New Mexico, and in 1656 at Jémez Pueblo.[24] By the time Fray Alonso de Posada assumed the joint offices of custodian of Franciscans and commissary of the Holy Office in 1661, the relations between church and state had been all but sundered. Posada wrote to his superiors about social conditions in New Mexico. He noted the lax morality among clergy as well as settlers; the low levels of literacy surprised him, as did the mixed racial and cultural ancestry of the population.[25]

In his first month in New Mexico, Fray Alonso began to take exception to social conditions throughout the colony. Concluding that native religious ceremonies had gotten out of hand, on May 22 he issued an order forbidding the performance of kachina dances and requiring the burning of all dance paraphernalia.

Peñalosa, the new governor, arrived in mid-August. Shortly after his arrival, he began collecting evidence of Don Bernardo's activities as part of Don Bernardo's residencia. It appears that initially there was significant cooperation between Governor Peñalosa and Fray Alonso as each pursued his respective investigation of Don Bernardo. Their collaboration did not escape the notice of López de Mendizábal, who sent his own messengers to Mexico City at the end of 1661 to complain that Peñalosa and Posada were in collusion, unfairly using the residencia and the investigation by the Holy Office to publicly discredit him.[26] Although the Inquisition's main inquiry focused on the governor, information about the running of the household and the couple's personal habits implicated Doña Teresa as well in actions that were contrary to the Christian faith, and that in the eyes of some of their accusers, pointed to forbidden Jewish practices.

Witnesses against Don Bernardo and Doña Teresa

In all, Inquisition officials heard from twenty-six witnesses who testified, often in great detail, about the misdeeds, scurrilous words, and scandalous behavior of López de Mendizábal and Doña Teresa. The sheer volume of materials relating to the investigation shows how thoroughly Fray Alonso Posada, as commissary of the Holy Office, sought to discredit and dishonor the governor and his wife. But that was not his only goal. He also captured information that he used later to file charges against other officials and his own clerics. Each person he interviewed seemed to implicate another, so that few among the colonists in New Mexico were left untainted by their lifestyle or their social connections.

Inquisitor Posada began his investigation by interviewing the outgoing governor, Don Juan Manso, the immediate predecessor of Bernardo López de Mendizábal. Manso, originally from the Asturias region of Spain, was only thirty-three or thirty-four years old. He gave his statement to the Holy Office of the Inquisition in Mexico City on January 13, 1661.[27] He swore under oath that his testimony against Governor López de Mendizábal was true, that he did not act out of hatred or ill will, and that he acted simply to clear his own conscience. This assertion hardly seems credible, as he and Don Bernardo had already become estranged over Don Bernardo's handling of Manso's residencia proceedings. Using the same formulaic introductory wording offered by many of the other twenty-five witnesses in promising to keep his testimony secret, he testified that the governor and his wife did not fulfill the obligations of the church. Although they lived near the church they were not regular in their attendance, attending only on sunny days in winter and days of holy obligation, and he had heard the governor say hateful things about the church.

The second witness, Fray García de San Francisco, the vice-custodian of New Mexico's Franciscan order, submitted his testimony in a letter. The fifty-nine-year-old friar was a resident at the church of San Antonio, in the Piro Indian community of Senecú south of Socorro, New Mexico. His testimony, written on May 9, 1661, recalled that it was "common knowledge" in the region that a Spanish maid who served in the governor's household in Santa Fe was distressed that every Friday she had to wash the feet of the governor and his wife and then dress them in clean clothes. He identified the maid as the wife of a certain Arteaga, and although he did not know the maid's first name, her name and the confirmation of this story was known by Doña Isabel de Pedraza, who lived in Santa Fe.[28] Fray García's testimony had been hand-carried to Mexico City by Fray Nicolás de Freitas, who was the third witness to testify against Doña Teresa. Fray Nicolás gave his testimony to the Inquisition officers in Mexico City on February 25, 1661. He offered the same testimony as Fray García, but added that because the Friday foot-washing and dressing in clean clothes "seemed to be a Jewish ceremony," the incident had caused a scandal—although he does not say who was scandalized.

Fray Alonso gathered additional testimony as he traveled the Camino Real through New Mexico. He summoned or received voluntary testimony from several priests and settlers living between Senecú and Isleta, New Mexico. Captain Tomé Domínguez de Mendoza was identified as the fourth witness to testify against the governor and Doña Teresa. He voluntarily met Fray Alonso at the church of San Antonio at Isleta Pueblo on May 21, 1661. He may have been responding to the edict of faith that had been read in the churches along the road, or he might have come to pay his respects to the father custodian. Captain Domínguez de Mendoza, thirty-six years old, was a retired military officer who was then a rancher south of Isleta Pueblo. His home was one of the most important *parajes*, or stops, on the Camino Real south of Isleta.[29] Domínguez de Mendoza was one of the men who had been rewarded with an encomienda and land grant by López de Mendizábal. But they parted ways over the governor's acceptance of the Pueblo dances and his disrespectful treatment of the friars.[30] Domínguez de Mendoza had become a staunch defender of the Franciscans. While most of his testimony was focused on the governor's failures, he commented on the couple's personal life as well. They washed their hair and feet and changed their clothes on Fridays, and this seemed curious to him. Further, he had learned from Bartolomé Romero of Santa Fe about a strange occurrence on Good Friday. Domínguez de Mendoza related an incident that several other witnesses would also describe, although none had actually witnessed it. As the religious procession passed by their home, where the governor and Doña Teresa were drinking cups of chocolate, she hastily gave him a clean cap to wear and they exchanged caps in what Romero had told Domínguez de Mendoza appeared to be a kind of ceremony.[31] Romero had repeated this story to Domínguez de Mendoza so often that he was sure that it was some type of evil ritual.

Witness Miguel de Noriega was summoned by Fray Alonso to testify against Doña Teresa twice. The first time was on May 25, 1661, in the convento of the church of San Antonio at Isleta Pueblo. Noriega, thirty-six years old, was a resident of Mexico City but had been stationed in New Mexico where he served as secretary to López de Mendizábal. He came from the coastal town of San Vicente de la Varquera in the Cantabrian region of Spain near Burgos. In his first testimony he stated that he "always" realized that the governor and his wife went to mass as though they had been forced to do so, and felt that they had very little fondness for the devotions of the mass. His later, written testimony was transported in spring 1662 to the Holy Office of the Inquisition in Mexico City by Noriega, in his capacity as the guard who accompanied the prisoners from New Mexico to Mexico City. Posada had assigned Noriega the task of recording anything of note that the prisoners might say during their trip. Noriega recalled several instances on the journey when Doña Teresa railed against the friars of New Mexico, calling them bad priests, bad Christians, heretics, and treacherous enemies of God. She longed for God's justice on them and implored that they be stuck by lightning, fire, and punishment from heaven. On Christmas Day, 1662, while on the trail near Río San Pedro, Noriega recalled that she was very agitated and tearful about the way she had been treated in New Mexico. Noriega reportedly consoled her with the assurance that the Holy Tribunal was fair and just, and in response to his gentleness she quieted down.

Fray Benito de la Natividad was the sixth witness called by Fray Alonso. He testified on May 17, 1661, in the church at Socorro Mission. Fray Benito was sixty-two years old and the councilor and guardian of the Socorro Mission. He declared that it was common knowledge as reported by one of the maids that the governor and his wife bathed on Fridays and put on clean clothes, giving rise to the belief that this was a "suspicious" ceremony.

By mid-September of 1661, Fray Alonso began a series of interviews in Santa Fe, where the accusations against the governor and Doña Teresa were spreading wildly among the military officers and household staff who served in the casas reales. Their testimony and the gossip that they spread contained some of the most minute details about what went on in the governor's household and about the relationships among the staff.

Captain Juan Muñoz Polanco appeared before Fray Alonso, without being summoned, on September 26 in the convento of the Immaculate Conception. Muñoz was thirty-two years old and a native of Santillana del Mar, in the archbishopric of Burgos, Spain. He, too, had heard from Pedro Arteaga and his wife that Doña Teresa washed her hair every Friday, year round, and that she spent all day Saturday adorning and grooming herself, which aroused much suspicion in the capital.

The news of the inquiry spread quickly beyond Santa Fe, and soon Fray Alonso was receiving voluntary testimony from visitors throughout the colony. Captain Diego de Trujillo, a rancher in the Las Huertas district of Sandia in the middle Rio Grande valley, came forth recalling some things about Doña Teresa that he had heard from a friend. Trujillo, forty-eight years old and from Mexico City, recalled that while he was visiting Captain Andrés de García, who lived among the Manso and Suma Indians on the lower Rio Grande, the caravan transporting the governor and Doña Teresa southward as prisoners arrived. In that sad transport there was a black woman, whom he identified as a slave owned by Governor López de Mendizábal. The woman, he said, believed that she had been delivered by God from the "hell" that her owners had subjected her to, including Doña Teresa's demands to be washed and "shaved" every Friday. Don Bernardo also did the same, but not every Friday. Further, the woman testified that on the day church edicts were issued, when people gathered from all over the provinces, neither the governor nor his wife went to church, though they were in good health.

Fray Nicolás de Villar arrived to tell his version of the transgressions of the governor and Doña Teresa. Fray Nicolás, forty-four years old, was the guardian of the Franciscan community at Galisteo Pueblo, and a native of the province of Guadiana in Nueva Vizcaya in northern Mexico. Through multiple links in a chain of hearsay, Fray Nicolás heard from another Franciscan, who heard from a trustworthy, but unnamed, person, about the "strange ceremony" that had occurred on that fateful Good Friday. Fray Nicolás had learned from residents of Santa Fe all about the governor and Doña Teresa's bathing and household routines. Given all of this, he considered them to be "persons suspicious in matters of faith."[32]

Sebastián de Herrera Corrales was the tenth witness to come before Fray Alonso. He was twenty-six years old and a native of the town of Conil de la Frontera in the province of Cadiz, Spain, who was stationed as an ensign in New Mexico. He, too, had heard from those who worked in the governor's household that a black slave owned by the governor and his wife had the chore of heating water every Friday so that her master and mistress could bathe and put on clean clothes on Friday nights.

Fray Miguel de Guevara, the eleventh witness, had also learned a great deal about the behavior of López de Mendizábal and Doña Teresa from residents of Santa Fe, who in turn had heard stories from the governor's household staff. Fray Miguel was the guardian of the church at San Ildefonso Pueblo. He was thirty-six years old and a native of Barcelona, Spain. He had learned from magistrate Captain Bartolomé Romero that a servant had observed the governor and his wife put down the chocolate they were drinking and don long smocks when the procession passed by their home one Good Friday. Further, he had heard from Captain Juan Griego, Captain Bartolomé

Romero, Doña Isabel de Pedraza, and Doña Ana, who lived on the Alamo Ranch (presumably south of Santa Fe), that they knew from a person in the governor's household that the couple washed and changed their clothes every Friday night. If they were unable to change their clothes on a Friday, they waited until the next, not changing their clothes on any other day of the week. When the notary taking the testimony fell ill, the hearing was continued until October 24. At that time Fray Miguel proceeded to testify that he had learned from Fray Diego Rodríguez that in 1659, when the governor and his wife were on the trail to New Mexico, they spent Holy Week in El Parral without ever fulfilling their religious obligations. Further, it was common knowledge that Doña Teresa sometimes went two or three months without going to mass, and that the governor himself would feign illness to avoid going to hear the edicts of faith read in church.

The same day that Fray Miguel concluded his testimony, Ensign Pedro de Arteaga gave his voluntary testimony against the couple. Through his wife, Doña Josefa de Sandoval, who was a servant in the household, Arteaga had access to intimate, detailed knowledge of how Don Bernardo and Doña Teresa lived. Arteaga was twenty-six years old and a native of Mexico City. He, too, lived in the casas reales, which enabled him to make his own direct observations of the governor and Doña Teresa. She was heard making slanderous comments about priests. For their amusement, she and the governor often asked their associate Juan González Lobón to repeat his story that concluded that "he would sooner be buried in Lucifer's hide than in a Franciscan habit,"[33] a pronouncement they found hilarious. Arteaga had heard Doña Teresa say that she did not want to go to confession because the friars revealed her confessions to others.

Arteaga described the special attention that Doña Teresa paid to her personal hygiene. He noted that she took special care to put on clean clothes every Friday, and to change the bedclothes and tablecloth. She washed her hair year round on Fridays, even when it was snowing, he noted with surprise. When she finished washing her hair, she would shut herself up in her room for about an hour, not allowing anyone to stay with her. Arteaga's wife, Doña Josefa de Sandoval, claimed that she must be cleaning her private parts, and was suspicious of why she had to do this in private when at other times she let Doña Josefa see all of her body. Doña Josefa also reported to her husband that Doña Teresa had another curious practice. She placed onion peels on the soles of her feet every day. He reported that he considered this a ceremony that made a bad impression on him, and that this must be a form of superstition.

Arteaga related in great detail the information that his wife had told him in 1661 about Don Bernardo and Doña Teresa drinking chocolate on Good Friday. Although Josefa had not seen it herself, she learned of the incident from Antonia, a Mexican Indian servant who was in the governor's quarters serving them chocolate.[34]

Arteaga reported that he never saw the governor pray, never heard him speak of a saint, nor carry a rosary, nor say grace before eating. When Arteaga cleared the table at the conclusion of meals, he would offer the words "Praise be to the Blessed Sacrament," and neither the governor nor his wife would answer with the expected reply of "Forever." In fact, Arteaga felt that Don Bernardo would turn his face away, annoyed. During a particular dinner in 1659, Doña Teresa was reported to have said that the church in Santa Fe did not have images as beautiful as ones she had seen before. No doubt true, given her wide travels in Europe, Colombia, and Mexico. But when Arteaga pressed her on the matter, asking for her opinion of what he considered to be a fine image of San Antonio, she said with amusement that the image looked like a local military man. Arteaga reported this as another example of her irreverence.

Arteaga had a poor impression of a book (not written in Spanish) that Doña Teresa enjoyed reading. He concluded that "'this must be a book by English heretics, and this woman must be of their ilk.' And that he held this suspicion [the more strongly] because he saw her lack of charity and her evil deeds." His final accusations concerned the way the governor and Doña Teresa treated their servants. He claimed that he never heard the couple order or advise their manservants or maids to go to confession or to mass. He also reported that one of their black slaves, Ana de la Cruz, was whipped, allegedly because she fasted on a Wednesday in homage to Our Lady of Carmel. When Ana de la Cruz asked Doña Teresa's permission to go to confession, to say her prayers, and to receive communion, Doña Teresa called her a "deceitful bitch" and told her to get out. Others saw the slave whipped as well. Finally, he recalled that the governor and Doña Teresa told him to scold his wife, Doña Josefa, for going to confession on the feast of St. Nicholas Tolentino (September 10) in 1660.

Posada seems to have taken nearly a month off before he began taking more testimony from witnesses in Santa Fe on October 26, 1661. Diego de Melgarejo was the thirteenth witness who testified, and he, too, appeared without having been summoned. A native of Puebla de los Ángeles in the Valley of Mexico, he was thirty-two years old and living in Santa Fe, where he worked as a servant in the governor's household. He declared with great specificity that he knew from Doña Josefa de Sandoval that every Friday Doña Teresa washed her hair and feet, and that every third Friday she washed her private parts. That every single Friday the governor and Doña Teresa put clean linen on their bed and their table. He testified that they used to shut themselves in their room to sleep and that no one was allowed to enter until they opened the door and called out, and only a little mulatto girl about nine years old was permitted to sleep in their room.

Melgarejo testified that he never saw Don Bernardo go to mass willingly, and that if he was summoned to go to mass he would feign sickness, as did Doña Teresa. He also declared that shortly after the governor came to New Mexico in 1659, he ordered his wife to have a slave girl whipped for fasting on a Wednesday in devotion to Our Lady of Carmel. Melgarejo admitted that he and Pedro Arteaga carried out the whipping by order of the governor and Doña Teresa. He went even further in his condemnation of their lax religious practices, alleging that they ate meat on Fridays, and that during Lent their fast was incomplete, as they continued to drink chocolate and eat toasted bread that was cut from a large loaf prepared especially for the purpose, implying perhaps that it was some kind of sacrament.[35]

Melgarejo recalled very specifically their behavior during Holy Week in 1659, while they were en route to New Mexico. He was surprised by their failure to perform the required holy obligations. He reported that Don Bernardo had few scruples about eating meat on Fridays, and that when Don Bernardo came from New Spain, he reached El Parral two days before Palm Sunday of the year 1659, and he recalled that Don Bernardo and his wife Doña Teresa and his whole household ate meat all through that Holy Week, without any illness to justify it. He recalled that Doña Teresa was somewhat indisposed and that neither Don Bernardo nor his wife fulfilled their Easter obligation that Holy Week and failed to take part in services, masses, or processions. He testified that they did not advise or order their servants to do so, except that Doña Teresa came to El Paso on the day of Corpus Christi to confess and receive communion, and Don Bernardo did not confess until the following

Lent. Further, he noted, the servants made their confession as soon as they arrived in New Mexico on their own initiative, not because Don Bernardo or Doña Teresa urged them to do so.[36]

On October 27, 1661, Fray Alonso summoned the fourteenth witness, Antonia Isabel, a forty-year-old Mexican Indian who was a servant in the governor's household. She was a native of Santa Fe and had knowledge of the Spanish language. Antonia told Posada that she understood she was summoned to tell the friar what she knew about the religious practices of Don Bernardo and Doña Teresa. She related that every Friday Doña Teresa washed her hair, and feet, and cleaned her nails, and she changed her clothes and bed linens without fail. Antonia never observed them praying the rosary, nor heard them speak about the saints or "edifying" subjects, and they never ordered their staff to make confession or attend mass. During Holy Week, she observed that Don Bernardo spent time in bed although he did not seem to be sick, and Doña Teresa was in fine health. Antonia gave the only eyewitness account of what transpired on Good Friday 1661:

> In the afternoon of Good Friday of this year, at about 3 o'clock, when she was about to serve chocolate to Doña Teresa de Aguilera and already held the cup in her hand in order to give it to the said Doña Teresa, who was seated at her husband's bedside, some as yet unbaptized Apache girls, two of them, came in [and] said, "The procession is passing by"; and then the said Doña Teresa rapidly got up and went to a chest that stood in the room, which might have been about a yard and a half in length, and, opening it, she took out a clean bonnet and went to the bed where Don Bernardo López de Mendizábal was sitting under the bedclothes in his shirtsleeves drinking chocolate, and she took off a bonnet he had on his head and put on the clean one and spoke some words to him that she does not remember well, which she thinks began with "Sir Lazybones," and she laid the other bonnet there on the bed; and this witness, who was there present, stood there watching all this, and there was no one in the said room other than the said Don Bernardo and the said Doña Teresa and this witness; which ceremony, taking place on Good Friday and while the procession was passing by, must, in the opinion of this witness, have been something wicked.[37]

Captain Bartolomé Romero was the fifteenth witness, and he too appeared without being summoned. He testified against Doña Teresa on October 29. Romero was a native of Santa Fe, about thirty-four years old, and married. He had heard from María de la Cruz, a servant in both his own household and that of the governor, that on Good Friday when the Lord's burial procession passed the house, Don Bernardo and Doña Teresa stopped drinking chocolate and put on smocks, though he was not sure of the significance of this exchange. He did not name his daughter-in-law, Isabel de Pedraza, as the source of his knowledge, although other witnesses did.

On the last day of October, 1661, Fray Alonso took the testimony of the sixteenth and seventeenth witnesses, Captain Pedro de Leiva and Doña Josefa de Sandoval, wife of Ensign Pedro de Arteaga. Leiva was a magistrate of Santa Fe and a native of Nueva Vizcaya. He was forty-two years old, married, and made his home at Las Salinas, southeast of Santa Fe. He appeared voluntarily to ease his conscience, though he seemed to know few details with any certainty. Leiva testified that during Holy Week, though he was not sure which day, when the religious procession passed by, Doña Teresa came to the door of her residence, and then went back inside to put a smock on her ailing husband as well as herself. He did not know what this ceremony was.

Doña Josefa's testimony was the opposite: detailed, precise, and damning. Fray Alonso had summoned Josefa to tell what she knew about the governor and his wife from her perspective as a member of their household staff. Doña Josefa de Sandoval, a native of the city of Mexico, was about twenty years of age and married to Ensign Pedro de Arteaga, and together they lived in the casas reales.

Regarding Doña Teresa's rituals of washing and personal care, she stated that:

> As a person who always served the said Doña Teresa, she saw that every Friday while she was with her and in her service she washed her hair and sometimes her feet every Friday, and as for washing her hair, she did not miss one; and that as soon as she finished washing her hair, the said Doña Teresa usually shut herself alone into a room, taking along water and saying that she was shutting herself in to clean her private parts, and that she would remain with the door closed for three hours, and during this time she did not allow anyone to enter there; and this raised such concern and suspicion in this witness that had she been able to spy on her she would have done so, but this was never possible because the said Doña Teresa took such care to ensconce herself.
>
> Further, she declares that she saw the said Doña Teresa put onion peels on her feet every day, and this witness does not know why; but once she asked her about it, and she replied that she applied them for her corns.[38]

Josefa found it strange that they slept alone and with their door locked:

Don Bernardo and Doña Teresa always slept alone and locked in their room, and the only person they allowed to sleep there was a little mulatto girl eight or nine years old who was used to their wicked ways; and even if they got up very late they did not allow anyone to enter the room where they slept until they called, and they were extremely upset and would whip the maids if they came to the room where they slept, and this witness noticed that this was something of special importance to them.

. . . and she noticed that every day while she served the said Don Bernardo and Doña Teresa, when they awoke and called in the mornings this witness would enter the bedroom and say, "Praised be the Blessed Sacrament! God grant Your Honors a good day," and that she never heard them answer "Forever," except that she says that a few times the said Don Bernardo would say "C" [maybe a hissing sound], without articulating a single word.[39]

In addition to their privacy concerns while sleeping, Josefa was curious about why Doña Teresa kept the drawer of her writing desk locked and why she laughed while reading a book in a foreign language.

Doña Teresa de Aguilera had a desk and took excessive care to protect the middle drawer, and although this witness often went to open the said desk, she was never allowed to see or open the middle drawer of the said desk; and she tried diligently to see what she had in the said drawer and was never able to see it because of the care they took that no one should open it, even though she saw and examined everything there was in the house.

Further, she declares that Doña Teresa de Aguilera had a book in the Italian language with which she used to entertain herself, and sometimes she would laugh, and she would say to this witness, "Look how pretty! I wish you could read and might understand this language." And she said that the said book was about love, but this witness does not know what it contained.[40]

Josefa was very specific about their indifference to their religious practices, having never seen them pray, or hold a rosary, or name a saint, and they were hostile to the religious behavior of their staff.

The said Don Bernardo and Doña Teresa never allowed this witness to go to confession or to hear an entire mass, but rather scolded her whenever she wished to hear mass or confess; and when she did go, they scolded her when she came back, saying that she was late; and she saw that they gave the same treatment to the other persons in their household and service; and one day she saw that a black belonging to the said Don Bernardo and called Ana was whipped because she wanted to go to confession in the company of this witness, and it seems to her this was on the feast of the Portiuncula [August 2] of the year '60.

. . . and when the said Don Bernardo or his wife saw a rosary around the neck of this witness or of any other servant in the house they told them they were hypocrites and that they should get those baubles off their necks.[41]

Further, she declares that as a person who was always present when the aforesaid Don Bernardo López and his wife Doña Teresa dined or supped, since it was this witness who served at dinner and distributed the food right in the room or hall where the table stood, she never saw, either at the beginning or at the end of dinner or supper, that they said grace of any sort; and that when this witness's husband, Pedro de Arteaga, or Diego de Melgarejo would clear the table they would say "Praised be the Blessed Sacrament," and she never heard them say "Forever"; and the said Don Bernardo, when he heard the said words, would turn aside his face and grimace, but he neither replied nor took off his hat or cap; and when they went to bed she never saw them make the sign of the cross or say "Praised be the Blessed Sacrament" or pray or perform any other action expected of a Catholic, and she saw them get up in the same way, without any indication of being Christians.

Further, she declares that the said Don Bernardo had little or no scruple about eating meat on Fridays, Saturdays, fast days, and Lent, and that when they fasted they did not change their way of drinking chocolate, because just as he drank it on days when meat is permitted, with two large slices of toasted bread in the morning and the same in the afternoon, he drank it on fast days, and so did Doña Teresa de Aguilera his wife.

Further, that she once whipped her black slave because she was fasting out of devotion to Our Lady of Carmel, and that on other occasions she saw her scold her for the same reason, but on this occasion when she was whipped, she knows that the said Doña Teresa de Aguilera ordered the said slave to take off her religious necklace or scapular, saying to her, "Get out of here, you hypocritical bitch, take off that apron of yours!" Further, she often saw the said Don Bernardo tell the Indians of this kingdom when they came to visit him, "Go on, you dogs, why don't you shoot those friars? What good are they?" And that when the said Don Bernardo went to church to hear mass he went as though forced to do so, and so did his wife Doña Teresa, and that he used to say that all that was needed for saying mass was a hut and a painted hide [*anta pintada*].

Further, she testifies that this witness heard Antonia, who was a cook in the governor's palace, say that in the afternoon of Good Friday of this year, as she was serving chocolate to the aforesaid Don Bernardo and Doña Teresa, when she informed her that the procession was passing, the said Doña Teresa rose from her seat and went to a chest and took out a clean bonnet and went to the said Don Bernardo in the bed, and taking off the filthy one he was wearing, put the clean one on him, saying, "Put this one on, Sir Lazybones," and that she threw away the one she took off him

Further, she declares that at the present time the said Don Bernardo and his wife Doña Teresa have some images stored among some rubbish in a pantry of their house, but she does not know for what purpose; and that on the occasions when she saw the aforesaid Don Bernardo and Doña Teresa unwell, she never heard them call on God or His Blessed Mother or any other saints; and having been on very familiar terms with the said Doña Teresa ever since she came to this kingdom, she never heard her say that she had a devotion for any saint.

Further, this witness declares that she never saw or knew the aforesaid Don Bernardo and his wife to be given to confession; and that many and various times she heard the said Doña Teresa say that she never wanted to confess when she was at divine services, because the priests and friars revealed confessions, and that she said this had happened to her at San Juan de los Llanos, and so she was speaking from experience.

And after further testimony dealing with Don Bernardo, Josefa concluded:

Further, she declares that on St. Nicholas's Day of the year '60, this witness having gone to say her prayers, they sent for her one, two, and three times, and that the third time they summoned her she went without finishing her prayers, and when she got home the said Don Bernardo and his wife scolded her, saying, why was she at church sucking on the saints; and she declares that it seemed both to this witness and to the other white servants that all the time they were in the household and company of the aforesaid Don Bernardo and Doña Teresa they were among heretics, since they never saw them carry a rosary or act like Christians. And this is the truth under the oath she has taken, and upon its being read to her she declared that it was correctly recorded, and that she does not testify out of hatred.[42]

Josefa's testimony began at 3 p.m. and must have run well into the evening. But the next day, on the evening of All Saints' Day, perhaps following mass, Posada was approached by Captain Juan Griego, who volunteered his testimony against the governor and his wife. Griego, the eighteenth witness, was a native and resident of Santa Fe for all of his fifty-six years. He told Fray Alonso that he had learned from Pedro de Arteaga and his wife, Doña Josefa de Sandoval, that the governor and wife changed their bed and table linens every Friday and that they washed their hair and legs. He knew that these things were of concern to the servants in the governor's household, but he did not know why.

Posada took a break for the next ten days and did not resume taking testimony until November 11, when he heard witnesses in the monastery of Santo Domingo Pueblo, where the Holy Office of the Inquisition was held in New Mexico. Esteban de Verdiguer was the nineteenth witness. He was a native of Santa Cruz de Topia and an employee and servant in San José de Parral, both located near Durango, Mexico. He was thirty-one years old and had been married in Mexico City. He testified that when the governor's caravan traveling up the Camino Real reached El Parral, the couple lay in their carriage in front of the church, with the curtains drawn, and heard mass from there. He found this lacked proper respect and decorum.

Fray Alonso does not appear to have taken any more testimony for several months, but in the interval he prepared his report to officials in Mexico City and dispatched it to the Holy Office in December 1661. Still, he interviewed five more witnesses in Santa Fe. The twentieth witness, summoned by Fray Alonso, was Fray Antonio de Ibargaray, who gave his testimony on March 6, 1662, in Santa Fe. Fray Antonio was a Basque from Bilbao, sixty years old, who served at the church of San Francisco de Nambe. He had heard from Captain Juan Griego, who in turn heard it from a former servant of the governor's, that the servant was tired of having to provide hot water for the governor to wash his feet and for his wife to wash her hair every Friday. And he noted it was common knowledge that they changed their clothes every Friday. More shockingly, Fray Antonio had learned from a woman named María Martín de Salazar of La Cañada that Doña Teresa collected her menstrual blood in a silver cup and kept it for an unknown reason.

Fray Tomás de Alvarado was the twenty-first witness. He gave his testimony to Fray Alonso, who had summoned him, on April 5 in the monastery of San Francisco in the town of Sandia. Among reports on other people, he offered testimony concerning the governor and his wife's behavior on Good Friday, using terms that indicated that Doña Teresa was agitated when the procession passed by, and that allegedly she was jovial as she placed a large white cap on her head and one on her husband's. Fray Tomás had not even in been Santa Fe at the time, let alone inside the casas reales, but "this kind of ceremony on such an occasion caused a bad impression on this witness and scandalized him."[43] He concluded his testimony by noting that it was also commonly reported that Don Bernardo and Doña Teresa washed their feet and hair and cut their nails before putting on clean clothes every Friday. He denounced this as a ceremony not practiced among Catholics.

Fray Alonso recorded the testimony of the twenty-second witness, Juan Esteban de Fagoaga, whom he had summoned, on April 8 in Sandia. Fagoaga identified himself as a native of the valley of Oyarzún, a region of the Basque province of Biscay. He was fifty-five years old, unmarried, and a resident in the Sandia jurisdiction. He reported, amid his testimony about other people, that he had heard the stories that the governor and his wife put on clean clothes on Fridays. Further, he had learned from Captain Francisco Javier that the servants in the governor's household reported a strange ceremonial exchange of caps while Doña Teresa and he were inside their home when the Good Friday procession passed their residence. Fagoaga became ill before he could ratify his testimony, and so in some haste, Fray Alonso rushed to his side on May 10 to have the testimony ratified.[44] Fagoaga died on May 18 and was buried in the Sandia church on May 19.

The last two witnesses that Fray Alonso heard in Santa Fe were Doña Catalina de Zamora, a friend of Doña Teresa, and María de la Cruz, Doña Teresa's servant. They were witnesses twenty-three and twenty-four, respectively. Each had access to Doña Teresa's intimate behavior and actions, and in some cases to her motives.

Doña Catalina offered her testimony on March 9, 1662, in the monastery of the Immaculate Conception. She had not been summoned, but came to ease her conscience. Doña Catalina was thirty-six years old, the wife of Sergeant Major Diego Romero. She had heard from Doña Isabel de Pedraza, who heard it from a black servant in the governor's household, that her master and mistress washed their hair and changed their clothes on Fridays, and that she hoped to God that the Holy Inquisition would come for them. She also testified to some risqué behavior between the governor and his wife and that Doña Teresa used magical powders to make her husband love her:

> She heard Don Fernando Durán de Chaves, resident in the judicial district of Sandia, say that he had heard that one Good Friday afternoon (she believes it was this last one), as the procession of the Lord's Burial was passing by, Doña Teresa de Aguilera got up and, taking a cap, put it on her husband Don Bernardo's head, who in turn put it on hers. And immediately thereafter the two fed each other chocolate with their mouths while dancing.
>
> Further, she declares that Doña Teresa de Aguilera y Roche told this witness that once she was given some powders to make her husband Don Bernardo love her, and that she sprinkled them by his feet and saw that the next day he behaved differently; and if she remembers correctly she

told her this in the month of October of the year '61 or '60 while the said Don Bernardo was occupied with the audit, but that she did not say where this incident with the powders had taken place, and this witness does not remember where it was.[45]

When later asked to ratify her testimony in September 1662, Doña Catalina rescinded her testimony regarding the events of Good Friday. Clearly she had heard something from members of the governor's household about that fateful Good Friday, but fearing that she was straying from the truth or uncertain of reporting something that she did not herself actually witness, Doña Catalina seems to have demurred from her previous report of the governor and his wife exchanging caps and appearing to dance with chocolate in their mouths as the procession passed by.[46]

Fray Alonso summoned María de la Cruz, a forty-year-old mestiza who lived in Santa Fe, to testify on May 28, 1662. She was an unmarried woman who had lived in the casas reales as a servant in the governor's household. She testified that she saw the governor's wife wash her feet and hair and put on clean clothes and tablecloths and bed linens every Friday. Although she never saw Doña Teresa pray, she saw Don Bernardo holding a rosary a few times, but she was not sure if he was praying. The household servants said that the governor and his wife must be Jews. She testified in some detail about the events of Good Friday, saying that Doña Teresa had not only put a cap on her husband's head but had tucked a smock under his chin as he lay in their bed drinking chocolate.[47]

Orders for the Arrests

In March 1662, Don Juan Manso carried a dispatch to New Mexico from the Holy Office in Mexico ordering the arrest of four of Don Bernardo's closest aides—Nicolás de Aguilar, Cristóbal de Anaya Almazán, Francisco Gómez Robledo, and Diego Romero—on charges of blasphemy and, in Gómez Robledo's case, being *judaizante*. It was almost a year since Fray Nicolás de Freitas had personally given a report to the Inquisition authorities on conditions in New Mexico and had hand-carried a letter of denunciation from Vice-Custodian Fray García de San Francisco. The orders carried to Santa Fe by Juan Manso also contained a secret decree appointing him as alguacil mayor for the Inquisition's New Mexico activities. The inquisitors—who already had accumulated accusations that Don Bernardo and Doña Teresa were *judaizantes*, among other things—waited to take action until Posada's reports were received some four months later.

Don Bernardo's associates Nicolás de Aguilar and Diego Romero were arrested at Isleta Pueblo on May 2, 1662, as they arrived in the company of Governor Peñalosa from a patrol to Moqui, in Hopi country. Francisco Gómez Robledo was arrested in Santa Fe two days later, and Cristóbal de Anaya Almazán was arrested at Sandia on May 14. All four were then confined in specially prepared cells at Santo Domingo Pueblo. On May 12, 1662, the inquisitors in Mexico City ordered the arrest of López de Mendizábal and Doña Teresa, although the orders would not be received in Santa Fe until mid-August 1662.

The broad scope of authority that the inquisitors granted to Don Juan Manso was formidable in its efficiency:

> We, Apostolic Inquisitors against heretical depravity and apostasy in this city and archbishopric of Mexico, the states and provinces of New Spain, Guatemala, and the Philippine Islands, by apostolic authority, etc., order you, Don Juan Manso, who serve as [*alguacil mayor*] or chief bailiff of this Holy Office in New Mexico, or such person as our commissary may appoint, that immediately upon receipt of this order you proceed to the city [*sic*] of Santa Fe in the provinces of New Mexico and to such other places and localities as may be necessary and seize the person of Doña Teresa de Aguilera y Roche, wife of Don Bernardo López de Mendizábal, resident of this city of Mexico, wherever you may find her, even though it be in a church, monastery, or other sacred, fortified, or privileged place; and that once seized and secured you bring her to the secret prison of this Holy Office and deliver her to the warden thereof, whom we order to receive her from you in the presence of one of the secret secretaries thereof and keep her in detention and secured as stated and not release her on parole or bail without our permission and order; and that you sequester all her property, chattel and real, wherever she may have it and you may find it.[48]

As Don Bernardo's residencia proceeded alongside of the unfolding Inquisition case, more than seventy complaints against him were received by his successor, Governor Peñalosa. Many of these were from members of the clergy and Pueblo Indians, but more than thirty were from individual colonists and soldiers. One was brought on behalf of the entire Hispanic colony by Captain Diego González Bernal, a member of the Santa Fe cabildo, Santa Fe's *procurador general*, or attorney general, and a former adherent of Don Bernardo's faction. Through his belligerence, greed, cruelty, and lasciviousness, Bernardo López de Mendizábal had succeeded in bringing disastrous consequences upon himself. After receiving the usual allegation that Don Bernardo planned to flee, Peñalosa had him imprisoned under house arrest in the Palace of the Governors. The residencia finally concluded in mid-December of 1661 and the results were sent to Mexico City. Based on the evidence, the civil authorities reporting to the viceroy absolved him of many charges but found him guilty of others. He was sentenced to forfeit eligibility for any office for eight years, to pay three thousand silver pesos to the Crown, and to resolve the claims made against him in the residencia. But the sentence did not relieve him of the charges that might be brought by the Inquisition, and so he and Doña Teresa waited for the assertion of those charges.

Orders from the Inquisition calling for Posada to arrest Don Bernardo and Doña Teresa were carried to Santa Fe from Mexico City by Diego González Lobón on August 18, 1662. After first meeting with Peñalosa, González Lobón left the same day for the *custodia*, or Franciscan offices, at Santo Domingo to deliver the arrest order. It was a moment that Posada had long wished for, but it took him another week to carry out the arrests. On August 26, 1662, around 10 p.m., the Inquisition representatives arrested Don Bernardo. Doña Teresa was arrested the following morning. At the time of his arrest, Don Bernardo was already being held under guard in the house of Pedro Lucero de Godoy, where he had been moved on orders from Governor Peñalosa. His detention allowed Peñalosa to seize goods belonging to Don Bernardo before the Inquisition officials did. Peñalosa tried to convince Doña Teresa to transfer her goods to him before Posada embargoed them, but she refused.[49]

Doña Teresa's arrest by the Inquisition authorities took place about 4 a.m. on the morning of August 27, 1662. Fray Alonso de Posada carried out the arrest, which the notary accompanying him recorded in somewhat voyeuristic detail as he described her anguish:

> On the twenty-seventh of the month of August of one thousand six hundred sixty-two, in the early morning about four, more or less, I, the Father Custodian and Commissary, Alonso de Posada, in the company of the *alguacil mayor* of the Holy Office, Don Juan Manso, and assisted by Father Nicolás de Freitas, Captain Antonio de Salas and the Armorer Joseph Jurado, went to the house where Doña Teresa Aguilera y Roche lives and has lived, and having opened the door of the hallway that is there with a passkey, were found in said hallway, Doña Teresa de Aguilera y Roche, seated on her bed. She was half dressed and there, next to her were

two beds. Doña Ana Robledo and Doña Catalina de Zamora were lying in one bed. And in the other, was Antonia Gonzalez, inhabitants of this Villa of Santa Fe who had gone to be companions to Doña Teresa. . . . And said *alguacil* having entered the hallway first, told Doña Teresa de Aguilera that she should surrender as a prisoner of the Holy Office by virtue of a special order which he had concerning her from Your Lordship. To this Doña Teresa, crying and showing her grief, responded by asking why, an important person like her, was being treated in this way. And saying that she was a Christian Catholic, and she did not know why she was being offended in this way. Turning her face twice toward an image of Our Lady, she asked for justice (with appeals) against whoever was the cause of outrages like those Our Lady had suffered. And that the Inquisitors would know who she was. And if they wanted to make her a martyr, to be done with it.

And then they told Doña Robledo, Doña Catalina and Antonia Gonzalez that they should get dressed and go to their homes. And they did this, taking their beds along with them. And with kindness, Doña Teresa de Aguilera was ordered to finish dressing. . . . And having put on a red cape, he brought her as a prisoner and put her in custody in a cell of this *convento* which is immediately after the second door of the *convento*, and which had a closed window and a single skylight among the beams.[50]

The morning following her arrest, Fray Alonso summoned and questioned his twenty-fifth witness, Fray Salvador Guerra. Fray Salvador testified that Doña Teresa had asked him many questions from her cell next to the main gate of the convento of the Immaculate Conception. She pleaded with him to tell her where her husband was being held and whether he, too, had been arrested by the Holy Office. Fray Salvador informed her that Don Bernardo was being held under guard in the house of Colonel Pedro Lucero de Godoy, but he interpreted her tears and anguish with suspicion. She wondered aloud whether her husband had also been arrested by the Holy Office, and on learning from Fray Salvador that he had not, she wept even more. She raised even more suspicion when, on August 28, she asked Fray Nicolás de Freitas to return to her house to retrieve a box. Fray Nicolás reported to Fray Alonso that she asked him:

"Have you gone to my house, Father?" And that he answered her, "No, Madam." And she went on, saying, "Well, go there tomorrow, and [in] a box of chocolate that stands at the foot of the bed try to find two letters stained with chocolate, and bring them to me, because my whole defense rests on them," which, the said father said, caused him to become suspicious and say, "Her conscience is accusing this woman, or these letters are something bad, and perhaps she aims to destroy them."[51]

Several days after their arrest, Don Bernardo and Doña Teresa were transferred to the Inquisition cells at Santo Domingo. It was from there that they and the governor's four compatriots left under guard on October 6, 1662, destined for the Inquisition cells in Mexico City. Fray Salvador again recorded her words and actions at this emotional moment as she called "to Heaven for justice against those who had brought her to this pass, and [declared] that she found nothing in her conscience that would reproach her before this Tribunal." Fray Salvador reported yet another encounter with her several days later while they were in the town of Sandia, where she attempted to pass notes to the governor through a servant girl. When Fray Alonso ordered the girl whipped, Doña Teresa attempted to intervene to save the child. Instead, an altercation between the friar and Doña Teresa led to a memorable moment that Fray Salvador recounted:

> Doña Teresa de Aguilera came to the step of the carriage and shouted, "Father, Father, listen to me, that girl is not to blame; I'm the guilty one, because I sent her. See they don't whip her, and I'll tell the truth." And when our father answered her, "Shut your mouth, Madam, and get inside," the aforesaid said, "May God's justice strike them all, because such scoundrelly behavior is intolerable. God grant they get their whipping in Hell, because no woman in the world has been treated with greater cruelty than I."
>
> And then our father commissary went to the step of the carriage and very earnestly told the said Doña Teresa to realize she was under arrest and that she should not send messages to anyone, because if she did not go very quietly he would have her put in a cart, and that if she was traveling in the way she was and was enjoying the comfort of her carriage it was because he had wanted to show her this kindness in view of her being a woman and frail, and why did she not obey the [order that under pain of] excommunication was given to her at Santo Domingo, not to communicate, by message or in writing, with any person whatsoever except only her two guards; to which she replied that it was true that she had sent Morcona to see her husband, and that if for this the father wanted to send her in a cart, he should do as he pleased, because she was prepared to die a martyr's death, and that if the [order of] excommunication is to be obeyed there must be an appropriate reason for it.
>
> All of which I certify to have seen and heard, because by order of our father commissary I have been paying close attention to this; and because it is the truth, and for the record, I executed the present attestation, affirming that the said Doña Teresa outdoes her husband in haughtiness, although not in deviousness.[52]

The governor was shackled in a prison cart, but even that did not stop him from outbursts against the fathers as he was led to his fate in Mexico City. For her part, Doña Teresa arrived at the gates of the Inquisition prison poised for the fight of her life.

CHAPTER FOUR

Charged with a "Haughty and Presumptuous Spirit"

DOÑA TERESA MET SEVERAL TIMES with inquisitors before she even learned the scope of the charges leveled against her. It was not until fourteen months after her arrest in the palace and more than six months after she entered the Inquisition prison in Mexico City that she was presented with the forty-one articles containing the accusations against her. The indictments were based on the testimony of twenty-six persons who were never identified to her. In addition to detailing her alleged failure to fulfill religious obligations, they also included allegations that her personal hygiene—bathing and changing clothes and linens on Friday nights—could be evidence of Jewish practices. Several witnesses were deeply suspicious about the contents of a book written in Italian that made her laugh aloud. Her oral and written testimony in response to the denouncements offers a rare view of the interior thoughts of this woman of privilege.

She testified nine times between May and October 1663, during which time the inquisitors gave her opportunities to clear her conscience and admonished her to reflect on her actions and deeds that could be grounds for repentance. In her first hearings she displayed a staunch defensive posture; in her view, she was wrongly accused by people with their own conflicts of interest and moral failings. She parried with the judges, criticized the friars and government officials in New Mexico for their deviousness and immorality, and asserted all the while her own pious beliefs and illustrious family history. During and after her third hearing, in June 1663, she occasionally requested paper and ink to make notes for her defense. She spent the time in her cell sewing, contemplating her travails, and reserving her harshest reflections for the failings of the priests, Governor Peñalosa, her servants, and her neighbors. In the excerpts of the admonitions and her first appearances before the court, the changes in Doña Teresa's tone of voice and the tenor of her demeanor are nearly palpable as she began to comprehend the severity of the situation and to endure the conditions of the Inquisition prison. In the later months of her incarceration she began crafting her own defense. Finally, in October 1663, the prosecutor presented the forty-one charges against her. Many of the counts included references to the governor's behavior and complicity. As the charges were read to her, she must have recognized that some of the accusations arose from testimony that could only have been offered by servants and close associates.

Entering the Inquisition's Secret Prison

The Camino Real—the Spanish royal road connecting the colony of New Mexico with its motherland in Mexico City—winds its way for nearly fifteen hundred miles. From the plaza in Santa Fe, the camino follows the Rio Grande, passing near or through the villages of Pueblo Indians where churches built under Spanish rule still mark the new religions and regimens introduced by Franciscan missionaries. Governor López de Mendizábal and his allies who were arrested by the officials of the Holy Office were placed into prison carts at the Inquisition headquarters in Santo Domingo Pueblo. Doña Teresa could not see her husband, but she could hear about his dismal state from the gossip of the guards and friars whom she overheard describing the reduced circumstances of a man many of them despised. They gloated over his degraded condition and distress, jeering at this humiliated figure chained in a prison cart. She knew that he was shackled in a cage, given neither mattress nor blanket, and forced to cover himself with saddle blankets used on the mules. His guards had been ordered not to refer to him by his title as governor, nor as Don Bernardo, but only as Bernardo López de Mendizábal, stripping him literally and figuratively of his status.[1] Doña Teresa rode in a carriage, attended by her own jailers who had been instructed by Fray Alonso de Posada to report on her words and actions as she too was taken south. The caravan would have crossed the *jornada del muerto*—the waterless stretch of road known as the journey of the dead—in the late fall of 1662 or early winter of 1663. At least they avoided the searing temperatures of summer along this deserted stretch of the trail in New Mexico. Then they would have passed through the *despoblado*, a sparsely settled area of the northern Mexico state of Chihuahua, and reached El Parral, where Doña Teresa might have recalled suffering a miscarriage four years earlier as they ascended the camino to New Mexico. By the time the prison train reached

Zacatecas, several of Doña Teresa's female servants were taken from her or had died from mistreatment. At its terminus the Camino Real entered into the Plaza Santo Domingo in Mexico City. There, at the very southern end of the trail, is the location that housed the secret prison of the Holy Office of the Inquisition.

Doña Teresa and Don Bernardo López de Mendizábal entered the prison on April 11, 1663. They appeared before the Inquisitor Inspector Dr. Don Pedro de Medina Rico and several other officials of the prison, including jailer or warden Don Fernando Hurtado Merino and the secretary of the proceedings, Pedro de Arteeta. Bernardo López de Mendizábal would never emerge, and Doña Teresa only after a spirited defense lasting almost two years. The Inquisitor Inspector Don Pedro ordered their first appearances and the careful inventory of Doña Teresa's and the governor's clothing and possessions (appendix B lists her possessions). Don Fernando would have been assisted by the provisioner of the prison in making the inventories as they carefully accounted for the items the accused would be permitted to keep and those that would be stored for the term of the trial or sold to support them while in prison. Once the inventory of their possessions was complete and they signed the inventory, they were removed to their respective cells. Don Bernardo was placed in cell 10, and Doña Teresa in cell 17.

In a report on proposed improvements to the prison written two years before Don Bernardo and Doña Teresa entered it, Don Pedro described the first floor of the building. On the right-hand side was to be the prison library where the inquisitors and prosecutors could find legal reference books. On the left side of the first floor would be the Chamber of the Secret, subdivided into three rooms. One room was where prohibited books were to be collected and locked in cabinets. Another was planned as a library and work space where the notaries could prepare the files for current cases, and the third room would house the completed case files and protocol documents. Don Pedro was troubled by the conditions of the cells, which he described as almost "uninhabitable" due to the cold and damp conditions, which caused the clothing and bedding of the prisoners to rot.[2]

During the intake process, Don Pedro described the governor and Doña Teresa, noting their physical condition, their clothing, and even the contents of their pockets. Medina remarked that Don Bernardo was well-dressed and evidently sturdy of body (*buen cuerpo*). Perhaps he was being wry when he referred to the governor as "a fine figure of a man." He was, of course, describing a man who had just descended the Camino Real from New Mexico on a journey of more than six months shackled in a prison cart. Don Bernardo's deteriorating health is mentioned throughout his trial record, although the cause is not explained. The pair would be permitted—in fact, it would be essential—to furnish their cells with their own possessions so they would have some level of comfort. By law they would have access to food, medicine, and other needs that they could afford, though not any that would be deemed excessive, as would happen with Doña Teresa's consumption of chocolate.[3] Throughout her long imprisonment, Doña Teresa made her needs known, and yet she never complained about the food or the medical treatment she received. She was billed for luxury items—for the chocolate and cordials she took as medicine and for relaxation, for the thread and fabric she requested for sewing projects, for cleaning her cell, for laundry service, and even for coal.[4]

While many of the possessions that Doña Teresa brought might seem out of place and too refined for a prison cell, some things that the governor brought into the prison in his apparent attempt to show that he was not a Jew were almost comical. He carried with him several crosses and rosaries as well as palm fronds that he claimed had been blessed and that he needed for his prayers. He also brought into the prison a book titled *The Christian Governor.* Curiously, among his possessions were three pieces of bacon or salt pork, one of which had a piece missing. It is tempting to speculate that maybe some of these items were planted in his possessions to see how he might react to them, or placed among his possessions by allies who were trying to assist his defense. He, like Doña Teresa, carried the makings of their favorite beverage: cups and containers used to store, prepare, and consume chocolate. The amount of chocolate that he carried was extraordinary: more than 180 small bars of chocolate as well as several lumps or balls of chocolate and several pounds of sugar. This was certainly more than he could consume. Perhaps he intended to use it to entice his jailers or in the hope that he could pay a fine and leave prison. He appeared dressed as a man of some refinement, carrying an assortment of religious and personal objects:

> Don Bernardo López de Mendizábal who is in the custody of this Holy Office, a fine figure of a man, age about fifty years, dressed in a gabardine of trimmed fur, and woolen knee breeches in the ecclesiastical style and he was examined to as to whether he was carrying any prohibited item, and there was found a bag of the sort for relics, and in it was a piece of white

linen bordered in gold, that he said was an altar cloth, and a small wooden cross, about the length and thickness of a finger, and a medal or seal [bula] of the Holy Cross, and a painted image of La Concepción, and a bundle of papers of three folded sheets, which he said were papers to be presented, and a little rosary and a rosary that looked like coioli [shell or nut] with a cross decorated with silver, and another thinner rosary appearing to be [coioli] bound in copper, and a mustache form or support [bigotera] of chamois bound in scarlet, and some fronds of palm that he said had been blessed, and he handed over the said rosary decorated in copper.[5]

In her first weeks in the Inquisition prison, Doña Teresa demonstrated some of the haughtiness that was characteristic of her behavior, or so her guards claimed. After she complained that her cell was unsuitable, Don Pedro agreed to have a different cell built that would be better suited to her station and her comfort:

> The said inquisitor inspector declared that whereas the said Doña Teresa de Aguilera has come from so distant a place and been a prisoner for so long a time, and, since she is a woman raised amidst much pomp and luxury, she solicited at the hearing when the aforesaid was received that she be placed in a comfortable and dry cell, because she had arrived maimed from her journey and it seemed to her that she would be permanently disabled and her life endangered if she were placed in a humid and uncomfortable cell, and for the said reason a cell newly constructed in the antechamber of the former secret prison of this Holy Office has been prepared, he would and did order that the warden place her in the said new cell.[6]

Ten days after Doña Teresa entered prison, the Inquisitor Inspector Dr. Don Pedro de Medina Rico ordered the possessions she had with her when she entered the prison to be delivered to her. These were the only items she could keep with her. The remainder of her goods were to be held in secure storage, to be released only by order of the Inquisition Tribunal. But she immediately began to ask for things she wanted from her embargoed possessions—a small tortoiseshell box in which there was a note that she wanted for her defense, a cloak, and more chocolate were among the items she pressed the court to deliver to her.

> There has been delivered to her everything she was wearing on her person on the day she entered the secret prison as a prisoner, and everything relating to her bed, to wit, two mattresses, two sheets, and the other objects pertaining to her said bed; and a smock decorated with colored silks; and

the mantelet of red linen, and the bodice of blue fabric; and the petticoat of Chinese damask; and the other petticoat of old linen; a towel in which it was wrapped; a small case with a key, and in it about three pounds of chocolate, and two copper chocolate jars, three small tablets of chocolate, two cups, one silver spoon, one pound of sugar, a small Moorish rug; a small brass basin; a small cotton chemise with wool adornments; a linen chemise; a petticoat with red embroidery; some tablecloths with openwork decoration; a very small box with a key, and in it a mirror along with all the small objects contained in the said box and having to do with coiffure and adornment of the head; half a loaf of sugar; and 40 tablets of chocolate; and [whereas] the other goods likewise inventoried at the time of the said entry into prison are in the possession of Don Fernando Hurtado Merino, warden of the secret prison of this Holy Office, he [the inquisitor] would and did order that the said Don Fernando Hurtado Merino keep it all in his possession and custody, without delivering it to any person whatsoever unless it be by order of this Tribunal.[7]

At this same hearing, she may have learned that three of her maids— Micaela, Isabel, and Inés—had been released by Don Juan Manso under orders of Viceroy Conde de Baños.[8] This does not appear to have been an act of kindness. Although Don Juan Manso acknowledged that the three women were not slaves, and all were free and Christians, he was ordered by Governor Peñalosa and the viceroy to deliver them to the viceroy's palaces in El Parral and Zacatecas, where they were released to serve the Condesa Marquesa de Baños.[9] Doña Teresa was permitted to retain two enslaved children: a six-year-old mulatto slave boy called Dieguillo, and Clara, whom she often referred to with great affection as a girl she treated kindly as if she were her own child.

The Admonitions

The governor's first appearance before the inquisitors was on April 28, 1663. Doña Teresa's was four days later. In the first hearing, prisoners would be asked to give their life stories and to recite their family history as well as their education. In giving her *discurso de la vida*, Doña Teresa testified emphatically that her parents, grandparents, and relatives were considered to be Catholic Christians without any racial taint. She emphasized that she was baptized, confirmed, and educated in the Catholic faith during her childhood in Italy. She testified under oath that she had always attended mass on feast days, and confessed and took communion once a year as the Church

Figure 3. *Woman before the Inquisition*, Constantino Escalante,
Mexico City, 1908.

required. She could recite all the appropriate prayers—in Latin and Spanish—and although she could read well, she claimed that she did not know how to write fluently. When asked if she knew why she had been arrested, she replied that although she knew the Inquisition did not arrest anyone without cause, as a good Catholic Christian who would die to defend her faith, she did not know why she had been arrested unless it was because her enemies had given false testimony, the specifics of which she did not know.

> She declared that she stands advised of the admonition given her; and if she had done or committed, or seen other persons do or commit, anything contrary to our holy Catholic faith, she would come on her knees to request pardon if the matter concerned her, or to declare what she knew, because she is a Catholic Christian and very proud of it; that she is sure that this Holy Tribunal would not have ordered her arrest without a reason, but that the reason must have been invented by her enemies; that she said so several times to the commissary in New Mexico.[10]

While asserting her innocence, Doña Teresa did not lose the opportunity to let the inquisitors know that she had reason to think that the friars and settlers who were responsible for her arrest had motive to wish her ill. She accused Fray Pedro Moreno, a lay brother of the monastery of St. Francis in Santa Fe, of telling others about the arrest of the governor and his wife and saying that they were "in for it now." Although Fray Pedro had not testified against her, she was correct in her belief that many friars were witnesses against her and the governor. She claimed to have heard Diego Romero, who was also arrested in New Mexico, and Rodrigo Rubín, the guard charged with transporting Romero, gossiping about the governor when they were traveling on the camino:

> And this confessor [Doña Teresa] also heard the said Diego Romero, when he was coming as a prisoner in a cart, say, "Have you ever seen such a thing, that that friar should come from so far off just to see the said Don Bernardo in shackles?"[11]

Doña Teresa asked to be advised of the charges against her, something she would not know until several more months and several more hearings had passed. When she was returned to her cell after the first hearing she was admonished to examine her conscience, to think carefully about the matter, and to tell the truth. Still in the dark about what charges she faced, she persisted in her denial, speaking about herself in the third person. "Let her be told how she is in error," she pleaded, "and she will truthfully declare the facts without adding or omitting anything." Following the hearing, the warden issued an order directing the registrar of inspections to purchase twenty-five pounds of chocolate on behalf of Doña Teresa and the governor and to deliver it to them at proper intervals. A month later she requested another twelve and a half pounds of chocolate and an equal amount of sugar. During Lent, and continuing because of her ill health, she would also receive a daily ration of wine. By the next year, her ration of chocolate was cut because the warden described it as an extraordinary expense to the prison, as the normal ration was only about one-quarter of what she had been granted.[12] In May 1664, her ration was fixed at eight pounds of chocolate and four pounds of sugar each month. She was accused of using the chocolate to bribe prison guards; in at least one instance she allegedly traded chocolate for embroidery thread.[13]

Doña Teresa returned for her second hearing, this time at her own request, on May 9. Her testimony at this hearing was likely still not what the inquisitors wanted to hear. She immediately launched into a lengthy description of items she was missing or that she needed, and then persisted in denying that she had done anything wrong. She told the inquisitors that one of the coconut-shell cups for drinking chocolate cracked when it was given to her on the journey south and had broken, and she kept the ornamental silver. She did not know what had happened to the silver, and she asked that the inquisitors determine what had become of the pieces. Again she asked for the small tortoiseshell box in which she had kept thimbles and needles. In that same box she had written on a small sheet of paper the amounts owed to her by several Santa Fe residents. She recalled that Francisco Javier owed her some twenty pesos, and Catalina Bernal, a widow, owed her about three pesos for chocolate and sugar. At the time of her arrest in Santa Fe she had asked Fray Salvador Guerra to find the note, but he had not given it to her. She pleaded with the inquisitors to find out what had happened to the note and to try to recover it for her. Fray Salvador had testified in New Mexico to Fray Alonso that she asked for letters kept in a box of chocolate, and Fray Salvador had found that to be suspicious. Clearly this was not the testimony that the tribunal was seeking, and again they admonished her to examine her conscience:

> She was told that she will recall that at the previous hearing she was admonished in the name of Our Lord God and His glorious and blessed mother Our Lady the Virgin Mary to search her memory and unburden her conscience by declaring the whole truth of what she may have done or said, or seen other persons do or say, that might have offended or seemed to offend against Our Lord or against His holy Catholic faith, the law of the Gospel that our Holy Mother the Roman Catholic Church believes, follows, and teaches, or against the rightful and free operation of the Holy Office, without concealing anything concerning herself or another person or bearing false witness against herself or another person; that in a second admonition she is now admonished and charged to the same effect, because if she does so she will do her duty as a Catholic Christian and her case will be decided as promptly and as mercifully as possible. Otherwise, justice will be done.[14]

And again she asserted her innocence and her faith:

> She declared that she has been and is a Catholic Christian, and she proclaims her intention to be, live, and die as one, without offending Our Lord; and she therefore neither feels nor knows herself to have done or said anything against Our Lord or His holy faith, nor has she heard or known

of another person who might have committed any of the said offenses; and thus she has nothing whatsoever to declare.[15]

Some sixty days after she entered the Inquisition prison she requested a third hearing. At this hearing, on June 12, 1663, she requested that she be given paper and ink so that she might write down whatever occurred to her when she was in her cell contemplating her acts and her fate. Her request was granted, and she was cautioned again to examine her conscience and declare the whole truth of what she might have said or done herself or heard or witnessed in the behavior of others that may have been contrary to the Holy Catholic faith. When she was called by Don Pedro de Medina Rico for her fourth hearing on June 15, 1663, she came with the first of several written statements she would prepare during her time in prison. The inquisitors may have been surprised by her precise recollection, not of her own alleged crimes against the faith, but of offenses committed by the faithful and the powerful in New Mexico. She began with Governor Don Juan Manso, the man who had crossed her husband several times, and who was also present at the time of her arrest in his capacity as bailiff of the Holy Office in New Mexico. Her first written response concerned the illicit relationship that the former Governor Don Juan Manso had with a married woman in New Mexico, and that a friar had baptized their bastard child twice. The first time, the friar baptized the child as the son of the biological father, and the second time, he recorded him as the son of the deceived husband:

> And she also stated that some things have come to her mind that make her uneasy, and in case they should concern this Holy Office she wishes to state and declare them; and what has come to her mind is that Don Juan Manso, former governor of New Mexico, who now came here as chief bailiff of this Holy Office escorting this confessor and her husband and other accused, had an unlawful relation with a married woman called Doña Margarita Márquez, wife, as far as she can remember, of Agustín de Caravajal, a resident of the town of Santa Fe in New Mexico who lives in a place near the said town called Los Cerrillos; and that the said woman became pregnant, and while her husband was out of town or away from his house, she gave birth; and as Fray Miguel Sacristán, a Franciscan friar who was guardian in the said town, was passing by, they called him so that he might pour water on the said child, baptizing him; and the said Fray Miguel did in fact baptize the said child, and the said woman did not inform her husband of the said baptism, and they arranged for the said child to be baptized a second time in the town of Santa Fe and for the said Don Juan Manso to be his godfather, in order to confute the said husband's

suspicions that the said Don Juan Manso was having an indecent relationship with his wife; and they did in fact bring the said child to the said town and arranged for the baptism, and the said Don Juan Manso, reluctant to be the said child's godfather while he had an unlawful relationship with the said child's mother and intended to continue having it, said to the said Fray Miguel Sacristán, how might this be, and how, when the said child had already been baptized, were they to baptize it anew, and the said Fray Miguel replied, "Go on, hush, you don't understand these things"; and they did in fact go to the christening.[16]

She wrote a long allegation against Inés de Anaya and her daughter, Ana Rodríguez, that detailed Inés's alleged indecent relationship with the father of another servant and her use of love magic made from menstrual blood and chocolate. Underlying Doña Teresa's written transcript were her suspicions and the intrigues that strained her relationships with the Hispanic and Apache Indian women who were servants in her Santa Fe home:

> Two women—one of them a servant of hers named Josefa, the wife of Pedro de Arteaga, now deceased, and she does not recall who was the other—told this confessor that when Inés de Anaya and her daughter Ana Rodríguez (and the said Inés de Anaya is married to a certain Rodríguez, and the daughter is also married, to Ambrosio Sáenz) were down by the river of the said town, they quarreled with María, the wife of Juan de la Vega, who just now came to this city with the carts; and the said Inés de Anaya and her daughter told the said María that she should keep still, that she was an Apacha, which means a descendant of Apache Indians, to which the said María replied that they were the sort of women who, when she was little, the said Inés de Anaya had relations with her father, Miguel de Hinojos, and that as she was a little girl, she would carry messages from her father to the said Inés, and that the aforesaid would wash the blood out of her chemises, which was her menstrual blood, and would make chocolate for her said father with it to keep him from leaving her. It may be that they told this to this confessor not because it is true but to please her, knowing that she disliked the said Inés and Ana because they were wicked. And this is what she knows and can declare to ease her conscience; and at this time nothing else occurs to her.[17]

Don Pedro ordered her back to her cell and told her to reexamine the matter and to tell the truth. When she requested her fifth hearing a week later, on June 22, she amplified her recollection about the baptism of the child sired by Don Juan Manso and the complicity of Governor Diego de Peñalosa in the cover-up of the two baptisms. She recalled, with characteristic certainty, that when Don Juan Manso was governor of New Mexico he swore oaths against the Lord. She remembered that Francisco de León took the name of the Lord in vain, but she delivered the most dramatic testimony against Fray Salvador Guerra. She recounted the rumors that Fray Salvador (Witness 25) had committed terrible crimes against the "Moqui" when he served in their village.

> She also heard that Fray Salvador Guerra, a Franciscan friar in the said kingdom, when he was guardian among the Humanas in the provinces of Moqui, had most cruelly whipped some Indians and after the whipping had poured boiling lard on them, and that one of the Indians died as a result of this punishment. She does not know what became of the said Fray Salvador Guerra after this.[18]

She concluded this fifth hearing by requesting that the Inquisition officials account for a leather case containing clothing that was not delivered to her in Mexico City. Again, her recall of the details of what was in the case may not have been what the tribunal hoped to hear. At a time when they were anticipating her admission of wrongdoing, they could hardly have cared about her lost clothing. But the clerk dutifully transcribed her testimony and she was ordered back to her cell:

> She also states that when she was brought to this Holy Office she brought along in a cart a large leather case containing some items of clothing, to wit: two petticoats of domestic wool with five adornments of black wool lace; one underwaistcoat of plain scarlet cloth; a woman's bodice of carmine damask with gold adornments on a green satin border; a coarse woolen petticoat belonging to her little mulatto, and some small chemises and bodices belonging to the said mulatto; and a small pillow and other items of small value; which case was being transported on a separate cart that Fray Juan Ramírez called Elena's cart, after a cook called Elena whom he was bringing on it; and when the chief bailiff was asked about this confessor's clothing, the said Father Fray Juan Ramírez stated that the said case was being transported on the said cart and the order was given to take it off, and the girl Cristina, the servant of this [confessor], said that it had been taken off; and when her clothing was examined in this Tribunal, she said that she was missing the said case, and the warden replied that it had not been brought; and now, when she asked the said warden for some things from the said case, he replies that it was never brought to him, and she mentions this so that it may be sought and brought; and for the time being she can think of nothing else to declare.[19]

On July 5, 1663, Doña Teresa requested another hearing, this time petitioning that the case be concluded rapidly so that potential New Mexico witnesses would not depart from Mexico City before they could come to her defense or at least speak to the substance of her claims against enemies in New Mexico:

> She declared that she has requested it [another hearing] in order to state that with the greatest care and diligence, unable to sleep, she has recalled her whole life and whether in the course of it she has said or done anything contrary to our holy Catholic faith, and by God's mercy she has found nothing of which to accuse herself, and she therefore believes that her suffering must be due to some false testimony brought against her by some persons in New Mexico because of hostility toward her; and because if this were true it will be necessary for her to offer her defense and she has no one on whom to base it other than the persons who at this time have come from New Mexico, who at present must be in this city, she asks and entreats this Holy Tribunal that her case may be resolved with dispatch before they leave, or that they be ordered not to leave until they have been questioned in her defense.[20]

After delivering this impassioned appeal for justice, she asked the tribunal again to give her the black dress and cloak that were among her embargoed possessions. She explained that while it was certainly rather formal for prison garb, she felt the black dress and cloak were appropriate for her present condition. The inquisitor inspector considered her request and ordered the dress brought to her, but denied her the cloak. He reasoned that the cloak provided by the Inquisition prison preserved her anonymity and was adequate coverage. When the jailers brought her dress, they also requested permission of the court to move her possessions to drier conditions as the holding place was low and humid.

When another month passed with still no resolution of her case, Doña Teresa requested another hearing, her seventh before Don Pedro. She was clearly desperate when she appeared on August 1 before the inquisitors. This time, she pleaded for expediency, given what she described as her precarious health and well-being:

> She declared that it is true that she has requested a hearing, in order to advise that she is disconsolate, because, as she suffers so from a heart ailment she has been more affected by her great affliction, and she is very sorrowful and distraught and has been on the verge of committing an irrational act imperiling her life.[21]

She again asserted her innocence and continued to defend her actions as a consequence of the danger and hostility she had endured in New Mexico.

Her testimony was becoming more and more agitated as she related how the friars had conspired to discredit her husband, and the attempts of Governor Peñalosa to extract more payment and property to conclude Governor López de Mendizábal's residencia. Doña Teresa's testimony at this hearing is a little confusing; it is sometimes difficult to distinguish when or where an event occurred or whom she is accusing of which crime. She accused Fray Luis Martínez and several other friars of murdering Indian women who failed to perform household tasks properly for them or who threatened to reveal sexual favors solicited and abuses committed by the friars. As she concluded what must have been an emotional hearing, she again asked for her cloak. Before ordering her back to her cell, Inquisitor Inspector Don Pedro tried to calm her with an oration on the fairness of the proceedings and a reminder of the importance of faith in the Lord:

> The Inquisitor Inspector told her that she should be very patient, bearing in mind that when this Holy Tribunal arrests someone, if it [turns out to] be due to falsehoods and knavery, this Holy Tribunal restores the reputation of the person who had been imprisoned as fully as he may request, and it is pleased and consoled at seeing that his innocence prevails and that those who testified against him are punished; and if perhaps there is guilt, one should consider it good fortune to undergo these travails to satisfy Our Lord; that she should trust in His Divine goodness, for an effort will be made to procure her relief in all things without any consideration other than that which we ought to feel for Our Lord.[22]

Doña Teresa asked the inquisitor inspector for a prayer book that was among her embargoed possessions and it was brought to her, but the cloak was not. On August 7 she asked for sewing supplies: four yards of fine buckram, twenty-five yards of imitation gold trim, one ounce of buff silk, four yards of narrow silk ribbon, some thread, and two dozen bobbins for making lace.[23] Perhaps she concluded that if she was not going to be given her cloak, she could embellish the one the court made her wear.

On the one-year anniversary of her arrest, August 27, 1663, Doña Teresa, who was described as being in a state of near despondency by Inquisition Secretary Pedro de Arteeta, asked for a hearing to plead again for resolution of her case and that of her husband:

> She stated that she has asked for this hearing to declare that this morning marked a year since this confessor and her husband Don Bernardo were arrested by order of this Holy Office in the town of Santa Fe in New

Mexico, and after so much time she finds herself lacking strength and patience to bear her confinement, the more so with the chagrin caused by her poor husband's, who she thinks must also be so lacking, all because of false testimony and their persecutors, which the friars in that kingdom have been and are.[24]

One month later she again appeared before the tribunal to correct two minor errors in her testimony, adding the name of someone she had not previously recalled, and recalling the correct name of another witness who had been arrested by the Holy Office. She implored the inquisitor to understand that as a women she might not know what she should have declared; a clever ploy but one that did not serve her. In her most expressive testimony, she asked for more paper and ink so that she could examine her conscience in her cell and write what was needed:

> She has also requested this hearing to beseech this Holy Tribunal to have compassion for her, who, though a woman of distinction, has suffered so long an imprisonment, coming as a prisoner from so great a distance in so long a voyage, and then in this Holy Office, without her case advancing; that she asks and entreats in God's name that she be succored in her travails; and some things that she must declare so that her case may be accurately investigated, she cannot declare before this Holy Tribunal because of the affliction she feels in its presence. [She asks] that she be given paper and ink so that she may consult her memory in her cell and write what is needed; and this is why she has requested this hearing. And the said inquisitor inspector told her to trust in Our Lord, that the truth will come out and that the delay in her case has not been deliberate but due to necessity, for the Lord commands us not to harm our neighbor, and the intention is to comply with this precept; and he ordered that she be given a fold of paper, ink, and a pen, so that she may write what she says she has to declare, keeping in mind Our Lord, who is pleased only by the truth; and if she should need more paper she should ask for it and it will be given to her; and she was in fact given the said fold of paper, rubricated by me, the present secretary, and the warden was ordered to give her an inkpot and a pen for six days.[25]

In early October she requested more paper to record her thoughts, and then on October 5, 1663, she requested a hearing to present her extensive writings—eight pages in all—to the inquisitor inspector. Presumably her growing tome was still not what the inquisitors wanted. There was no confession of her sins, no admission of her guilt. This time she presented claims against Manuel de Noriega, who had been her guard in New Mexico and on the road south. He was called by Governor Peñalosa twice to testify about what Doña Teresa might have said or done while she was in custody. Noriega had been a secretary to Don Bernardo until he became a scribe for Governor Peñalosa. He was also the guard assigned to Doña Teresa and accompanied her as far as Zacatecas, where he became ill and had to stay behind. She testified that he had sworn to remember everything she had said and she feared that he had given false testimony against her. She wrote of her despair when, after being held in a dungeon at Santo Domingo for a month and five days, she was released to Noriega, an enemy of her husband. She recalled Noriega's imprudence and his threatening manner when he rebuked her for scolding a slave named Magdalena, and wanting the Holy Office to know how badly behaved their guard had been, she testified against him:

> The day that I scolded her he came to me angry because I was doing so, and among many other indignities and discourtesies he heaped insults on me, and coming up to the step of the coach and with each word saying, "Do you understand me?" spending a long time insulting me, foaming at the mouth and leaning toward me as though he wanted to attack me, until, because of this rudeness and his many threats against me I told him to be advised that the custodian had informed him . . . and that if he did not show me the requisite respect, I was gathering witnesses to complain to this Holy Tribunal about everything. And in short, Your Honor, the guards served only for this and to stroll about and do as they wished.[26]

Noriega became the thirteenth witness to testify against her. She also wrote accusations against Diego Melgarejo, a former servant in her Santa Fe household. She claimed that while on the road, Melgarejo sent her word that if there was any testimony attributed to him, she should know that he did not speak against the governor and Doña Teresa, and that he did not know how to read or write. But, of course, he was one of the witnesses who testified against them, giving details of their eating bread on fast days and meat on Fridays, and that they washed their clothes and bathed on Fridays. She wrote that when Governor Diego de Peñalosa spoke to her in the church in Santa Fe, he assured her that if they paid one thousand pesos to Don Juan Manso, he would drop the case against them. And, she stated, Governor Peñalosa suggested that she transfer their property to him so it would not be embargoed by the royal treasury or taken by the friars. She wrote of the desperate attempts she had made on behalf of her husband for him not be turned over to the friars, but to be allowed to go back to Mexico City in the caravan. She claimed that after the audit of Don Bernardo's property was made, Governor Peñalosa increased his fee to settle the residencia, requesting a huge payment of ten thousand pesos in property. She composed her response passionately, quoting the oaths and curses that her friends had heaped on Governor Peñalosa on the night of her arrest in Santa Fe:

> And according to what was told to this confessor by Antonia González, a widow, resident of Santa Fe, the said Don Diego [Romero] called this confessor and the said Don Bernardo Jewish dogs, so saying in the house of Antonio de Salas in the presence of the wife and daughters of the aforesaid, and she does not know whether of other persons as well. And she also declares that the night when the said Don Diego was in the house of this confessor, while Doña Catalina de Zamora, wife of Diego Romero and resident of Santa Fe, was with her, as the said Don Diego walked about the great hall he said to this confessor, "Ah, my esteemed Doña Teresa, if I could help it, I'd give the blood of my veins; a curse on the duties of office here in the Indies!" And then the said Doña Catalina said fairly loudly, so that the said Don Diego could have heard it, "A curse on you! How is your office to blame for your evil deeds? After you have thought them up and carried them out and been the instigator of them all, now you want to give satisfaction. God give you the punishment you deserve!" But the said Don Diego did not reply to this, if perchance he heard it.[27]

Doña Teresa accused the friars of trying her for the crime of being the governor's wife. She reported that they threatened witnesses into providing false testimony, and that they mocked and humiliated her and the governor at every chance following their arrest:

> Fray Fernando de Monroy said in Juan Griego's house, which he said twice on separate occasions. One time Josefa, the wife of Pedro de Arteaga, told me about it; and the other time—a few days, two or three, before we were arrested—Antonia González, who was present in Juan Griego's house, said that he said he hoped to God that he would see even my chemises publicly sold on the square; and they say that Juan Griego said to him, "But Father, in what way has Doña Teresa offended your reverence?" And he answered, "In no way at all," and he repeated, "Well, why do you hate her like that?" and he had replied, "Well, hasn't her husband quarreled with me? Let her pay, too, since she is his wife."[28]
> . . . when Domingo González the Galician told us that someone had gone to his house to summon his wife and him, but especially her, to go testify against us, and he asked that person, what was his wife to testify to, when she did not know me and had never seen me except in church, and he said, "How do you want her to testify if she doesn't know her?"; and he

asked whether they had testified, and that person replied that they had, all of them, and they were many; and he had replied, "Well, that's your business, and you will bear the consequences," and he had replied, "No, the fathers say that the Tribunal of the Holy Office does not reveal its witnesses; a fine thing it would be if everyone knew who the witnesses were. Who would then testify in matters as grave as those of the Inquisition? And so that their identity may not be known, they never reveal it."

. . . the day after I was arrested Fray Nicolás de Freitas could find nothing better to do than come to peek through a hole in the door and laugh uproariously, all the while running back and forth to do this; and not satisfied with this, he came in to tell me, with a great show of piety, "Lord, Lord, how the mighty are fallen!," repeating it many times along with other things in the same vein; and much the same happened to me with Fray Salvador Guerra and Fray Alonso de Posada.[29]

She implored the tribunal to believe her, as she wrote the truth and acted from the depths of her Christian faith:

And it is so sure a fact that all the [testimony] they have brought against us is malice, Your Honor, and not offenses of ours—for by the grace of God we are Catholic Christians and would give a thousand lives before doing or saying anything contrary to our Holy Catholic Faith—that by God's mercy it allows no doubt whatsoever that this is the wickedness of the enemies we gained from resentment of the exercise of the King's justice, because my husband blocked offenses against God where so many are committed, and acts of treason against the King, of which past punishment is evidence, and the old malice and hatred continue; and the opinion of the residents shows that what I am saying is true.[30]

She ordered more paper be brought to her on October 13 and continued to explain the injustice and conspiracy against her. She described the attempts of their allies to reach them with information about false statements they were forced by Peñalosa or the friars to make against Don Bernardo and Doña Teresa. At the end of October 1663, fourteen months after her arrest, she pleaded with the inquisitors to have someone knowledgeable advise her:

I ask and beseech Your Honor that neither now nor at any time it be to my detriment if in this document or that [submitted] the other day or in any other thing, I should err in the manner of writing or in the words, or if I should do so in anything else, because I am an afflicted, disconsolate, unhappy, and solitary woman who, Your Honor, is undergoing the greatest travails and sorrows, in addition to misfortunes that no human creature has ever undergone or suffered, and I am not accustomed to them and have no one who might advise me what I ought to do or how to do it, nor do I understand any subject in any way or manner.[31]

Charged with Imprudence, Apostasy, and Heresy

Doña Teresa was given one more opportunity, on October 26, 1663, to clear her conscience. She presented another note to the court docket in which she accused Governor Don Diego de Peñalosa of fomenting false testimony against her and her husband among their household staff and others in New Mexico.[32] Her declarations against Peñalosa were added to the dossier that would become the basis for his trial before the Inquisition in the coming years, but she offered no compromise or admission of her own guilt. And so on October 27, Inquisition Prosecutor Dr. Rodrigo Ruiz de Cepeda Martínez y Portillo lodged the long-awaited criminal complaint against Doña Teresa. Ruiz no doubt read the charges to the court, and seated on a hard chair or bench before the tribunal, Doña Teresa would finally hear the accusations. She still did not know the names of the witnesses, but the observations could only have come from servants, close associates, and those who she already knew were mortal enemies of her husband or held a grudge against her. Some of the charges were lodged against Doña Teresa alone, and others against her and Governor López de Mendizábal, although he was also tried separately. In many ways, the governor was tried twice, in his own right and as her husband in this case. Before reading all forty-one counts, the Inquisition prosecutor opened with a summary of the charges:

> Although the aforesaid is a baptized and confirmed Christian and as such has enjoyed the privileges and prerogatives that good and true Christians ought to and do enjoy, she has apostasized from our holy Catholic faith and the law of the Gospel, wickedly and perfidiously contravening the declaration she made at her holy baptism and turning to observance of the defunct and obsolete law of Moses, observing the rites and ceremonies of Judaism and believing that she would be saved thereby, and committing other offenses indicative of her impudence and apostasy, and not complying with the precepts of our Holy Mother the Roman Catholic Church at the times when she was obliged to do so to the scandal of the Christian people, and preventing other persons from complying with the said precepts and punishing a member of her household because she observed her performing acts of piety, of which I accuse her in general, as well as of impenitently and perjuriously denying her guilt.[33]

Counts 1, 2, and 3 related to her personal hygiene, and in some cases also referred to Don Bernardo's ablutions. Count 1 accused her and her husband of observing a special ceremony of washing on Friday evenings. Doña Teresa in particular seemed to make a special ritual of washing her hair, cutting her nails, and changing the linen on the beds on Friday. The prosecution judged it suspicious that she would lock herself secretly in her chamber for hours, "pretending that she shut herself in to clean her private parts." Prosecutor Ruiz linked his suspicions to his conclusions, arguing, with circular reasoning, that her seclusion "must be judged unfavorably because of the stigma that falls on her because of that Judaic ceremony." In count 2, they were further accused of not washing on any other day; they bathed so faithfully on Fridays that "this constitutes a strong indication that they were observant Jews . . . as they wished to celebrate the following day, Saturday, as a holiday." Further, the prosecution stressed,

> [On] Saturdays she would habitually adorn and groom herself as though to mark and celebrate and observe the day; and since this is the one that in the defunct law of Moses was to be observed, and that its followers respect so punctiliously, it is clear that this accused is one of them and shares in the errors of the Judaizers.[34]

Counts 4 and 5 accused the governor and Doña Teresa of drinking chocolate on the afternoon of Good Friday in 1661. Drawing from the testimony of their household staff and the web of witnesses who had testified about this incident, the charge claimed that partaking in chocolate on such an occasion was a demonstration of their irreverence. The prosecutor summarized several different witnesses here in relating these two counts, focusing on the couple's indifference to or perhaps mockery of the procession, the uncharacteristic speed with which they stopped their chocolate drinking, and the speed and timing with which Doña Teresa placed a cap on Don Bernardo's head, and, as was stated by some of the witnesses, the couple may have even donned smocks.[35]

The next count, number 6, related to the grave offense of her owning, reading, and laughing while reading a book in a "foreign and unintelligible language." Because the language was not Spanish, and because she could have read "ordinary books" in Spanish for her devotions or entertainment, the inquisitors suspected that the book might contain things or teachings contrary to the Catholic faith, and could have been heretical. In their view, Doña Teresa's lack of charity and her behavior, including her laughing while reading and her condemning another who could not read this work, constituted wicked deeds. They argued that the book was allegedly about love and was written in Italian, but until they examined the book to determine that it did not "contain polluted teachings reproved by our mother the church," they would let the accusation stand. She stood accused, it seems, of following and professing heretical ideas that they might find in the book.

Count 7 dealt with the allegation that while she and her husband were in El Parral during Easter of 1659 they failed to comply with the Church's mandate to make a yearly confession and take communion. The accusation led to the conclusion that their scandalous behavior seemed to rise from an obstinate wish to repudiate the efficacy and necessity of the holy sacrament. They were specifically accused of heresy arising from the Thirteenth Council of Trent concerning the Sacrament of the Eucharist. Counts 8 and 9 elaborated on the events of what the prosecutor termed their "voyage" north to New Mexico. Count 8 concerned the failure of the governor and Doña Teresa to leave their coach to celebrate the service of masses that took place in the Holy Week celebrations. It was further noted that they kept the curtains drawn in their coach while it was parked in front of the church. This was cited as evidence of their irreligious and irreverent spirit. Count 9 claimed that others noticed this failure to attend mass or to hear the service, in contravention to the teaching of the Church, which requires that they show gratitude for the benefit of redemption.

Their lack of devotion to the Catholic Church, as well as their mockery and contempt for the monastic order, were the substance of Count 10. Governor López de Mendizábal and Doña Teresa were known to have shown great amusement when they heard a story told by Juan González Lobón, who allegedly said that he would sooner be buried in Lucifer's hide than in the habit of St. Francis. Evidently they had heard the story some years before they arrived in New Mexico, but often called on González to retell this story for their amusement and as a mockery of the faithful.

Count 11 stemmed from a comment that Doña Teresa made in August 1659, during a dinner, when she said that images in the church in Santa Fe were not as beautiful as ones she had seen elsewhere. Her comment was that the image of San Antonio de Padua was not handsome but looked like a local official. This exchange was seen as being irreverent toward San Antonio and suggested that she failed to show proper veneration for the saint.

Doña Teresa and her husband were accused in counts 12 and 13 of failing to be diligent examples to their staff in matters of religious practice. They were accused of not requiring staff to attend confession and communion, and of failing to reply with customary praise for the Blessed Sacrament when they were offered the opportunity on waking or receiving the benefits of food. Not only did they not cross themselves, they did not say grace before meals, and the governor seemed to grimace when the staff clearing the table praised the Blessed Sacrament. They seemed, this charge concluded, to exhibit "execrable vices" showing no signs of being Christians. In count 19, the prosecutor reported that when they awoke and a servant greeted them with pious greetings, Doña Teresa never answered as prescribed with the word "Forever," and Don Bernardo seemed to respond with a hissing sound. The prosecutor concluded that this was "blameworthy and not very Catholic in spirit."

Sleeping alone in their private quarters was the basis of count 14 against Doña Teresa and her husband. Only a young servant girl was permitted to sleep in their room, and they never allowed anyone to enter their bedroom without first calling out to be admitted. They even allegedly whipped their maids if they entered the room without permission. The prosecutor granted that sleeping alone in their quarters was not a crime in and of itself, but in combination with their other actions it was suspect:

> Although this action is morally neutral and insufficient in itself to arouse suspicion, yet it does not dispel the suspicion that arises from the wicked qualities of this accused and her husband, for it is easy to understand that the said care could be a stratagem to avoid being observed in the evil deeds that they might engage in when alone.[36]

Counts 15, 16, 17, and 18 focused particular attention on the abuses that Doña Teresa or the governor committed against the servants and enslaved persons on their staff who requested permission to attend communion or mass. In one case they were accused of whipping a black slave who fasted on a Wednesday in devotion to Our Lady of Carmel. They evidently ordered her to remove the religious scapular she was wearing, calling it an apron, and then beat her, calling the woman a deceitful and hypocritical bitch. Such language and actions convinced the prosecutor that Doña Teresa had a "perverse spirit." Further, count 16 claimed that they sometimes berated the servants for going to church or scolded them when they came back late. In one memorable instance on Christmas Day in 1660, they allegedly sent others into the church to fetch a maid from her prayers. In sum, they placed so many obstacles in the way of devotions for their staff that the prosecutor concluded "that they considered the devotions of the Christian people to be something of no consequence, which is powerful evidence of the evil doctrines harbored in their breasts."[37] In count 21 the prosecutor recounted the accusation, made as well in count 18, that they scolded another servant for her religious devotion. This, the prosecutor found to be evidence that they were "impious, injudicious and scandalous."

Count 20 claimed that in October 1661, one of the servants found that the accused and her husband kept some images of the saints in a pantry where they also kept rubbish. This was listed as clear proof of a heretical act showing lack of veneration for the saints. Count 22 stated that neither the accused nor her husband were ever heard to call on the intersession of the Lord, nor the Blessed Mother, nor did Doña Teresa ever speak of devotion to any saint.

Their obvious disdain for the Church and their failure to attend mass with any regularity gave rise to the charges leveled against them in count 23. It noted that they "went to mass as though obliged against their will," that it was common knowledge in Santa Fe that months went by between their attendance at church services. Further, in this count the prosecutor noted that neither illness nor inclement weather nor distance from the church could account for their failures to observe the obligations of the faithful, but rather their actions were blameworthy and indicated "contempt for the precepts of our Holy Mother the Church."

Counts 24 and 25 concerned their failure to observe the rules of abstinence on holy days and during Lent. The prosecution charged them with mockery of the precepts and described in detail how the governor and Doña Teresa drank chocolate and ate toast that was made from a special loaf. Here the prosecutor may have been implying that the bread itself was part of some unnamed Jewish rite.[38]

Count 25 alleged that they ate meat during Holy Week in 1659 when they were in El Parral and continued to eat meat on Fridays in Santa Fe. The charge concluded with a strong accusation that their failure to abstain from eating on holy days and their rare presence in the church were proof of their alignment with heretics:

> It seems they agree with the heretics who reject the choice of foods that our mother the Church has made for fast days and Fridays; and the violation of the Church's precept accords with the transgressions of paganism in failing to render the required obedience to the Holy Apostolic See and rejecting the approved rites and customs of our mother the Church, [and]

gives rise to the said suspicion, which with an accused like this one, is powerful, when in addition, as is her case, she rejects the holy sacraments of the Church, not partaking of them when she was obliged to do so, and her rare presence in church, circumstances that reinforce the suspicion that eating meat on fast days raises against one who does so, and this is noted by the learned men who deal with this subject.[39]

In count 26, Ruiz again used their failure to confess and their disdain for the clergy as proof of heresy, and used increasingly inflammatory language to show Doña Teresa's own words—about her failure to confess to priests who might reveal her confession—as evidence of her crime. He also argued that if a priest revealed her confession she could have asked the Holy Office to investigate this lapse, something he believed she might have done simply for the pleasure of further impugning the reputation of the clergy:

> She never wanted to confess when she was at services because the priests and friars revealed confessions, and that this had happened to her at San Juan de los Llanos, and so she spoke from experience, in which one sees cunning heretical trickery, namely, to cast blame on the ministers of the Church so that this accused might extenuate and conceal her own blame-worthiness; and it shows the special hatred that those of her stripe feel toward the clergy, loathing them because they are most especially dedicated to the worship of God.
>
> . . . and furthermore the insincerity of the said excuse is plain to see, for if what God forbid had happened, since that is a matter to be investigated by this Holy Office, this accused would no doubt have mentioned it at her hearings, if not out of obligation, then for the pleasure that the punishment of such a clergyman would have brought her; and the fact that she has not done so shows that this is a false calumny that she brings against the said clergyman.[40]

In Count 27, Prosecutor Ruiz takes her to task not only for her "bad habit of speaking ill of the priests," but because she gossiped about a priest who she claimed had died with his mistress and their eleven or twelve children around his bedside. This charge argued that she inflicted injury on the said priest and also that she believed she could defame her neighbors with impunity.

Counts 28 and 29 accused Doña Teresa and her husband of failing to inspire their household with the fear of God, reverence for the teachings of the saints, and compliance with the precepts of the Church. They stood accused of failing to show devotion of any kind, and of their special disregard for the rosary. She was accused of shutting the rosary away in her desk, and the governor of telling people who were wearing the rosary to "get those baubles off their necks." In sum, their words of contempt were scandalous and "hurtful to the pious ears of the faithful."

And reminded of her desk, Ruiz lodged count 30 against Doña Teresa for securing the middle drawer of her desk. This charge does not cite a specific cause of action, but seems to be an indicator of her hiding something in that drawer. Ruiz did not deem that the person who consistently tried to open the secured drawer might herself be guilty of a crime or something highly suspect.

Counts 31 and 32 charged Doña Teresa with the practice of magic and making a compact with the devil, heady matters that the Inquisition was especially on alert to recognize and prosecute. Women's use of chocolate, herbs, and menstrual blood to produce powerful love magic was a practice that many colonial European women learned from their maids in Mexico and other New World colonies. Doña Teresa too was accused of possessing powders with unnatural efficacy and of collecting her menstrual blood for her nefarious acts:

> This accused has added that of practicing magic and superstition, because in the month of October of the year '60 or '61 she told a certain person that she was once given some powders that would make her husband Don Bernardo love her, and that this accused scattered them by his feet and saw that the next day he was changed, without saying where or in what place she practiced the said superstition or sorcery, which comprises a pact with the Devil, in addition to the false belief that this accused showed herself to have in the said powders, attributing to them an effect that they could not by nature produce.
>
> And the preceding count [31] is corroborated by the reports that this accused would collect her menstrual blood and keep it in a silver cup for an unknown purpose, and none can be supposed other than one having to do with superstition or witchcraft, for no more favorable one can or should be thought of for keeping such filth.[41]

In count 33 she was accused of being insincere and therefore suspect for putting onion peels on her feet. She testified that it was for the relief of corns, but the prosecutor deemed this explanation immaterial.

Count 34 dealt again with the defiant posture Doña Teresa and the governor took toward the Church. On September 25, 1661, a general edict of faith was read in Santa Fe that urged all persons who "had reached the age of puberty to attend under pain of anathema." This edict invited all who had sinned against the Church, or knew someone who had, to come forward and ease their conscience. Neither Don Bernardo nor Doña Teresa was ill, according to the charge, but they failed to attend this holy day of obligation, and the prosecutor concluded that their absence showed a lack of respect for the commands of the Holy Office and a failure of faith.

When Doña Teresa was first confined to a prison cell, as she wept in anguish over her fate and that of her husband, she committed the acts that were the grounds of counts 35 and 36. Her tears and inquiries, as well as her request that one of the priests bring her a box of letters from her home were taken as signs of guilt and more pointedly of concealing crimes that might have fallen under the jurisdiction of the Holy Office. The prosecutor gave what was represented as a verbatim quote, undoubtedly based on the testimony of Fray Salvador Guerra. He had used the same words in his testimony about Doña Teresa's first nights in custody when she implored the friar to tell her if her husband had been arrested and where he was being held. The charge also referred to the curiosity she aroused in Fray Salvador when she pressed him repeatedly to return to her house to bring her the two letters she kept in the box of chocolate at the foot of her bed.[42]

Throughout the testimony and accusations against Doña Teresa ran a recurrent leitmotif: she was characterized as cruel, uncharitable, and harsh in word and deed. And yet, the charges in count 37 stem from her trying to save a girl from being whipped for carrying messages from Doña Teresa to "a certain person close to her," presumably her husband. While in the pueblo of Sandia on October 9, 1662, Fray Alonso ordered a girl whipped for carrying a message from Doña Teresa to this unnamed person. When Doña Teresa stepped forward to save the girl from the whipping by accepting blame, it was not interpreted as an act of kindness, but as more evidence of her disobedient and defiant manner. In many ways the language of this count is a summary of the charges and the behavior that the Holy Office found so objectionable in Doña Teresa, a woman who would not submit to authority or demur even in these most dire circumstances. Count 37 charges that her strident behavior and "womanish chatter" were among the most serious allegations she faced.

> She was insufficiently compliant with church authorities and . . . that [she] seem[ed] to deny the coercive power vested in this Holy Tribunal and its ministers, and that falsely suggests that contumacy and disobedience do not suffice to merit lawfully imposed punishment, in addition to

which the foregoing words are seen to be injurious to and contemptuous of the ministers of this Holy Tribunal and their orders, and show this accused to be proud, haughty, and obstinate.[43]

Counts 38, 39, and 40 point to her continued challenges to the authority of the Holy Office and the insults she hurled at the friars while she was en route to Mexico City. At least part of her fury stemmed from having glimpsed her husband's prison cart while they were traveling on a winding section of the Camino Real, but in the prosecutor's mind the insults were evidence of her spiritual imperfection and her inability to understand that the Holy Office would not have arrested her had she not committed sins. The charge condemns Doña Teresa for her "scandalous imprecations, born of a haughty and presumptuous spirit." The charge concludes that she had notably and brazenly offended the Catholic Church,

> and although this accused has been repeatedly admonished in charity and with fatherly loving kindness to declare and confess the truth, she has not done so, persevering in her insolent denial, so that she is not only unworthy of but incapable of receiving the compassion habitual in this Holy Tribunal.[44]

As the prosecutor summarized his case in count 41, he found Doña Teresa accused of offenses she concealed or suppressed with malice, and of committing crimes that could only have stemmed from her observing the forbidden rites and ceremonies of Judaism, and of practicing witchcraft and superstition. If that was not enough, he added to the list of charges her insults and injury to the Holy Office. Then, in accordance with the instructions of the court, the prosecutor sought the permission of the inquisitors to use torture to extract confessions.[45] He asked that she be condemned to a sentence of anathema and that the greatest and most severe penalties be applied to her punishment.

> I accuse her forthwith, both of observing the rites and ceremonies of Judaism, and of being profoundly suspect in matters of faith, and of having an unfavorable opinion of the holy sacraments and of their efficacy and of the power of the keys [of heaven and hell] that resides in the Church, believing that the prohibition of meat on Fridays and fast days is not binding, and as a practitioner of witchcraft, superstitious, insulting to the clerical estate and to this Holy Tribunal and its procedures, and as impenitent, insolent, and unconfessing. For which reasons I ask and beseech Your Honor to receive this my indictment, and issuing a sentence accepting my

account as truthful, declare my intent to be adequately proven and this accused to have committed and perpetrated the crimes of which I have accused her, therefore also declaring her to have incurred a sentence of anathema, condemning the said Doña Teresa to the greatest and most severe penalties imposed on such offenders by the common law, the bulls of the Apostolic See, and the instructions and writs of this Holy Office, executing them on the aforesaid, relinquishing her person to the secular arm and justice, and declaring that her property has incurred confiscation from the day on which she committed the said crimes of Judaism and applying the said property to His Majesty's treasury, as punishment of this accused and as an example to others. Furthermore, should my intent not be considered adequately proven, and not otherwise, I ask and beseech Your Honors to order that the said Doña Teresa de Aguilera y Roche be put to the question with torture, to be continually and repeatedly applied to her person until she may fully declare and confess the truth. I ask that justice be done, and I swear as prescribed by law that this my accusation does not spring from malice, and if I should do so more formally I submit it as so done, and in all things necessary, etc.[46]

With this dramatic conclusion, Dr. Rodrigo Ruiz de Cepeda Martínez y Portillo signed the charges and consigned Doña Teresa's fate to her defense team and the tribunal of the Holy Office. Doña Teresa had listened to the reading of the charges for several days when Ruiz concluded on October 29, 1663. She and her defense lawyer were given three days to consider her first response. By the time Ruiz had finished reading this writ, could she have even been listening to the litany of sins, transgressions, judgments, and attacks on her character? The record does not contain a description of her demeanor at this moment, but she must have been stunned by the power of this writ. She began almost immediately to craft her oral and written defense.

Plate 1. Young Woman with a Harpsichord, artist unknown,
Mexico, 1735–50.
(Denver Art Museum Collection, gift of Frederick and Jan Mayer, 2014.209.
Photograph courtesy of the Denver Art Museum.)

Plate 2. Our Lady of Sorrows, with paraffin face and hands,
clothing of silk and gold thread.
(History Collection, New Mexico History Museum, Department of
Cultural Affairs, Santa Fe. Photograph by Blair Clark.)

Plate 3. Enameled chinoiserie sewing box with silver handles and a carved
wooden spool for thread.
(History Collection, New Mexico History Museum, Department of Cultural Affairs,
Santa Fe. Photograph by Blair Clark.)

Plate 4. Escritorio, early 1700s writing desk with drawers.
(Courtesy of the Museum of Spanish Colonial Art, Spanish Colonial Arts Society, Inc.,
Santa Fe, New Mexico. Gift of Mrs. H. M. Greene. [1956.89.] Photo by Jack Parsons.)

Plate 5. Puebla blue-on-white-style Majolica chocolatero.
(History Collection, New Mexico History Museum, Department of Cultural Affairs,
Santa Fe. Photograph by Blair Clark.)

Plate 6. Chocolate cup, coconut hull with silver handles and base.
(History Collection, New Mexico History Museum, Department of Cultural
Affairs, Santa Fe. Photograph by Blair Clark.)

Plate 7. Copper chocolate pot
(courtesy of Josef Díaz and Dr. Malcolm Purdy)
and Japanese Imari porcelain cup
(History Collection, New Mexico History Museum, Department of Cultural Affairs,
Santa Fe; photograph by Blair Clark).

Plate 8. *Birth of the Virgin*, Luis Juárez, painting on copper, circa 1620. The painting shows a Mexican house interior with canopied bed and Moorish rug. (Denver Art Museum Collection, gift of Frederick and Jan Mayer, 2011.425. Photograph courtesy of the Denver Art Museum.)

Plate 9. Window of a Palace of the Inquisition
cell, Mexico City.
(Photograph by Gerald González.)

Plate 10. Talavera-style Majolica inkwell.
(History Collection, New Mexico History Museum,
Department of Cultural Affairs, Santa Fe. Photograph by
Blair Clark.)

CHAPTER FIVE

Taking Matters into Her Own Hands

AFTER FINALLY LEARNING THE CHARGES against her, Doña Teresa responded orally to the inquisitors at several hearings in late October 1663. She began with a restrained but powerful assertion. "Yes," she replied under oath, promising to testify and reply truthfully, "she was Doña Teresa Aguilera y Roche, but she did not know if she was the person mentioned in the indictment, because she was a Catholic Christian."[1] As she responded to the charges, count by count, she called on logic, memory, belief, and passion to explain her version of the events outlined in the accusations against her. Following her oral response she was afforded an attorney and was presented with the evidence against her. Doña Teresa was asked to choose an attorney from two identified for her by the court; however, with characteristic strategy, she also requested paper and pen to prepare her own response. In all, through more than a dozen hearings, and long delays caused by the illness of her attorney, she maintained a strong resolve, though at times the words she delivered before the court betrayed her unsteady emotions.

Responding to the Charges

The general instructions governing an Inquisition hearing anticipated that at this stage of the proceeding, the accused might persist in her innocence and simply deny the charges. But the instructions noted that the response phase was important because doing it any other way would result in "confusion and adds little clarity."[2] Doña Teresa used her response to bolster her arguments, denounce her still-unnamed detractors, and passionately proclaim the strength of her Catholic faith. She began her oral testimony on October 26, 1663.

Responding to the first three counts relating to her personal hygiene, she denied that she habitually bathed on Fridays, and asserted that when she shut herself in her room, it was only to wash her hair. She elaborated that she would not wash anything else, including her feet, nor would she cut her nails. She testified too that she often changed her clothes, especially her chemise, which she might change as often as three times per week, but denied that she participated in any special religious ceremony or observance while attending to her bath. She complained about the cold in New Mexico; it was even colder than Flanders, she asserted. As a result her hands often pained her, making it necessary to retreat to her quarters. She protested that she always combed her hair on Saturday, as all women did, since they would not have time to do so before mass on Sunday. She was emphatic in professing her faith and denied that her personal hygiene was "done so to observe the Law of Moses or any other, because she has been and is a Catholic Christian and would give a thousand lives for the holy Catholic Christian religion."[3]

In response to counts 4 and 5, regarding her lax observance of Good Friday, Doña Teresa painted a predictably different interpretation of the events than the accusations leveled by her servants. She claimed that she and the governor spent the first of the three Good Fridays when they lived in New Mexico in church. On the second Good Friday, she said, the governor was ill with gout and she suffered pain in her feet from the cold and so did not go to church, but she spent the day seated next to their bed reading the Passion of Our Lord Jesus Christ. During that afternoon, Doña Catalina de Zamora, wife of Diego Romero, came in to see them and remarked how good it was that Doña Teresa was reading the Passion. The only other people who were with them were two Indian servants who would not have known what they were doing. She testified emphatically that the Christians employed by them would have been in church, and that those servants working in the house would not have understood the significance of anything she and the governor were reading or doing. Further, she noted that there was nothing unusual in her husband changing his bonnet:

> Some unbaptized Indian women who, being still uncivilized, were incapable of noticing any of the things mentioned in this count, because all the Christian slaves and persons of her household had gone to church; and afterwards many people came in, because the procession had already gone by; and then they drank chocolate, because before there had been no one to prepare it; and she has no memory whatsoever of having got up to fetch a clean bonnet or putting it on her husband; and if she should have got up to fetch it and should have put it on him, it would have been by chance, so that he should have a clean bonnet, and for no other purpose or reason.[4]

Further, she observed that no one passing on the street could have seen them changing their clothes because the interior rooms were not visible from the street. She repeated fervently that she was a Catholic Christian and would live and die as such.

In reply to count 6, she defended herself for reading and laughing over a book written in the Tuscan language. She admitted that she owned a book written in Tuscan, and that she read it on occasion so that she would not forget the language that she learned as a young child. She identified the book as Ariosto, and said that it contained the story of Orlando Furioso. She described it to the court as a book of chivalry, containing "enchantments and wars, and sometimes she had to laugh while reading those things; and that the said book was left at her house, in the same room where she slept, in a little basket or sewing box."[5] She assured the inquisitors that the book did not contain anything contrary to "our holy faith," thus aligning herself strongly with the Catholic Church. The epic poem by Ludovico Ariosto, an Italian poet, contains forty-six cantos in thirty-eight thousand lines of verse. It is a story of unrequited love set amid the battles of Charlemagne, Orlando or Roland, and the Franks against the Saracens. Doña Teresa must have found it endlessly engaging, with its winding storyline and references to the landscapes of her Italian childhood.[6]

Doña Teresa then responded to counts 7, 8, and 9 regarding her alleged failure to attend mass in Parral while they traveled to New Mexico in 1659. She admitted that she did not make confession or receive communion during the time, but not out of contempt for her Christian obligations. On the journey to New Mexico she became gravely ill as they crossed the Río Florida, and when they reached Parral she suffered a miscarriage. She was so ill that she could not say whether or not Don Bernardo confessed or received communion. She fulfilled the obligation of attending mass when they reached the country of the Mansos farther north on the day of Corpus Christi, which would have been about two months later. She also admitted to hearing mass behind the closed door of her carriage, but not out of disrespect. When she was too ill to leave her carriage, she closed the shades out of modesty and for privacy. Then she could kneel on her bed and hear mass through the windows of the coach. She did not intend to offend the Lord's mercy, and if she had, then she said, "Let Him rather take away her life."[7]

As to count 10, she denied that her amusement over the words of Juan González Lobón, who said that he would sooner be buried in Lucifer's hide than in the habit of a Franciscan, was a form of blasphemy or mockery of the holy order. Rather, she explained, she and Don Bernardo found Lobón's words and deeds so nonsensical that they laughed at his antics. She also denied, as claimed in count 11, that she said the image of St. Anthony in the church at Santa Fe looked like the cabo (a military corporal), someone who was well-known in Santa Fe. She dismissed the idea, saying she had never said nor even imagined such a thing.

She denied the allegations of count 12, that she would not permit her servants to hear mass, make confession, or receive communion. Quite the contrary; she claimed to have taken them to church with her and witnessed their communion. Through Josefa, the servant in charge of the kitchen, she had notified the servants and slaves that they could eat no meat on Easter unless they had been to confession and taken communion. She claimed, contrary to charges in count 13, that she always responded to her servants with proper pious words:

> When her maid Josefa would come in to prepare chocolate in the morning while this confessor and Don Bernardo were in bed, she would say, "Praised be the Blessed Sacrament. God grant Your Honors a good day," and they would answer, "Forever," and they said the same when the table was cleared; and it would be hard for anyone to see whether they crossed themselves when going to bed and when getting up, and that they did always cross themselves and praised Our Lord.[8]

She concluded the first day of testimony by denying count 14 regarding the allegation that she had whipped a maid for entering the room where she and the governor slept. She stated for the record that her maids slept in her dressing room and that they could go in and out of the room through the bedroom. Further, she noted that Clara, the young maid who was even with her in the Inquisition cell, was like a daughter to them and that she always slept in their room. She then asked the court somewhat rhetorically, "Why should the maids have slept in her room?" As the clock struck noon, she was ordered back to her cell to reexamine the matters and to return the next day to resume her testimony.

When she returned to the courtroom on October 27, 1663, she was asked if she had anything to add to her previous testimony. She only added, in reference to count 1, that she would shut herself in her room every month or month-and-a-half for cleanliness, and that even her husband was curious about why she was spending so much time there. She continued to respond to each count, beginning with count 15, her explanation of why she objected to her servant's devotion to Our Lady of Carmel. Doña Teresa explained at great length that she was not cross with the maid for her devotion to Our Lady. She was stern with Ana, an enslaved black woman, because she lied, was negligent in her duties, and was careless with the religious scapular that pictured Our Lady of Carmel. Ana also had claimed that she was pregnant, and until Doña Teresa learned that this too was a lie, she insisted that Ana take care not to fast in her devotions for fear of harming her unborn child.

Counts 16 and 17 had to do with Doña Teresa and Don Bernardo's failing to serve as good role models in teaching their servants reverence for the ideals of the Church, and denying the servants time to attend to their devotions. She denied that she was lax in attending to their religious devotions and cited as examples two mestizo servants, Juana and María, who had been with her since she came to New Spain from Cartagena, as well as other servants—an unnamed light-skinned mulatto, as well as Mariana and Isabel, also mulattos—who had lived with her and were now in the service of others in Mexico. She was certain that the women could all testify to how she lived her life, "because by the grace of God she is a baptized Christian."[9] As to her failure to notify one of her servants promptly that it was time to offer her devotions, Doña Teresa replied that with so many servants she could not attend to the details of all their obligations. Nor, she claimed, did she ever prevent a servant from confessing and taking part in her devotions to any saint.

She denied the claims made in count 18 and said she never sent anyone to the church to fetch a servant to make her chocolate. She related in some detail the sequence of events and likely explanation for the servant's recollection and claim against her:

> On the eve of one St. Nicholas's day, . . . [her maid Josefa] wanted to go to confession and communion the next day, and this confessor told her by all means to go, and to pray to Our Lord for her, and that she did go; and when late that day she returned, she said that on the afternoon of the said day she wanted to go to say her prayers, and this confessor told her to go; and when it got to be very late, Don Bernardo her husband said to this confessor that it was time to have chocolate, and this confessor replied that it was and ordered it to be prepared, without remembering whether the said Josefa was in the house or abroad, thinking that she might by then have returned, until her girls told her that she had not returned, that they had already sent for her, and this confessor replied, "Leave her alone; have the Indian Antonia come, and she will make it, or I'll make it"; and the

Indian did come, and just then the said Josefa came in, and the Indian said to her, "Well, you're back," and she replied, "Yes, since they sent for me, and I had already finished and was talking to some women"; but neither this confessor nor her husband scolded her or said anything to her. The people in the kitchen may have sent for her urgently; this confessor can only have said that they should make chocolate, because the said Josefa usually made it, and it is a gross falsehood to say that this confessor or her husband kept her from going to confession and communion.[10]

Doña Teresa offered a curt rejoinder to count 19, her alleged failure to respond to Josefa with proper pious greetings when the maid entered her bedroom. Doña Teresa asserted that both she and Don Bernardo would reply appropriately, sometimes in a loud voice and other times more softly depending on how sleepy they were. She also denied the accusation in count 20 that she kept images of the saints in a pantry with the trash. Doña Teresa assured the inquisitors that she kept images of the saints properly and piously housed on an altar at the head of her bed and that Don Bernardo put an image of one of the saints on his desk.

In reply to count 21, Doña Teresa began to allude to some of the intrigues that had made life so difficult for her in New Mexico. This count alleged that Doña Teresa had implored another person to scold or whip a servant for doing her religious devotions. While denying that she would ever have done such a thing, she pondered aloud whether it might have been Josefa who made this claim and who might have acted out of hatred for her mistress. Or perhaps it was Doña Catalina de Zamora who made this false accusation in retaliation for Doña Teresa's scolding her for serving as procurer and performing other worse "evil deeds" for Don Bernardo.

She continued to swear her devotion to God, his saints, and the strength of her faith in responding to counts 22 and 23. If she failed to attend mass it was only because she was ill, as she was often "incapacitated" by the climate of New Mexico. But in those circumstances she would offer prayers in the parlor of her residence. She added that after her husband was removed as governor, his successor, Don Diego de Peñalosa, moved her seat to the chapel where the wives of former governors sat. He added insult by seating her next to a light-skinned mulatto woman with whom he was having an illicit relationship. For this reason, and because she had no coach then to take her to church, she would attend to her devotions in private.

Concerning the couple's alleged failure to fast during Lent and on holy days, as counts 24 and 25 contended, Doña Teresa offered a learned discussion of why they might have eaten meat and not fish, and why they could drink chocolate on fast days. They and their servants ate meat while they were in Parral on that fate-filled journey north because there was no fish, and because it was all that was offered to them by their hosts, and that Fray Diego Rodríguez had been consulted on the matter:

> Don Enrique [a member of the caravan] asked a servant of the said Don Bernardo whether they would eat meat or fish, and when the said Don Bernardo heard this he asked Fray Diego Rodríguez, a missionary father and member of the Order of St. Francis who was traveling with the said Don Bernardo, what he should reply, and the said Fray Diego said that it seemed to him that being in someone else's house they should eat what they were given, as it seemed to be difficult to eat fish there, and thus they continued to serve the meat; and on the Thursday, Friday, and Saturday of Holy Week the said Don Bernardo said that it was a hard thing to eat meat on those days, and so they brought them fish; and on the said three days this confessor ate things that were neither meat nor fish, although she was ailing and had permission from her doctors to eat meat all through the year and was forbidden to eat fish; and this is what happened, for the reasons stated, and not out of contempt for the precept [of the Church]; and in Santa Fe they never ate meat on days when it was forbidden.[11]

She countered that the way they prepared chocolate did not violate the obligation for abstinence. She elaborated that the chocolate contained only water and not water mixed with atole (cornmeal). Further, she consumed only a small slice of bread or a smaller piece of toast that she shared with the servant boys and their little dogs.

Her defense of the preparation of her favorite beverage reflects back to a long-running Church debate about the proper place of chocolate in the foodways of Spanish colonists in the New World.[12] The first instances of chocolate that Spanish chroniclers observed in Mexico were in the early sixteenth century with their first contact with Maya and Aztec peoples. Hernán Cortés described, in his letters written to the king of Spain in 1519, the value placed on cacao beans in Mexico, so important in trade that it was used as money and collected in tribute payments. Some fifty years later Bernal Díaz, an eyewitness to the fascinating mix of warfare and ethnographic discovery that characterized the first years of Spanish rule, wrote The Conquest of New Spain. He recalled the ritual of preparing a frothy cacao drink consumed during elaborate feasts that were offered daily to the Aztec leader Moctezuma (Montezuma).[13]

Chocolate, as prepared by the Mayas and Aztecs, was not immediately adopted by Spanish settlers into their New World cuisine, and it does not seem to have been exported to Spain until at least a generation or more after the conquest. By the end of the sixteenth century, however, the Church began deliberating over its proper use. Spanish women reportedly had a particular passion for the bitter drink, and its deep brown color cast it among foods that were considered offensive, if not downright sinful, and therefore forbidden. For a time, Jesuits ruled chocolate a drink, not a food, and therefore drinking chocolate was not forbidden during Lent or days of fast. Dominicans took the opposite view. Franciscans, through the works of Fray Bernardino de Sahagún, reported in detail on the Aztec cultural use of cacao and chocolate. By 1636 the properties attributed to chocolate became the subject of rousing moral disputes after publication of a treatise in Spain on the subject of chocolate's properties, preparation, and moral effects. It was considered food if it was prepared with milk, eggs, or maize, as these ingredients added nourishing substance to a mere beverage. Another round of debates in the middle 1640s permitted maize, but not breadcrumbs, chickpeas, or other species of beans. If water was the only ingredient added, chocolate was to be treated as a beverage, like wine, and therefore was permitted during days of fasting. This still did not end the theological discussion, when in the 1730s an unnamed Carmelite theologian raised the issue of intent.[14] If, his treatise argued, chocolate made with water was taken to quench thirst or for medicinal purposes, it was not seen as breaking the fast. But if chocolate was taken as a form of nourishment, then indeed the fast was broken and it was therefore sinful. While the Carmelite treatise noted that chocolate was known to have medicinal properties, its author was more disturbed that chocolate aroused sensuality.

The Church ultimately settled the issue. Drinking a simple mixture of chocolate and water during certain hours with the right intent was not a sin, but the Church and Inquisition officials took a different view of women who became disruptive or volatile after drinking chocolate, or those who used it for immoral purposes. From the earliest descriptions of Spanish women's exposure to chocolate, there was the persistent suggestion that chocolate was to blame for unruly and sexualized behavior. One fascinating study of Inquisition records from seventeenth century Guatemala was able to demonstrate that among women of color—primarily mixed-race European and Mayan women, as well as black women—who were tried for crimes of sorcery and witchcraft, chocolate was considered a medium for producing spells and controlling the behavior of others.[15] Spanish and criolla women shared chocolate recipes and turned to their cooks and maids to prepare such powerful concoctions. Chocolate mixed with menstrual blood or bathwater was said to produce a highly potent aphrodisiac that would make the most wayward man return to his home, hearth, and bed. One woman used a chocolate concoction, ground with worms, to keep her man from straying. One Guatemalan mulata woman was accused by her husband of using chocolate to bewitch him into performing household duties that were normally assigned to women, such as cooking, and boiling water for their daily chocolate drinks.

In some cases, women who drank chocolate became publicly unruly, abusive, and even violent toward their men and toward authorities. In a well-known mid-seventeenth-century case, the bishop of Chiapas tried to stop women from drinking chocolate during mass and was beaten severely by a group of angry women. Apparently, when he again attempted to enforce the restriction, they poisoned him. Civil authorities joined the ban on chocolate consumption in church. Doña Teresa rallied several points in defense of her chocolate consumption—it was made without nutritional additives, she argued, and was consumed, with proper intent, in the company of others after the religious procession passed. Doña Teresa concluded the second day of testimony in response to the indictments and was returned to her cell at noon, after being admonished again to reflect on her behavior.

Her third hearing, on October 29, 1663, began with her declaration that she had nothing to add to previous testimony. She was cautioned by Inquisitor Inspector Dr. Don Pedro de Medina Rico to be attentive, specific, and truthful in resuming her responses. She began with an energetic defense of her behavior and attitude toward the clergy as presented in counts 26 and 27 against her. She again claimed that she went to confession and communion as often as she could when not prevented by illness. In defense of her husband, she countered that Fray Nicolás de Freitas, the guardian of Santa Fe, denied her husband access to any confessor and forbade other friars from attending him. She and her husband knew from repeated experience that he could not trust Fray Nicolás because of the friar's "vexatious temperament." She claimed never to have spoken ill of the priests, whom she held in great veneration, and, she added, her honor alone would not have allowed her to speak against them. She observed, without judgment, that while she was living in Mexico the priest Don Nicolás Pardo died without confessing because he did not realize how ill he was. Neither she nor her husband meant any disrespect by making this observation in conversation with others. As proof of their regard for the clergy, she related in detail events that had taken place when her husband served as the *alcalde mayor* (mayor or chief executive officer) of the area of the state of Veracruz, Mexico, called Huayacocotla. She recalled Don Bernardo's attempts to reconcile the Indians of the town of Chicontepec in the state of Veracruz with the priest who served there.

Since she had previously offered testimony on her insistence that household staff comply with their holy obligations, she denied the charge that she failed to inspire them as related in count 28. She dismissed count 29, her alleged disregard for the rosary as "egregiously false."

> [She] has habitually recounted the lives of saints and carried a rosary. It is true that when she went to mass she would take along a rosary of greater value and afterwards store it with her clothes, but she always carried another in her pocket, and neither she nor her husband have ever rebuked persons who wear a rosary around their neck or called these persons hypocrites or referred to the rosaries as baubles.[16]

She denied count 30 as irrelevant and false. She neither forbade nor permitted her servants to open the middle drawer of her desk, but she recalled that at appropriate times she gave them her keys to retrieve something that she needed from among the papers kept there. In reply to counts 31 and 32, her use of magic and making a compact with the devil, she flatly denied the truth of such things. She never possessed or dreamed of using any magic powder, nor would she have used herbs and menstrual blood to allure her husband, because as a Christian she relied on the wise counsel of the Lord. She affirmed that at times her husband had caused her distress, but she appealed to the Lord through prayers and masses to reform Don Bernardo's behavior. Placing onion skins on her feet, the substance of count 33, had nothing to do with magic or Jewish ceremony, she replied. It was simply the only remedy she had for treating and protecting the corns on her feet.

Count 34 denounced the governor and Doña Teresa for failing to appear in church to hear the reading of the general edicts of faith issued by the Holy Office in Santa Fe. She admitted that they did not attend the reading, not for any lack of respect for the Holy Office or for the Church, but because Don Bernardo was truly ill, and as previously stated, the cold in New Mexico incapacitated her as well.[17] Count 35 accused her of concealing her husband's crimes and made veiled reference to her heated argument with Governor Peñalosa over his requested bribe to suspend the investigation of Don Bernardo. To the inquisitors this was proof that she knew her husband was likely to be arrested, and her feigning ignorance of their peril was a deliberate attempt to mislead the inquisitors. She denied that she had concealed evidence of Don Bernardo's and her own crimes. Further, she believed that her husband "was not arrested by it [the Holy Office] justly, but because of false testimony against him." She reported that the friars who came to see her incarcerated in Santa Fe ridiculed her weeping, and she believed they had come to see her solely to ascertain if she would reveal any evidence of their alleged crimes against the faith. Inquisition officials also copied her testimony relative to count 35 for evidence in a prospective trial against Governor Peñalosa.

Count 36 concerned a box of letters from her sequestered property that she had asked for in her Santa Fe cell. She had asked Fray Nicolás de Freitas and Fray Salvador Guerra for the box, but neither responded to her request. Count 36 presumed that the letters might be evidence of her guilt and charged her with concealing crimes. In her response, Doña Teresa explained that among the letters were two that were of interest to Governor Peñalosa. In a complicated rendition, Doña Teresa denied that anything in the letters, which concerned a lawsuit that her mother-in-law, Leonor de Pastrana, had initiated some years earlier, or that she herself had written to people in New Mexico, had any bearing on the charges against herself or her husband.

She was obviously moved as she denied the accusations of her alleged disrespect for the clergy contained in count 37. She admitted that she had received a message from her husband through a Mexican Indian girl who was traveling with her as they left Santo Domingo. Doña Teresa confessed that she had disagreed with Fray Salvador Guerra because he whipped the girl for carrying the message. She also seized the moment to expose how cruelly he had treated her on their travels south to Mexico City.[18] She did not dispute that on occasion when, because of a turn in the road, she was able to see the prison cart in which her husband was chained, she cried out in anguish. But she disputed the accusation in count 38 that her reaction was in any way a challenge to the authority of the Holy Office or disrespect of the friars. Rather, she movingly stated:

> As an honorable woman of distinction who felt the misfortunes of her husband, she cried out against those who had borne false witness against

him; but she said nothing against the friars because at that time she did not yet know that they had instigated the prosecutions.[19]

In response to the final three counts, numbers 39, 40, and 41, she continued to deny that she questioned the fairness of the Holy Office, concealed the truth, or was unwilling to admit her guilt. She was adamant that she had told the truth and that she recognized her obligation as a Catholic Christian to do so under oath to God and while standing before the Holy Office. She made a passionate plea for clemency of the Lord and the Holy Office. The inquisitors gave her three days to review her indictment and then, with the attorney she selected from among those approved by the Holy Office, she was expected to return to respond formally to the charges. She asked for a relative of her husband to be appointed as her attorney, and when this request was immediately denied, she selected Don José de Cabrera as her defense attorney. But she also requested and was given paper to make her own notes related to her defense.

At the next hearing, on November 6, she was asked if she had remembered anything else to add to her declaration. She recalled some details about her household servant Josefa's personal character and unsavory behavior as well as that of the maid's husband, Pedro de Arteaga. Her testimony was duly recorded, and as she was ordered back to her cell she asked for a book that she had brought to the prison. It was called the *Libro del perfecto cristiano*, or the Book of the Perfect Christian.

Her Defense Begins

The attorney Doña Teresa selected, Don José de Cabrera, did not remain for long in her confidence. Less than a month after she had selected him to represent her, she asked the inquisitors to appoint instead Don Alonso de Alavés Pinelo,[20] an attorney from Mexico City. At the hearing on November 19, 1663, Doña Teresa told the inquisitors that she had become aware that Cabrera had represented parties in lawsuits against her husband, and she believed it was not in her interest to have him as her attorney. She asked for more paper on which to make notes. The Inquisition had a specific procedure and rules for supplying paper to prisoners of the Holy Office. Papers were to be counted, signed, and stamped with a seal when given to the prisoner, and also when returned to the court. Such writings were to be made part of the trial transcript.[21]

Once her new attorney was sworn in, the formal defense of her case began with a reading of the transcript of the previous hearings in which she had responded to the charges. Her attorney was sworn to secrecy and charged with providing a conscientious defense:

> The said Dr. Don Alonso de Alavés was placed under oath as required by law, under which oath he promised that with all thoroughness, care, and diligence he will defend the said Doña Teresa de Aguilera and will allege and declare all matters in which he may believe her to be in the right, and if he should believe her not to be in the right he will inform and correct her, and that he will maintain secrecy in all things, not saying or revealing anything to anyone.[22]

Doña Teresa may have had cause for some immediate concern about her new attorney. Once he was sworn in, he was called away on other matters, and so the reading of the charges against her was put off for another day. On November 27, 1663, Doña Teresa listened to the charges against her for the second time. She would need her attorney to help her craft the written response that would be filed by her attorney, and also to prepare her for the oral defense she would tender. Her reply to the second reading of the transcript contains a few more details that now and then display her cleverness. She does not elaborate on all counts, however. At times her written responses are rambling and confusing, but on occasion they offer insight into what she believed motivated her detractors. Some of the personal admissions that Doña Teresa offers to the inquisitors, no doubt prodded from the depths of her despair, reveal surprisingly intimate details.

She answered the charges in counts 1, 2, and 3 by relating several new details about occasions when other women in New Mexico had seen her washing or arranging her hair on days other than Fridays. She was emphatic in stating that there was no special significance to washing her hair one day or another. Only the "urgencies" of the following day determined when she washed it, as it often took two days to complete her coiffure, given the pain she suffered in her arms. Further, she noted,

> And if I had done so in order to celebrate it as this count [3] says, I should have put on ribbons, flowers, and roses; and since I did not do so, it is plain that what is being alleged against me is false, because I did not put on anything but what I normally wore at home, like a person acting without special care or any special aim, and I also used to do this at night, because that was simply when the occasion arose or I had time.[23]

She demonstrated her resolve and her dramatic use of language in defending why she sometimes heard mass from her carriage while the entourage was in El Parral in 1659, as charged in count 8:

> I used to hear it from the carriage, almost always dressed, and this I did to protect myself from the sun and wind, as a delicate woman distressed by everything, especially with such a long and slow voyage, always exposed to the inclemency of the weather and extremes of temperature unbearable even for a bronze statue; and as the Catholic Christian that by God's mercy I am, I could not have done so for any other reason.[24]

Concerning count 13 and the accusation that Don Bernardo seemed to grimace when holy words were spoken, she explained that those who made this claim might have been too inebriated to know or understand what they saw because they purloined and drank wine from bottles and then filled the bottles with water.

> And that grimace that those servants say Don Bernardo made was raising his eyes to heaven to give thanks to the Lord who gave us these things, as He Himself, who knows all things, can witness. And it is not surprising that those servants did not see or hear aright on those occasions, because they used to go about feeling faint because of the bottles that occupied them, because they used to pour the contents out of the bottles and make up the lack of wine with water.[25]

She elaborated again on why drinking hot chocolate and eating "some bit of toast" during Lent was not an infraction:

> The truth is that during Lent and the other days designated for fasting by our Holy Mother the Church, we fasted like Catholic Christians, and we have always done so; and if some bit of toast was served with the watered chocolate it was for the reason I have declared, and to say that they were two slices of toast is as false as everything else. The loaves were like the others, and let Doña Catalina be asked whether when she baked, which was once a week, she made more than two loaves with lard, and if they seemed a bit larger this is because the lard makes them rise more than usual. And when they say that if one slice broke another was served in its stead, I should like to ask anyone who says so by whose order it was done.[26]

She was even more precise on the events of that fateful Good Friday as related in count 4, as she recalled the timing of her actions and the names of those present at different times on that afternoon. She described a domestic scene, not that of a secret ceremony as portrayed by witnesses who had learned of the events from others who saw or had only heard the information third hand. There was nothing special, she claimed, about giving Don Bernardo a cap, as he always slept with a cap on his head, and they could not have exchanged smocks, because they only owned one smock. As for drinking chocolate they did not do that alone but were joined, after the religious procession went by the palace, by a group of friends:

> I declare that what I seem to remember happening is that when I entered the room—I do not recall whether when I reached the bed or before reaching it—Don Bernardo told me, "How is it that you haven't given me a cap, because this one is filthy"; and he told me this because of the people who were going to come after the procession had passed, and because he had been asking me for it for a day or two, and since during those days I had been busy with feeding the poor I had not given it to him, and after that because I was so tired from there having been no one to help me on that occasion and my having to do it all myself, because of which I had forgotten about it although he had asked me for it several times; and this time I went at my usual pace and without the haste that they say and wish to impute to me, and took it out of one of the linen chests where it was kept and gave it to him, and I said nothing to him but took the dirty one, and I think I threw it on a table, and I sat down at his bedside and took the book and started to read about the Passion of Our Lord Jesus Christ; and as I was doing so, nearing the end, I was informed, as I have stated, that Doña Catalina de Zamora was coming, and this I was told by the Apache girls who were at the front door; and she told us that just as she was coming in, the procession was passing through the square, and she had been walking with it and had stopped because of a pain in her foot; and she said she was coming to see me, and I asked her how the sermon had been and she told me that it had gone well, and I told her that I had read it there, because that book was one of Lenten sermons; and then after a bit Diego Romero came, and her husband Pedro Lucero and [her] father, and then her sister Doña Inés, and a little after this I ordered chocolate to be prepared, and Antonia the cook prepared it, and there were other people there, but I do not remember who they were; and let Doña Catalina be asked whether the girls were at the door when she came, and whether she left the procession as it passed, and whether she found me reading and my husband praying with his rosary, and all these people were always around the house in a bunch, like the keys.[27]

She vehemently denied that the "Tuscan" book that she read was heretical in any way. She poignantly described how she learned to appreciate the beauty of reading aloud, and the joy it brought her father to hear her read in Italian, her mother tongue:

> Your Honor, concerning the book, besides its being the one I have said and my owning it and reading it only to avoid forgetting the language, which was why it was given to me by my father, who sometimes made me read to him from it in order to distract him from his worries when he was imprisoned in the castle of Santa Cruz in Cartagena; and one time when I did not feel like doing so I asked him whether he did not know how to speak that language and read it, and he answered me, "Ah, child, you don't know what a difference there is between my speaking and reading or understanding it. Even though I hear it, I don't pronounce it [properly] when I read it, because it is not my mother tongue, and when you read, you do, and that is why when you read it I understand it and enjoy being entertained for a while." And being such a good Christian, he would not have allowed me to read it if it were a bad book.[28]

Doña Teresa was proud of her ability to read, and according to her reply to charges in count 22, she often read to the women in service to her from the book *El perfecto cristiano*, as well as a lengthy list of other prescribed Christian teachings and bulls, including:

> St. John Lateran and St. Roch and St. Anthony of the Rosary, about the Passion of Our Lord Jesus Christ, from my certificate as a slave of the Blessed Virgin of the Rosary and the corresponding prayer. . . . I distributed among my servants stories about Santa Juana de la Cruz. . . . [I] read to them about the great benefits granted to them and read them the bull of the Holy Trinity.[29]

She summarily dismissed count 25 by saying that neither she nor Don Bernardo ever ate meat on days when it was forbidden, not even when they were sick, nor at the end of their time in New Mexico when they were in such dire circumstances. She blamed her servants for twisting her words, and denied the charges in count 27 that she ever spoke ill of the priests. Further, in response to count 29 regarding her alleged ridicule of the servants for wearing rosaries or scapulars, she elaborated that several of the priests, even Fray Salvador, could affirm that she herself wore a holy rosary, and she had asked the father to bring her the one in the petticoat that she removed in the haste of dressing during her arrest. In response to the accusations in count 30 that she locked her desk drawer and never let anyone open it, she provided a long list of those who had opened the drawer at her orders, and others whom she suspected might have opened the drawer to steal from her:

I declare that it is so false that, when the occasion arose, I sent even outsiders and strangers to open the said desk without any prohibition whatsoever; and even when I was out of that room, as occurred when I had evicted Pedro de Arteaga and his wife from my home, and Doña Catalina de Zamora was visiting me in the parlor on a small platform [estrado] that I had there for the summer—and other times Doña Ana de Robledo along with her, and on occasion her daughter Doña Francisca, sometimes all of them together and at other times only some of them—when it was time to serve chocolate I used to send a mestizo called One-Eyed Cota, because she had lost the use of one eye, who would by chance be there, to go and bring the fabric for skirts from the desk they mention, and at other times, when I was sick, she would go and get them, so that although this woman was not a member of my household and although she came only to see our maids or when we called her for some special purpose, without being forbidden to go wherever she wanted she would open it and could see whatever she wished. And if I should have hidden papers that I had in it from Josefa, which is so false, it would not have been surprising, because she was such a thief, Your Honor, that even the bull of the Holy Crusade was not safe from being stolen by her.[30]

Doña Teresa offered for the record excerpts from a letter that she had received from Governor Diego de Peñalosa.[31] She used the letter to discount the charges raised in count 35 concerning her tearfully asking her jailers in Santa Fe whether her husband had also been arrested by the Inquisition officers. The vitriolic tone of Don Diego's letter was evidence, at least to Doña Teresa, that he harbored deep animosity toward her and would have reason for speaking ill of her and her husband. She also may have cited the letter to show the corruption that surrounded the change of governors and the residencia that Don Diego was conducting to examine her husband's term in office. The extracts of the letter that she read and Doña Teresa's interpretation of her own testimony follow.

"How many tears, how much grief, how much alarm and sorrow would Your Ladyship have avoided if, from the first day that I came to hold this office of governor, Don Bernardo had believed the truths I told him, which, because they were true, he took as offenses in his irascible way." Which, Your Honor, shows the truth of what I have stated that he said to us and gave us to understand from the first day, about an arrest; and farther on in the body of his letter he says, "On my honor, I shall do all I can for Your Ladyship, as you will see, although you did not believe what I told you in the church, so perhaps you will not trust me now either." . . . And then he told me twice that he was expecting the father custodian that night, and that by the next day they would have examined everything belonging to my husband down to his slippers, I don't know why, I suppose it must have been to look for papers that he was so eager to find. That is what I attributed it to.[32]

Doña Teresa disputed further the claims made in count 37 that she was censured by the priests on while the trail south. She claimed that she did not know that she was under threat of excommunication, but still that she obeyed everything that was asked of her. She even disputed the claim, made in count 38, that she could see her husband's prison cart on a winding portion of the road near El Ancón, on the lower Rio Grande in New Mexico. She claimed, in fact, that it was not a winding road but a straight road, which seemed to contradict her earlier testimony that her anguish on the trail was caused in part by being able to see her husband chained in his prison cart because of the curves in the road. In voicing her defense she testified that her anguish was not directed toward the friars, it was caused by the treatment of her husband on the trail south. She concluded her testimony with a strong defense of her faith and insisted that her appearance before the tribunal was evidence in itself of the strength and depth of her faith.

> I have come before a holy tribunal, with great confidence that the Christian spirit and sense of justice of its judges will render justice to me and defend my innocence, as can be seen, Your Honor, in the firmness and valor with which I appeared before this holy Tribunal; and it is so true that I have never said anything contrary to this, that I have never even thought it; and when the chief bailiff came out to Guadalupe I said as much to my maids, when they did not want to be separated from me, as he can testify, and I consoled them with this, as with something so certain and in no way subject even to a shadow of doubt.[33]

The hearing continued on November 27 and 28, 1663, with the reading to her attorney of the claims against her. Doña Teresa was cautioned to admit the truth without bearing false witness against anyone. Although she had listened to the claims against her in previous hearings, the evidentiary portion of the trial was now about to begin, with Prosecutor Dr. Don Rodrigo Ruiz de Cepeda Martínez presenting the specifics of the evidence against her at hearings on December 6 and 13, 1663. Her reply to the initial admonishments was clear and concise: if witnesses testified falsely against her and Don Bernardo it was because of the conspiracy that Governor Don Diego de Peñalosa and the friars had formed against her and her husband. She took the stand again on December 17 and added more details about the conspiracy between Fray

Juan Ramírez and Governor Peñalosa. She recalled that on their initial ascent of the Camino Real, several of the accompanying friars claimed that Fray Juan carried a commission of the Holy Office, and that he ordered the friars to keep a close watch on the behavior of the married men and women and their blood relatives and those who shared bonds of *compadrazgo* as godparents. Perhaps to attest to the acuity of her recollections, she remembered further that Don Bernardo had had his retinue build a raft of felled trees to cross the then-swollen Rio Grande.

Doña Teresa recalled that Don Diego counseled her, days before their arrest, that she and Don Bernardo should leave New Mexico. He advised that Don Bernardo should appoint a lieutenant governor to hear the audit and to let the friars handle the audit of his administration. Don Diego thought Don Bernardo was "crazy" to remain in New Mexico while the audit was being conducted. At the conclusion of her testimony and the reading of the evidence on December 20, 1663, she was given pen, ink, and paper, and by the terms of the proceedings she was given six days to prepare notes for her response.

Her Written Indictment of New Mexico

Doña Teresa requested a hearing on January 9, 1664, to tender her brief to the court so that it could be conveyed to her attorney. It was a document comprising seven folds or folios, totaling twenty-eight pages,[34] in which she responded to charges by people whom she imagined might have testified against her. The close-lined pages of her writing constitute much more than a defense; they vividly reveal Doña Teresa's view of frontier life in New Mexico. It was, of course, colored by her current status as the imprisoned wife of a governor who was deeply despised by colonists, friars, and other colonial administrators. Although the witnesses were not identified to her by name, she must have known from the intimate details of the charges that the accusations were leveled by people who served in their household, her friends, and others who served her husband or were damaged by her husband's administration. She named, reproved, and discredited more than seventy Hispanic citizens and referred to the strained relationships she had with about a dozen servants—Indian people of several tribes and pueblos, as well as mixed-race individuals she called mulattos or blacks. All were people whom she surmised, sometimes correctly, had testified against her. She described New Mexican society as a colony where corruption, moral

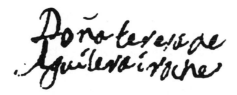

Figure 4. Doña Teresa's signature from her 1663 testimony.
(Archivo General de la Nación, Mexico City, Ramo Inquisition, vol. 596, exp. 1, folio 147.)

laxity, and intrigues reigned. She named specific members of the clergy but indicted all of the friars, whom she accused of failings of faith and heinous actions that ought to be considered in weighing their testimony against her and her husband. Her writing retains the same dramatic, vivid language and rambling discourse as her oral testimony. Yet the document, for all its accusations, criticism, and descent into vituperation, contains deep insight into the social mores and political factions that historians have long characterized as church and state conflicts of the seventeenth-century colony. In fact, the conflicts sprang from many other sources as well—economic disparities, racial and social class tensions, financial misappropriations, and a range of issues including sexual exploits; the abuse of servants, native peoples, and women; and labor relations—that have a surprisingly contemporary ring.

In a society as small as New Mexico was in the mid-seventeenth century, the discontent was far reaching. Settlers were linked by bonds of marriage and proximity and through webs of extended kinship and commerce. Santa Fe was even smaller, described by Don Bernardo himself as "38 adobe houses"[35] and by Doña Teresa, more troublingly, as a place where she perceived constant threats and quite palpable forms of enmity and disrespect from the neighbors, servants, soldiers, and even friars. Her formal, written testimony was read to the inquisitors over several days: January 10, 15, and 21, 1664. In some cases the people she named had been witnesses against her, but she named and implicated many more. In most cases, she referred to individuals and then to their extended kin networks—spouses, the adult children of those named, the in-laws, nieces, nephews, other collateral kin, and a complicated tangle of political allies. Her recollections of perceived and actual slights, instances of insubordination by her servants, and the surprising number of women with whom Don Bernardo had had sexual liaisons support her testimony that she had long been prisoner not only of the Inquisition, but also of the household in which she lived in Santa Fe. Appendix C is a complete translation of her lengthy written rebuttal and response to the inquisitors.

Allies, Conspirators, and Lovers

Doña Teresa contends in her rebuttal argument to the inquisitors that the testimony collected by Fray Alonso and offered to the Holy Office by Governor Peñalosa and other witnesses was tainted and prejudicial. She began her written statement by observing that Don Juan Manso was her and her husband's enemy, a word she uses often throughout the document. Don Juan, then acting as the *alguacil mayor*, or chief bailiff, of the Holy Office in New Mexico, presided over her arrest and that of her husband. It was Don Juan who had directed that their goods be seized and embargoed, and Doña Teresa remained bitter about the confiscation of her belongings. She noted, in regard to her claim that Manso was not a credible witness, that Don Bernardo had previously conducted the residencia, or audit, of Manso's term as governor (1656–59). Manso, she asserted, held a grudge against them, as he had claimed that Don Bernardo improperly seized household property and stores that Manso had amassed during his administration. Indeed, the process of the residencia that allowed people to present claims against any governor at the conclusion of his term created an opportunity for collusion and filing false claims. At the time of Don Bernardo's residencia, three governors—Manso, López de Mendizábal, and Peñalosa—were living in the small community in Santa Fe. Their competing interests and the interests of those who rallied around each of the governors to try to bolster their claims are a prevailing theme in Doña Teresa's written reply.

Doña Teresa added a more provocative detail to her reply. Her indictment of Manso touched on the nature of extended kin networks and sexual assignations that ran through the small colony. She argued that Manso was resentful because Don Bernardo had had relations with Ana Rodríguez, a woman with whom Manso was also involved. And that Don Bernardo had quarreled with Ana Rodríguez over the behavior and treatment of her nephew, Pedro de Valdés. Doña Teresa was correct that Manso had testified against her. He was the first witness called by the inquisitors in January 1661, but his testimony seems to have been limited in scope. He stated only that Don Bernardo had said hateful things against the Church, and that the couple were lax in their Christian duties.

Neither Pedro de Valdés nor Ana Rodríguez were witnesses, though both seemed to be enemies in Doña Teresa's mind.[36] Her indictment of the pair led to a broader declaration of her suspicions about their relatives and friends, as she widened the scope of who she thought might have testified against her. Valdés was the *teniente general*, or lieutenant general, to Governor Peñalosa, and in that capacity he had inflicted many indignities on Don Bernardo and Doña Teresa. Further, he was connected to a powerful local family—that of Juan Griego, whose daughter had been Valdés's lover.

> Pedro de Valdés, in case he should have testified, is our enemy for all the same reasons as Don Juan Manso, and because like him he [Don Bernardo] held him under arrest in the town hall, and in addition to that because he kept him from entering the house of Juan Griego and I believe ordered him not to do so because of the scandal that he caused with his [Griego's] daughter. And after he returned there [to New Mexico] with Don Diego, who made him his lieutenant general, he has inflicted so many annoyances and vexations on us that it is impossible to explain them all or recount them except by saying that he is and has been our mortal enemy.[37]

Juan Griego, she claimed, lacked credibility because of a long list of reasons why he might have hated Don Bernardo and Doña Teresa. He had served as the governor's Tiwa language interpreter until he was relieved of those duties by Don Bernardo, something that earned the governor and Doña Teresa the enmity of the extended Griego family. She implicated one of his sons-in-law in financial misdealing for his failure to account satisfactorily for property that Governor López de Mendizábal had ordered him to deliver to El Parral. Another Griego son-in-law had complained about the governor sending him out on expeditions and escort duties, service that many colonists complained about during Governor López de Mendizábal's audit. Further, the governor had scolded Griego for his inability to control the immoral behavior of his sister Catalina Bernal and his daughters. Doña Catalina, it seems, had even sold one of her daughters to Juan Manso. Griego, Doña Teresa reported, had told Don Bernardo that if he wanted the support of many people, he too should get involved with women of New Mexican families—an activity in which Don Bernardo apparently needed little persuasion. It had also worked for Juan Manso, or so it was reported by Doña Teresa. She also suggested that Griego's father may not have been much of a Christian himself. She reported that at the time of his death he "died with a shoe in his mouth," and his face to the wall refusing to be reconciled with the Church. Evidently she was implying that not only did Griego have many reasons to report false information, but that he was the son of a heretic and therefore not a reliable Christian. Doña Teresa excoriated more than a dozen other members of Griego's extended family under the assumption that they too might have filed claims against Don Bernardo and herself.[38]

> Juan Griego, if he should have testified . . . , has been our enemy since we went there, because Don Bernardo removed him from his position as interpreter, something that he and all his family greatly resented, considering themselves deeply offended. . . . He used to tell [the governor] that if a man wanted to have defenders there all he had to do was get involved with a woman of some family, whereupon all those of that family would defend him, and this was why they all defended Manso . . . ; and with all this, not only are they and have they been mortal enemies of my husband, as they are, but mine as well, all of them, as they have shown in all things without my having given them any occasion for it, and as the Griegos and the Bernals never fail to show.[39]

Doña Teresa turned her pen on other allies of Manso. She described his ally Francisco de Javier, brother-in-law of Pedro de Valdés and son-in-law of Juan Griego, as a smooth-talking scoundrel who flattered, swindled, and then slandered his way through their lives in a variety of schemes before Don Bernardo threw him out. Likewise Diego del Castillo, another son-in-law of Griego, caused them no end of grief. She criticized Miguel de Noriega, who had been her guard and tormenter, suggesting that he was not credible because of his own querulousness and evil disposition. He was, she claimed, among their greatest enemies.

In another section of her reply, Doña Teresa sought to undermine any testimony that might have been offered by the members of the influential and extensive Domínguez and Durán y Chávez families. She stated that Tomé Domínguez de Mendoza [Witness 4], was a member of the faction aligned with Fray Salvador de Guerra and earlier had been Governor Manso's lieutenant governor and captain general. When Don Bernardo arrived in Santa Fe, he replaced Tomé with Tomé's brother, Juan Domínguez, another veteran soldier, administrative officer, and local militia leader. Juan's wife was Isabel Durán y Chávez, apparently the daughter of Pedro Durán y Chávez, who in a kind of widening arc of suspicion Doña Teresa asserted were enemies by the fact of their marriage and kinship. Tomé was appointed lieutenant governor by Governor Peñalosa when he left for Mexico City in 1664 and therefore was one of Peñalosa's henchmen. Another Domínguez brother, Francisco, carried notification to Don Bernardo's brother in Mexico City—and thereby to officials of the viceroy—concerning Don Bernardo's imprisonment during his residencia, setting up the prejudicial environment for the audit as well. Doña Teresa pointed out that Tomé's loyalty to Manso and Peñalosa, and the connections between the Domínguez and Durán y Chávez families, made them unreliable and biased witnesses. She then implicated other Domínguez relatives—including the Pérez Granillo family, whom she accused of being enemies because of a disagreement with Don Bernardo over a shipment of goods.

Diego Romero and his wife, Doña Catalina de Zamora [Witness 23], were also labeled as unreliable witnesses by Doña Teresa because of false claims they had made during the residencia and audit of Governor López de Mendizábal's administration by Peñalosa. Doña Catalina had been asleep in Doña Teresa's bedroom alongside Ana Robledo on the night that Manso and Fray Alonso made their arrest. Yet as close a friendship as the women once shared, Doña Teresa even exposed a rumor circulated by a priest in the colony that Don Bernardo "had had something to do with Doña Catalina in a bean field."[40] She widened the network of potentially unreliable witnesses by casting aspersions on the character of Doña Catalina de Zamora's brothers and other members of her well-connected family, whom she now numbered among her fiercest enemies.

The Household Conspirators

Doña Teresa discredited many of the women, several who happened to be of Pueblo and Apache ancestry, who worked in the palace kitchen. She accused them of a range of offenses including stealing, immorality, and pimping for the governor. One was Catalina Bernal, sister of the likewise denounced Juan Griego. Doña Teresa argued that Catalina Bernal's relationship with Manso may have been the reason she offered—or was forced to offer—false testimony.

> I do not know whether Catalina Bernal has filed some claim in the audit; if she should have testified, and likewise her daughters if they should have done so, they are our enemies. She is the sister of Juan Griego and our enemy for all the same reasons as he, and furthermore, since we went there she has joined up with Josefa, because she used to come to my house to prepare some remedies for me, which is why she had occasion to do so, and she was quite ready by her nature to fall in with her wicked ways and

habits, and so, to make use of the opportunity, she would come prepared with some empty space under the petticoat or hoopskirt that they wear, with a sack for when chocolate was being ground, and she would pretend to be adjusting her dress and would slip in the tablets;[41] and those who ground it, because they had heard me complain about how little there was, informed me and passed me information and complaints so that I should not blame them, in addition to which I saw it myself; and there was nothing she would not deal with in the same way, because of which I scolded her and shamed her a few times, but this only served to make them dislike me more. And this woman also pimped one of her daughters to my husband, and I saw it one night when she came in disguise through the garden gate to look for him, and finding me, who was surprised at her coming that way, and more so because she had left for home only shortly before, I asked her what had happened to her, why was she coming like that; and seeing her agitated I suspected something bad, and she, to deceive me, pretended to ask for sweets and bread,[42] and he quickly ordered it to be given to her; and because I suspected something wrong I looked into it and they told me that the daughter had remained outside, and for this reason among many others they all hate me.[43]

Pedro Atreaga [Witness 12], his wife, Josefa de Sandoval [Witness 17], and Diego Melgarejo [Witness 13] were thoroughly condemned in Doña Teresa's written reply. She considered Josefa the leader of all the wickedness in the palace household, and her husband, Pedro, a gambler, a thief, and a procurer. In sum, all were the greatest mortal enemies of the governor and his wife. The couple stole from the governor's storehouses to supply parties staged in homes in town where they would dance and sing through the night. Don Diego Melgarejo would join them at their revelries to learn news about the goings-on in the López de Mendizábal household.

Pedro de Arteaga, in case he should have testified, and Diego Melgarejo, who is [also] our enemy. The latter is our enemy because on the way to New Mexico Don Bernardo scolded him several times for offenses that he committed, arrested him, and had him in irons for days because he gambled away even his wife's rations. Because of their wicked inclinations, and because of Miguel de Noriega's [Doña Teresa's jailer and transport guard] lies, they left me at El Parral; and when they were brought back they confessed it and greatly regretted being brought back, and from then on they always hated us greatly, as they showed on all occasions. And when, on reaching the town [of Santa Fe], we took them into our house for the love of God because we saw them out in the open, this only served so that they might steal from us, at which we caught them many times, with the food that they were sending to the households they were supporting on the outside; and no granary or pantry was safe from them, and they even threw sheep, tied with ropes, over the wall at night, not satisfied with the four that they killed every week and the seven cows, all of which they consumed, and because it was entrusted to them, and several times I was told that they were supporting half the town; and for these reasons we often chastised them severely, without their mending their ways.

And likewise this man [Arteaga], and all of them with him at their head, procured some women for my husband, because of which I saw myself in such straits that much harm could have come to me; and a person who learned of it, moved to compassion, advised me, and sent me advice through another person, that I should bear it and be patient, lest something should happen to me that would bring on a convulsion and deprive me of my sanity or my life because of the threats that I would sometimes hear they were making against me. And so after endless annoyances I succeeded, almost by violence, to have them expelled from our house, and I greatly wished to have them expelled from town; and even after their expulsion they always did whatever they could against me; and for these and many other reasons all these have been and are my mortal enemies. And this Arteaga is a claimant in the audit. And in addition to this Don Diego attached this man to himself and after giving him other positions made him a mayor, although they say that on his mother's side he is a mulatto or has some such blood. And these men were much devoted to Manso. And so is she and all of them.[44]

Josefa, whose surname I do not know, the wife of Pedro de Arteaga, in case she should have testified, is our enemy and, like her husband, a leader in all the wickedness committed in my house by my servants and of the hostility they all felt toward us. And this she is for all the reasons stated concerning her husband and Diego, besides which she was herself a woman who spoke badly and had no sense, who was inclined only to whatever was or might be bad, which is why I had constant trouble with her from the first day on; and since their provocations were countless, so also did I scold her countless times, and more so since from the time of our voyage there she could not stand us, both because my husband kept hers under arrest for many days, and because one night on the pretext of coming to see me to give me I don't know what treatment, although I had told her that afternoon when she was with me that I did not want to do it, that [night], telling her husband she was coming for that purpose, she went to the tent of a man who was traveling with us, and because she was seen, Don Bernardo found it out and gave her a public dressing down, and if her husband had been a different sort of man things could have gone badly for her, and she so resented it that she complained greatly about it to me. And because of all this she came to hate us intensely.[45]

It was not only Josefa's gossip, thefts, and loose ways that caused this tension, it was that she joined her husband, Pedro de Arteaga, in procuring women for the governor. Doña Teresa wrote in detail about the depth of her hatred and mistrust of Josefa and Pedro, and how their reciprocated ill will might have infused their testimony against her:

> I learned that she was an accomplice and helped in the procuring that her husband carried on for mine and did what she could to further it, for which reason I chastised her countless times, since I did so whenever I had one of the constant fights I had with my husband because of them, because of the great risks to which they exposed me, such that, wicked though she was, she told me aghast one day while I was quarreling with my husband, "Lord, madam, if I weren't seeing this I wouldn't believe it no matter who told me." And I answered her that I owed that to her and her husband and that if he came before me I should stab him with one of the knives with which he used to set the table, and she told him; and they all did what they wished and hated us, until, to avoid greater troubles, I succeeded in having them thrown out of our house, and I greatly wished to throw them out of town, something that they deeply resented.[46]

Doña Teresa named several other household servants she suspected had testified against her because they acted as part of Josefa's gang. Among those she assumed had testified against her was the Indian cook Antonia—perhaps the Apache woman called elsewhere Antonia Isabel [Witness 14]. The cook had been a servant of Manso, and so from the beginning of her time in the palace, she was disrespectful and devious. Antonia Isabel's husband was a muleteer, and he and others who served as carters were said to hold a grudge against Don Bernardo and Doña Teresa because the governor had punished them for unnamed offenses. Two more Indian cooks, Ana and Juana, Doña Teresa alleged had had sexual relations with the governor. The cooks caused her so much trouble that Doña Teresa admitted that she wished the kitchen and all who lived in it would burn. She dismissed any potential testimony from María Zuñi as invalid, as Doña Teresa disdained the woman for being "savage and completely inept," and she could only have been coerced to offer testimony innocently.[47] In a similarly harsh manner she rejected any testimony that might have been offered by her black servant:

> My black woman, in case she should have testified, is our enemy because she is a slave, as they all are enemies of their masters; and besides I punished her frequently for her insolence and idle chatter, carelessness and negligence and also gluttony, and because ever since we were on the way

there she allied herself with Josefa and they were great friends, so much so that we even saw them [plead] to go together in one cart and kiss each other, for which reason we scolded them severely, and also for their inattentiveness, not to put it another way; and because of this great friendship, as soon as we reached town she began to help in everything that she did and covered up for her; and when I found something out I would have her whipped for it, and then the two of them got together to grumble about us, something they never stopped. And this slave's cleverness allowed her to practice such deceit that she pretended to be pregnant, wrapping herself in rags to create a belly, and she would pretend to faint, affecting to fall and sometimes holding on to the walls.[48]

Doña Teresa wrote with deep hatred for Petrona de Gamboa, her brothers and parents, all of whom she accused of serious crimes and of trying to remove Doña Teresa herself from her place in the palace and in the governor's affections:

Petrona de Gamboa and her parents and brothers,[49] in case they should have testified, are our enemies. This woman and her parents were brought to my house under arrest because of a girl whom her mother had beaten to death; and when, because she [Petrona] said she was a virgin, I ordered her to sleep in a room farther inside the house than mine, where my maids slept, what she did was to pry loose a board from one of the windows and go out that way and go to sleep with whomever she wished, although I did not learn of this until later; and they also told me that the slave accompanied her, because they were great friends, and it is a fact that she could not have done this without her consent because she slept there; and in the morning they came back through the same garden and window. I scolded this woman on different occasions and chastised her and her mother because she vehemently denied having committed the murder, and because of my pity for the poor victim I could not stand her. Another [time I scolded her] because, when Noriega was standing there talking to Don Bernardo, she pretended to be passing by and tried to take hold of his hand; and after they left I spoke to her as her brazenness deserved. And later I did so because I was advised not to let her go out in the morning because she had often been brought back from his door. And because of her quarrels and squabbles with other women on various occasions. And because of other shameless actions that I saw and learned of, because she was of the type to go after anyone. After the trial of her parents Don Bernardo ordered her to go with them. I afterwards learned that while she was in our house, and outside the house, she had had relations with him; and when I was informed of this I learned that he would bring her to a room to see her, and when I had asked for the key to get rid of this difficulty and ordered Ana Carima, who was her aunt, that she should not come to my house because I should skin her alive with whippings, because when she came on the pretext of seeing me she would see him there before or afterwards, and when I had asked my husband whether this was right, and other things that as his own wife I had to say, and he [was] blinded by the deceit and felt it as they all do, and for this reason I came to have more quarrels with him than I can say; and when she learned of them because her go-betweens and Josefa told her about them, because she was one of her gang and party, as one for whom her husband pimped and she covered up, she came to be so insolent that often, when he and I were standing at the parlor door toward nightfall like two silent statues, with him resenting my watching over him, and as I did so I heard this woman come to the front door where the servants were, and especially after Arteaga had been thrown out by Diego Melgarejo, who, as he was there, tried to drive her out, even shoving her, but he could not do it, but like a weaver's shuttle or a mad dog she would constantly rush in and out furiously as though giving him to understand with those actions that why was it that he did not drive me out and allowed me to keep her from seeing him; and when he saw that I was weeping because of the threats that he had made to me on account of her and others and I dared not speak a word lest they grow even more insolent toward me, I went out to shout at Diego, what did he want, some armor, and pretending not to recognize her, and for all they both did, she paid no heed, because of which I used to speak of her as she deserved, and it was all reported to her, and she hated me intensely. And this woman and her mother, who, once she knew about it, served as her go-between as best she could, used to send one of her sons so brazenly that in my presence he came to ask him for something, and I scolded him several times, speaking ill of them, and he told them about it and for these reasons they hated me no end. And one time I took off after him calling my servants to beat him and others with a stick.

This woman seemed like a shadow or goblin, and there was no place I could be but she would show up, in the garden and everywhere; and since I had to resent this, they brought upon me every day countless very tiresome and dangerous conflicts with my husband, which was what she provoked him to because of their great hatred of me. After Peñalosa, or Don Diego, came there he attached this woman to himself, and through her all her family, because after countless incidents she and her family came to hate my husband; and although she spoke ill of him she got him to marry her to his coachman, and she sued him on account of her honor, and her father [sued] for his having condemned him, if I remember correctly, for the death of his wife; and for these and other reasons all of these are and have been our mortal enemies, and especially mine.[50]

The chaos and conspiracies that took place within the palace extended outside its walls. The testimony offers a view of colonial life in Santa Fe at variance with the assumption that the seventeenth century was an epoch of piety and deprivation. Doña Teresa recalled that Juan Muñoz Polanco [Witness 7], a soldier in Santa Fe, might have testified against them because the governor had scolded him for having relations with the daughter of Catalina Bernal and for spending wages that he should have taken home to his wife. Further, there was the matter of some debts that might have caused Polanco to lodge a complaint against the governor in the audit. In darker commentary, she alluded to gambling debts, murders, and incestuous relationships that the governor had adjudicated among colonists, which might have led them to offer testimony against herself and Don Bernardo.

Condemning the Friars

Doña Teresa reserved a deeper conviction that the friars must bear the burden of culpability for bringing about the arrest and unhappy circumstances that Don Bernardo and she endured. Father Custodian Fray Alonso de Posadas, she believed, was the enforcer and was surely behind the Inquisition proceedings against her and her husband. He had been their enemy from the start of their journey to New Mexico. During a visit to the palace, when Fray Alonso had come to warn Don Bernardo about the limits of the governor's authority, Doña Teresa testified that she and her mother-in-law, Doña Leonor de Pastrana,[51] were scandalized by the gossip and threats that they heard uttered by this man of God.

> And the things he told me about this matter and others were so many that they make a long story, as he told me countless bad things about everyone and I defended them vigorously; and he eventually left, and, scandalized, I said to my husband's mother, who was present—although, not knowing any of them, as she hardly knew any of those who were in this city, she had remained silent during the conversation because she did not have the information that I did about people there or my knowledge of those here—"Madam, if we were to go to confession and said that we had said these things, would this friar not order us to ask those involved for their forgiveness?" And, crossing herself, she answered me, "Yes indeed." And I asked this about the women there who carried on illicit relations, and although I did not know them I did so on behalf of their husbands who were here. And sometimes she would ask me afterwards whether that father had come back, who later saw my husband and told him the same

things or others more or less. And, finally, since then he bears me ill will; and after he went back there as custodian Don Bernardo had some differences with him that he will be able to explain better than I, because I do not remember them well, and for this reason he has been and is the enemy of both of us.[52]

She characterized Fray Alonso as "plundering" the missions for his own benefit, and of Don Diego and the friars of playing cards and gambling until the wee hours of the morning. She went on to discredit Fray Salvador Guerra [Witness 25] as their "most mortal enemy," and Fray Nicolás de Freitas [Witness 3] and his ally Fray Juan Ramírez as enemies of long standing. She accused them of exceeding their authority and interfering in matters that pertained to civil justice, as well as cruel treatment and excessive punishment of native peoples in their missions, which Don Bernardo had tried to stop.

Fray Salvador Guerra, in case he should have testified: Almost since we went there he has been our most mortal enemy possible. I have already mentioned his reasons for this, and if there are others, Don Bernardo will know and [tell] them, as he is better informed of these matters than I; I only know what I chanced to hear there at times, that although I had not offended against him in any way, he would speak about me as he wished and has on all occasions shown his hatred for me. Fray Nicolás de Freitas, in case he should have testified: He has been our mortal enemy since the time of our journey there, firstly, because he is one of the favorites of Fray Juan Ramírez and [because] of his [enmity]. He showed this on one occasion, when one afternoon a soldier and one of the carters were fighting with knives, and when Don Bernardo saw it, he [Fray Nicolás de Freitas] went there and got out of the cart in which he was riding and began to argue about their being arrested, in order to defend the carter, although Don Bernardo told him that he had judicial authority over them; and finally I went there and said to two more-sensible friars that were there that they should go and take him away, and they answered me that they were keeping quiet because they had no reason to get involved in something that did not concern them, what did they have to do with the stabbings, and that the father was doing it because of the custodian's indulgence toward him; and from that point on his ill will was even greater. Later, in New Mexico, because of whippings with a leather whip, which they say is a severe punishment, and shearing [the hair of] the Indians and other things of which the poor natives complained several times, and for other reasons that my husband will also know and explain better than I, he is and always has been our fierce enemy, and mine, too, although I have done nothing to him or given him any reason whatsoever.[53]

She names another dozen friars, decrying their lifestyles, the harsh treatment and demands they made on native people, and their "shameless slander" of her and the governor. She condemns all of the friars in New Mexico for their claims against the governor during the audit for cattle lost, not because of any fault of his but because of the severe winter. In her concluding statement, she responds directly to the charge that she failed in her Christian duties:

> And as for what they say about not seeing me pray or knowing me to have any special devotion, and so that this may be seen clearly, and as a Christian, which by the grace of Our Lord I have been, am, and shall be, a member of the following confraternities: first, in that of St. Peter and St. Paul; in that of Jesus, Mary, and Joseph, and I had its bull, and likewise in that of St. John Lateran, and I had its bull; and that of St. Anthony; and that of St. Roch; and that of St. Augustine, and I had its bull and wear its girdle and am inscribed in its register of members; and with the Dominicans as a slave of the Blessed Virgin of the Rosary, and I had the certificate as a slave and an assigned time for the rosary, and the truth of this can be seen in the books of these confraternities; and wherever I have been, I have tried as best I could to comply with all of these devotions and say their prayers in keeping with the places where I was, and in addition I have always prayed the ten-bead rosary of the Passion of Our Lord Jesus Christ, for which so many blessings are granted, and I had a list of them and of the great ones that are granted for a thousand beads.
>
> And likewise when Fray Diego de Santander read the first edicts I handed him the liturgy of the pure and immaculate conception of Our Lady and that of the glorious patriarch St. Joseph, and some litanies of the sweet and adored Mother of God and the list of the five greatest sorrows of the Blessed Virgin, all of which were among the things that the edict said this Holy Tribunal had ordered collected, and as a faithful and Catholic Christian and as such obedient to its commands, although these were among my favorite devotions, I was the first to turn them in. And I have always said these prayers and others and also the lesser office of the Blessed Virgin, and in it I have long recited the penitential psalms and the graduals and other devotions, and by their means, by the mercy of Our Lord and His Blessed Mother, I trust that His holy mercy will deliver me from my false accusers and for His sake bring me to a safe harbor out of so many torments, for His greater service.[54]

CHAPTER SIX

Reaching Conclusions

AFTER DOÑA TERESA FILED HER REPLY, the inquisitor inspector, Dr. Don Pedro de Medina Rico, ordered a reading of that document with her attorney, Dr. Don Alonso de Alavés, present so that he might assist her with her case. Following court procedures, Don Alonso would never meet alone with his client, and all proceedings would be read aloud and witnessed by the inquisitors in the presence of the notary, who would record each step. At the conclusion of the reading, Doña Teresa added a detail that revealed that she was aware of a disagreement among the friars in New Mexico about the advisability of the case against her and Don Bernardo. She recalled being told by several people in Santa Fe that on the day the edicts of faith against her and the governor were read, Fray Diego de Santander was concerned that the case against them would not hold. He feared that the friars would suffer repercussions for their part in lodging the complaint if it were found to be false. Finally, Fray Salvador Guerra, previously deemed by Doña Teresa as one of their greatest enemies, agreed to serve as secretary of the proceeding.

> And she added that on the day when the edicts of Our Holy Faith were read in the town of Santa Fe, people were saying, and in particular Pedro de Leiva, Diego Romero and many others, and Doña Catalina de Zamora, wife of the said Diego Romero, told her that on the afternoon of the same day there was great excitement and celebration among the friars in the sacristy of the church, and that Fray Diego de Santander was saying, "Fathers, for Heaven's sake, let us not rush into anything but remember that we are friars and priests, let us have regard for our estate and in something that later on we cannot prove or carry off, and then it backfires on us and we suffer for it," and that on the next holiday after that of the edicts, this was also said, and although she does not recall whom she heard say it, she believes it must have been the same ones she has mentioned and some others, because it was said publicly and in the same words, with the said Fray Diego de Santander adding, "Now, my fathers, since I cannot remedy this and am no party to it and can do nothing, I do not want to get involved in something that afterwards we cannot prove or that turns out to be to our disfavor and I suffer some damage from it,"

and so he did not wish to be secretary, and that other friars had replied to him to let it be, that someone would be sure to do it, and that there was Fray Salvador de Guerra [*sic*] and he would be secretary, and that the said Fray Salvador de Guerra said that he would be.[1]

She testified that all of the servants in the palace household were mestizos, mulattos, and Indians, and, in fact, most of the population in New Mexico were people of mixed race as well as diverse cultural heritage. Mixed "blood," as Doña Teresa so dismissingly referred to her servants and New Mexican neighbors, was in her mind the cause of their deceitful ways and their working against her and Don Bernardo. She insinuated that their mixed "blood" alone was motive for them to lie or for their testimony to be tainted.

In mid-February 1664, a month after she had presented her written, detailed reply to the inquisitors, Doña Teresa requested a hearing to press for an expeditious conclusion to the trial. By then she had been a prisoner for seventeen months, and she feared that her attorney was proceeding too slowly and seemed too inexperienced to know what to do to conclude the case. She was careful, however, to show proper respect for the Inquisition procedure and the ultimate judgment of the Lord.

> She . . . beseech[es] . . . this Holy Tribunal to summon her attorney in order to discuss with him some matters conducive to her defense. She was told that on many distinct occasions her attorney has been ordered to come and bring his defense, and that it seems that not being experienced in what he ought to do, he is proceeding very slowly, because he has always replied that he is working on this matter and has not been able to do so more quickly, and when he was pressed to do something he has replied that he will take care of the matter by tomorrow, Friday; that since he is an attorney without experience in such matters he has been granted this delay, but that care will be taken to pressure him. And the said Doña Teresa de Aguilera de Roche [*sic*] said that she is not pushing her attorney to prepare her defense quickly, preferring rather that he study it very deliberately and that it be presented fairly and judiciously, that what she wants is for her defense to be presented and that if she should be guilty, she be punished, and that if she were not, she should be declared innocent, because she trusts in the Lord that He will defend her, because she always has been and is very zealous for His holy faith and she is more ready than she can say to die for it a thousand times.[2]

When there appeared to be no action on her case, she requested another hearing on March 4. Dr. Don Pedro de Medina Rico declared that the resolution of her case, and all cases pending before the Inquisition, was a priority.

He assured her that her attorney had been hindered in her defense only by the press of other matters and illness. She was told to expect to see him back on the case within six to eight days. One week later, she asked Medina Rico to read her reply again, and to assist her in preparing whatever might be needed to move the case along. And so, on March 17 and 18 her reply was read to her once again so that she might amend it or add to it. Medina Rico reminded her that her attorney was a person she chose and not one registered with the Holy Office. He admonished her that she was the only person who could speak to the facts about the charges. She was clearly distressed and pleaded with the inquisitors to assist her because, she protested, she was a woman with so many obligations, afflictions, and sorrows that she did not know how to proceed with her own defense. She reacted with apparent exasperation to counts 4 and 5 pertaining to the charges that she and her husband engaged in some type of ceremonial exchange of smocks while drinking chocolate on Good Friday.

> In reply to the fourth count she declares that the entire charge is false, because she . . . her husband are Catholic Christians by the grace of Our Lord Jesus Christ, and as such know only how to be Christians, and nothing about a ceremony and things that are not done in our holy Catholic faith, and since they are not done in it they do not do them; and that she has replied several different things to this charge, and the reason is that with the deep affliction caused by such false testimony she does not know what has been said, but that this, and nothing else, is the truth. And this is her reply. And then she said that what she says is the truth is that the said count is false, and this is her reply. To count 5 she replied that the content of the count is false, and even if they had many smocks they would not put them on as a ceremony, because as Catholic Christians there was no reason for them to do so.[3]

Her attorney, Dr. Don Alonso de Alavés, finally submitted a brief in her defense on March 20, 1664. He explained to the court that while he had advised Doña Teresa that he could conclude the case definitively showing that some evidence was false and fabricated, she insisted that she be present and that she could prove her defense. Alavés cautioned her that in order for her to mount a proper defense she would have to be able to impugn witnesses and would have to have recourse to New Mexico witnesses, all of which would delay the resolution of the case. She replied by suggesting that if she had access to her husband, and if the court considered the written responses she supplied in October 1663 and in January 1664, her defense could be concluded quickly. The inquisitors ordered the written testimony to be supplied again to Alavés, and her attorney filed his brief in her defense, which concluded, in pertinent part:

> I, Doña Teresa de Aguilera y Roche, lawful wife of Captain Don Bernardo López de Mendizábal, with full knowledge of the content of the criminal indictment brought against me by the prosecutor, accusing me of apostasy against our holy Catholic faith and the law of the Gospel, and adherence to that of Moses, and of witchcraft, which are the chief subjects of his brief, although in it he also alleges other offenses derived from the foregoing, declare that despite the said indictment and everything stated and implied therein and despite the exaggerations intended to give substance to the offenses imputed to me, Your Honor should be pleased to declare the said indictment to be inadmissible against me, or at least to absolve me and acquit me thereof, fully restoring my standing and reputation, because of what is shown in the record and can be inferred in my favor, which I cite, and explicit law, and because what is alleged against me, both in the said two chief points of the indictment and in the charges of various faults and offenses that are amplified in support thereof, is not proven or attested to in the record as required for a conviction; and the truth, and what Your Honor will always find to be clear and evident, is what I have declared at my hearings, which I present as lawful and peremptory basis for my defense; and that by the grace of Our Lord I am and have always been a Catholic Christian and observer of the holy law of the Gospel, obeying it faithfully and devotedly, and I therefore deny in their totality the said indictment and the inferences and hyperboles made therein and the offenses that in the prosecutor's brief are said to prove insolence and apostasy.[4]

The brief reads as a collaboration between the accused and her attorney—a compilation of legal reasoning, complete with footnotes and legal references, provided by Alavés, and details about the likely witnesses and the fallacy of their reasoning that could only have been inserted by Doña Teresa. For each of the forty-one counts, the reply prayed that evidence be dismissed because it was either hearsay, inconsistent, uncorroborated, or lacking in any substantiation that the practice was related to forbidden Jewish rites. In response to count 1, that the governor and Doña Teresa washed themselves, changed their clothes, and performed personal hygiene that appeared to witnesses as evidence of a Judaic ceremony, the reply brief argued that

> for all that the malice and plots of the witnesses tried to belabor this point, there is no proof of this even being a Jewish ceremony, in regard to which

the manner in which the witnesses testify must be taken into account, [and] the uncorroborated nature and defects seen in the record with regard to them and their testimony, because Witness 2, in the first and only count, and Witness 6, in the first and only count, declare, one, that it was public knowledge, and the other, that he heard it said, that a Spanish maid whom my husband and I had in our household was asked by another person where she was going and had replied, "To that torment, to that ordeal," for one witness uses one term, and the other another, because my husband and I had taken it into our heads that every Friday she was to wash our feet and give us clean clothes; and this is no evidence or proof, because they testify on the basis of rumor without the requisites that the law prescribes for this type of evidence, and, what is more, concerning matter incapable of being the subject of rumor, because in the last analysis it amounts to what one single person is supposed to have said, and thus these are not even hearsay witnesses, which at any rate are of no importance, because they say that they heard it from others who related it to them as a suspicious ceremony, and nothing is added to this, nor is there any change in the terms of the testimony.

    . . . Your Honor will see in the course of my replies to the other counts, they are driven by their rancor to give contradictory testimony, and even self-contradictory, with evident care that displays their state of mind; and it is proper procedure and a clear legal principle, especially in this case which deals with proving heresies, that the witnesses are to be beyond all objection, which is not the case with those whose person or testimony is subject to impeachment, so that as a consequence the circumstances on the basis of which the charge or count has been advanced disappear.[5]

Each rejoinder points out the inconsistencies among the witnesses. In the few cases in which there were eyewitness accounts, she notes that their hostility and the clear evidence of their imperfect memories suggest there was a conspiracy among those who opposed her husband, or who despised her, and that in other instances the testimony was an obvious fabrication.

Her defense of reading is a surprisingly contemporary-sounding argument against banned books. She contended that the inquisitors had no basis on which to declare her reading heretical simply because her servants found her reading to herself and laughing out loud to be strange. Further, there was no basis for concluding that she was reading a forbidden work.

No book is presumed to be prohibited without proof that it is, especially in this kingdom where the vigilance of this Holy Tribunal is so keen in the examination and expurgation of books and in the confiscation of those that ought not to circulate; and once it is shown what book it is and that it is permitted, it is not the obligation of the accused but of the initiator of this action, which is the prosecutor, to prove that it is condemned, for even with those that are condemned and are in someone's possession, the accepted view is that in order to support a presumption of heresy two things must be established: first, that the books are by a heretical author; second, that their possessor knows it, and it is still disputed among the doctors of the law what sort of presumption results from this; but in this instance there can be none, nor any book in the Italian language, since I know it, nor is it my fault that the servants who saw me read are ignorant.[6]

Several times in the defense brief, their reply appears to be a reminder to the court that presupposing that a crime or misdeed took place does not, in fact, prove it. Doña Teresa and Alavés make this point repeatedly and caution the court about using the malice and poor reasoning of the witnesses to make a rash judgment.

Further, because count 23, in its first part, states that it was seen that I and my husband used to go to mass as though against our will and forced to do so, and that although we gave it [them] to understand that this was because of the discomfort caused by the cold and snow, the witnesses suspected that it did not arise from the said impediment but from our lack of inclination, whereby there is alleged before the court a purely internal act known to God alone, which is our inclination; and for the witnesses to affirm this without presenting any evidence, signs, or outward indications that would lead to it, whereas the cold and snow are a clear and visible reason why going to mass should be burdensome, for the witnesses to disregard this reason and to have recourse to their malice is to form a rash judgment.[7]

The brief closed with her plea to the inquisitors to conclude the case and to spare her the pain of anathema that was requested by the prosecutor:

I ask and beseech Your Honor that despite the allegations of the said indictment you be pleased to absolve me and release me, restoring to me my former character and repute, which will grant me favor and justice, which I request, and I swear to God and the cross of this brief, and if I should take another more formal and juridical oath, I hereby take it and consider it taken, and in all things necessary, etc. Furthermore, even admitting the allegations of the prosecutor, I state that the merits of the case provide no basis for his request for torture, because I have testified in my reply to each of the said counts, and so may it please Your Honor to declare the said request to be inadmissible.[8]

Delay in the Proceedings

Once the defense brief was filed, Doña Teresa may have hoped for a rapid conclusion to her case. But just over a month after filing her defense brief, Doña Teresa asked for another hearing to offer testimony about the behavior of one of her jailers, the assistant warden Juan de Cárdenas. This additional testimony did nothing to help her. On the contrary, it added to the complexity of the situation and for a time created the appearance that Doña Teresa might have colluded with her jailer. On April 22, 1664, Doña Teresa asked to be heard by the inquisitors. It is hard to imagine why she thought that the testimony she offered about the relationship between her own father, Don Melchor de Aguilera, and the father of jailer Juan de Cárdenas, or about the information that Cárdenas had conveyed to her about her husband and the other prisoners brought from New Mexico, could possibly have helped her case. When the activities of Juan de Cárdenas came to light, Doña Teresa endured another round of hearings.

She testified again on April 28 against Juan de Cárdenas. This time she recalled that he had told her about the pending charges against Fray Alonso de Posada and other friars for their own failures of faith. Fray Alonso had fallen out with Governor Diego de Peñalosa, but according to Cárdenas, the good father was found to have "conducted himself like an angel" during his questioning by the inquisitor inspector.[9] While Cárdenas may have carried useful information to her, he also had confused her with his cryptic and dramatic utterances, and she was never sure whether he was telling her useful information or attempting to deceive her with suggestions about what she ought to say to the inquisitors. At other times she could not decipher if he was accurately reporting to her what other defendants from New Mexico had testified about her and Don Bernardo.

She was called to three additional hearings on May 9, 10, and 15, 1664, about her interactions with Cárdenas. At one point during her incarceration, Cárdenas had told her to press the inquisitors for a rapid conclusion to her case, to expose the wicked behavior of the friars in New Mexico as well as the antics of the servants in her household, and to press the panel to reunite her with her husband. She was confused about why Cárdenas told her these things. She was unsure if he was acting as a legal advisor or simply carrying gossip to her. She revealed his words to the inquisitors, it seems, so that she could not be accused of concealing information from the Holy Office.

The said Cárdenas came to this confessor's cell a third time and told her, "Now, as soon as your attorney comes, ask that your case be submitted for judgment, and do not in any way consent to anything else, because that will be to your disadvantage; pay attention to what I tell you, that you request only that they settle it and that they reunite you with your husband, because otherwise it will go badly for you, and you are ready to die defending yourself, come what may, and say it all like this, and let us see."[10]

Her spirits were broken by the delay in her case. She failed to understand how the Inquisition's deliberation of her case was proceeding, and over the spring of 1664 she grew to mistrust Cárdenas's messages and advice to her. He did little to assuage her fears, but told her she was "the most distressed, sorrowful, tormented, and afflicted woman the whole world had ever seen or could see."[11] Her distressed state did not improve even after she disclosed the torment that Juan de Cárdenas had caused her, and in mid-June she asked for another audience with the inquisitors to tell them more about his strange behavior. At times Cárdenas appeared to be carrying messages to her from her husband and from her attorney about strategies for her defense. At other times he seemed to be advising her himself on the best course of action. Her attorney was not communicating with her directly, it seems, and he failed to appear for several hearings. When another month passed with no word from her attorney, the inquisitor inspector issued a summons ordering him to appear. Alavés responded to the inquisitor's summons stating that he was still too ill to take part in the proceedings. On June 17, 1664, the secretary of the Inquisition notified Doña Teresa that her attorney had asked to be excused from that hearing as well because of his continuing illness. She elected to wait for him to return rather than continue with the hearing.

Another month passed, and she appealed to the inquisitors to hear her appeal for three novenas to be said for her: one to the Blessed Virgin of Guadalupe, another to St. Joseph, and the third to the Holy Spirit. She also asked to be given the print of the Immaculate Conception that she had had with her in New Mexico.[12] When she was asked what she wished to do, since her attorney had still not appeared, she replied that she knew no other, nor would have confidence in a new attorney at that point in the proceeding. Then she commenced another long diatribe against Juan de Cárdenas and the many times that he had visited her with confusing and contradictory advice. As she returned to her cell she was admonished yet again to examine her conscience and to reflect on the truth. (Plate 9 shows a prison cell window of the Palace of the Inquisition in Mexico City.)

The Defense Rests with a Powerful Admission

In early September 1664, Doña Teresa named Dr. Alonso Alberto de Velasco, a jurist and priest experienced with the ways of the Inquisition, as her new attorney. He appeared with her before the inquisitors on September 12, 1664, after swearing to carry out her defense with diligence in every lawful way.[13] This required that the case file be read to him, and so they continued over the next several days to read the transcript of testimony and defense documents. Doña Teresa added several stories to the record, not about her own actions but against others from New Mexico, including her own husband. She added a titillating story about love magic involving Francisco de Javier and Ana de Anaya, neither of whom had actually testified against her. She had previously identified Javier as a scoundrel and had assumed that Ana de Anaya had spoken against her because she was a member of the family of Juan Griego, the Tiwa language interpreter fired by Don Bernardo.

> Francisco de Javier, a resident of the town of Santa Fe, husband of Gracia Ana, the daughter of Juan Griego, had an unlawful relationship with Ana de Anaya, wife of Andrés López Zambrano, both residents of Santa Fe, which woman is generally held in very low esteem in terms of chastity, because she maintains improper relationships with many men, and although her husband often beats her with a stick she does not reform, because it is believed that she has bewitched her husband, as such women often do; and the said Francisco de Javier used to wear around his neck a little tube covered and tied with cotton thread, and although his wife had tried to take it away from him, he had never permitted it, and on one occasion the tube came open and a lizard fell to the ground as though in a faint and without running away, and when people saw this they were amazed and killed it and took the said tube away from the said man without his resisting it as he had resisted before; and from that point on he ceased to love the said Ana de Anaya and gradually abandoned her.[14]

In defense of count 31, Doña Teresa had previously dismissed love magic as something she would not have needed because of her faith in the Lord, even at those times when Don Bernardo's numerous affairs caused her so much consternation. Love magic was a superstition condemned by the Church and something Doña Teresa had disavowed several times in her testimony. Seemingly her point here was to show the superstitious nature of the "mixed-blood" New Mexicans, while she herself held to the ways of a Catholic Christian.

She went on to say that while they were in New Mexico during Holy Thursday of 1660 she recalled that Francisco Gómez Robledo, who was a magistrate in Santa Fe, was in church with several local officials for mass. She now remembered that he declined to take part in the adoration of the cross and seemed, in fact, to have reddened and grimaced watching the ceremony. She also told the court that Juan de Cárdenas told her that people had said Gómez Robledo had a tail, something that was thought to be a Jewish deformity, and perhaps his Judaism was the reason that he declined to take part in the adoration.

Though her many hearings and written statements, Doña Teresa had still not admitted to any misdeeds of her own. Then at the hearing on September 12, she broke into tears and with much grief she made an admission to the Lord and the Inquisition. It may not have been what the inquisitors had hoped to hear, and certainly did not relate to any of the charges against her, but it must have had quite an impact on the judges. She admitted to sodomy, a sinful sexual practice, by her husband. Sexual relations among married couples were not beyond the reach of the Inquisition. Sodomy—along with homosexuality, bestiality, incest, masturbation, and fornication among unmarried men and women—was considered a nefarious sin and an actionable offense. Bigamy, polygamy, witchcraft, and love magic were also punishable crimes. The Inquisition was particularly attentive to cases where women expressed sensuality—unless it was to unburden their conscience in the confessional or to seek repentance. In New Spain, the Inquisition was attempting to assert the sanctity of marriage and the religious obligations that lay at the foundations of the institution of marriage. The Inquisition's reach to control sexual norms was needed here in the far corners of the Spanish empire where isolation and temptation could coincide.[15]

Doña Teresa had described so emotionally, so palpably, how she was wounded by Don Bernardo's dalliances with other women, and she had testified to widespread immorality among the colonists. She had defended her ancestry, proudly touted her educational background, and pointedly displayed her religious devotion. But now, she admitted her own failure, and there was no doubt that sodomy was a sin and a cause for Inquisition proceedings. She tearfully related that her husband had reassured her that sodomy was not a sin, it was lust, which he defended as a norm. She learned otherwise when she called Fray Diego Rodríguez to her home to hear her confession. She saw his immediate reaction to her confession and how agitated he became by her admission. Earlier in her trial she alluded to her fear that a priest had violated the sanctity of the confessional by revealing what she had told him in confidence and in repentance. Now she had to tell the whole story of Don Bernardo's lust and her participation in sin to the panel of inquisitors.

The said Don Bernardo sought to penetrate her with his reproductive organ through the rear orifice, and when this confessor resisted, saying that this was a sin of sodomy, the said Don Bernardo said that he did not believe it was, because he had heard it said that it was lust, and this confessor told him that she has heard many say that it was lust but not a sin of sodomy, but that she did not believe it, that they were only saying that because they were men; and the said Don Bernardo did in fact penetrate her somewhat with his reproductive organ through the rear orifice, but he did not ejaculate; and when she showed that she was greatly upset by this, he tried to calm her; and this might have happened two or three times, but, as she has said, he never ejaculated in the said rear orifice; and although the said Don Bernardo sought on other occasions to do the same thing and thought that he was actually doing it, he was only doing it through the natural front orifice, because this confessor tried to deceive him, squeezing in such a way that he would think it was the rear orifice, so that he believed it. And when this confessor was getting ready to go to confession, she asked the said Don Bernardo, as a man who knew, how she should confess that transgression, whether she should call it lust or sodomy, and the said Don Bernardo told her that he was not sure, but that the best thing was to confess it as sodomy, that it was better to say it like that in case it might be so, than to deny it and burden the conscience; and this confessor being indisposed and twice unable to go to church to confess and receive communion, and because their confessor was Father Fray Diego Rodríguez of the Order of St. Francis, and because the said Fray Diego Rodríguez had had two serious quarrels with the said Don Bernardo about releasing a prisoner called Diego del Castillo, and because the said Fray Diego has a harsh temperament and she feared that if she confessed to him in church and came to confess the said sin, he might react violently and it might be noticed in the church, it seemed to her best to ask him to receive her confession at her house, and he did come, and when she came to confess the said sin, the said Fray Diego Rodríguez became agitated, and it seemed to her that he wanted to stand up, and she therefore grasped his robe, begging him to be calm, and to calm him she said that that was a sin of lust, and he replied that it was not of lust but of sodomy, and although she realized that it was, she told him, to calm him, that he should understand that it was not sodomy, but a sin of lust, trying to cajole and flatter him, and nonetheless he said it was a sin of sodomy, and he did in fact receive her confession and give her absolution.[16]

She was certain that Fray Diego must have revealed this transgression and had used it against them. For her part, she was fearful and ashamed that she had submitted to such an act, but she did it, she claimed, to calm her husband and so as to not meet with any more discord from Don Bernardo. She continued with this line of testimony on September 15, when she noted for the inquisitors that she was a chaste and virtuous woman, but that she felt obliged to obey her husband. She feared that this was a sin for which she could be punished harshly by the Holy Office, as other women had, and so once again she pleaded for clemency.

> In view of all this she requests and beseeches this Holy Tribunal to exercise mercy and clemency in this case with this confessor, since she has herself testified and denounced in the belief and certainty that this Holy Tribunal is exactly informed about this, for the reasons she will state presently, and because she has heard that on various occasions other women, not of her rank, have been imprisoned for this same reason by this Holy Tribunal, and nonetheless this Tribunal, holy, benign, and merciful as it is, dealt with them with mercy and clemency, even though her case lacks many of the circumstances that she has heard were present in the others, because they have acted by their own will and over a long time, and this confessor has not, but by her misfortune and completely against her will and unable to avoid it and not having sinned thus again, nor will she, although it might cost her her life, wherefore she again requests and beseeches of this Holy Tribunal what she has requested, and all the more because the noble, merciful, and pious person of the inquisitor inspector forms a part thereof, of whom she again requests and beseeches it for God's sake and that of His Blessed Mother; and that since she has heard that her imprisonment and that of Don Bernardo López her husband are due primarily to this cause.[17]

She went on to name others to whom Fray Diego might have revealed her confession, including Governor Peñalosa. She evidently believed that the charge of sodomy was the reason for their arrest by the Holy Office, and that other reasons were added to the charge because it was taboo to talk about sexual matters. She observed that it could only have been revealed by her confessor, thus making him liable, as well, for a breach of faith and trust. Her testimony became more and more rattled and convoluted, until she was ordered back to her cell.

On September 16, 1664, the day after Doña Teresa's revealing testimony, Don Bernardo died in his cell while still awaiting the conclusion of his own investigation by the Holy Office. Whether Doña Teresa knew this, and that he had been buried in unconsecrated ground, is not entirely clear from the documents.[18] Her trial continued on September 17, and again on September 20, with no mention of her husband's death. She does, however, focus on refuting the charge that she had engaged in Jewish practices while adhering to her schedule of bathing and changing her clothes and linens. She placed some of the blame on Don Bernardo for failing to help her to understand what might have been inadvertent offenses. She admitted that while it was true she had groomed herself, put on clean clothes, and changed bed linens on Fridays—which had become a matter of general public attention in Santa Fe—she stated that on one occasion when she was discussing all of this with her husband, she had a bitter disagreement with him because he had not warned her that the Jews bathed on Friday. And in his own contrary way, he had specifically told her that washing whenever she liked was no Inquisition matter for a Christian.[19] What he meant by this statement, if he ever really made it, is an intriguing allusion. One wonders if he ever talked about the charges and reconciliation to the Church that his maternal grandfather had faced in his trial before the Holy Office in 1603.

Doña Teresa continued to respond to the broad range of charges against her at eight more hearings in October and November, adding minor details and observations about those who might have testified against her. On November 21, 1664, her lawyer, Don Alonso Alberto de Velasco, rested his defense, although he did so noting that Doña Teresa was not sure if the defense should rest. When she was offered the closing statement to sign, her wrists trembled so much that she had to ask Don Alonso to sign the closing statement for her.

> With his counsel and consent she stated that the witnesses examined against the said Doña Teresa de Aguilera seem, with one or two exceptions, to have been examined and ratified in New Mexico; and although this conforms with the instructions of this Holy Office and with the law, they were undoubtedly examined by some friar of the Order of St. Francis, concerning which two things must be noted: first, the great hostility and quarrels that the record shows the said friars to have had with Don Bernardo López de Mendizábal, which must have produced ill will and hatred in them toward the aforesaid and toward the said Doña Teresa and her household, for which reason it is very likely that the commissary, in the examination and ratification of the witnesses, did not proceed as dispassionately and disinterestedly as he would have done were he not of the same order and monastery as the said biased friars; secondly, that

for witnesses to be fully credible and trustworthy the law very properly requires the judges to question them in person in order to discover, by their mien, the manner and form of their declarations, and the way they respond to cross-examination, the truthfulness of their testimony and their feelings and motive in giving it; and some learned men even teach that all of these circumstances should be noted and included in the record, so that, if the judge who questioned the witnesses should not decide the case and it should be given to another, this new judge may examine and know all the circumstances that demonstrate the truth or falseness of their testimony and the credence that should be given them; and although it is true that due to the impossibility of the witnesses' appearing to be questioned before this Tribunal, because of the great distance between here and New Mexico, they were questioned before the commissary as is customary, the aforesaid circumstances must be taken into account when deciding this case, and [raise] suspicions that demonstrate little or no trustworthiness in the witnesses, so that they should not be given the faith and credit they might be given had they been questioned before one of the inquisitors of this Tribunal; and this she points out on the advice of the said her attorney for its pertinence to her defense, in addition to the arguments that she has advanced in her written defense; and concerning the hearings at which she was again read the indictment and all her replies, and the presentation of evidence, she has nothing new to allege.[20]

Was She or Wasn't She?

Doña Teresa returned to face the panel of inquisitors one more time, on November 29, to inform them that she believed the record complete and that she would add information only if an appeal of their decision was necessary. While she awaited their deliberations, she consumed her usual monthly ration of eight pounds of chocolate and four pounds of sugar. The inquisitors met for several days in mid-December and then on December 19 they issued their opinion. More than two years had passed since her arrest, and after nearly another twenty months in prison, the inquisitors voted to suspend the case.

In the Holy Office of the Inquisition in Mexico, on the 19th day of the month of December of the year 1664, during an afternoon hearing for the examination and discussion of religious cases by the Inquisitor Inspector Dr. Don Pedro de Medina Rico (and the Inquisitor Licenciado Don Juan de Ortega Montañés was not a judge in this case because he had been its prosecutor), and as ordinary of the Diocese of Guadiana and New Biscay,

Father Juan Ortiz de los Heros, of the Society of Jesus, censor of this said Holy Office (as authorized representative of His Lordship Don Juan de Aguirre, bishop of Guadiana and New Biscay, to which I, the undersigned secretary, attest), and as expert counselors Dr. Don Andrés Sánchez de Ocampo and Licenciado Don Juan Manuel de Sotomayor, knight of the Order of Calatrava, judges of the royal audiencia of this said city, the case for heresy against Doña Teresa de Aguilera y Roche, a native of Alessandria oltre il Po, wife of Don Bernardo López de Mendizábal, governor of New Mexico, was examined; and upon completion of this examination, and having conferred about the matter, they unanimously declared that the case of this accused should be suspended for now, and that she be enjoined and admonished to live in keeping with the obligations of a good Christian; and that upon payment of her expenses and board, the confiscation of her property be lifted and her person be released. And this was the signed decision and order of Dr. Don Pedro de Medina Rico, Juan Ortiz de los Heros, Dr. Don Andrés Sánchez de Ocampo, Licenciado Don Juan Manuel de Sotomayor. Done before me, Don Pedro de Arteeta, secretary.[21]

The decision of the judges was read to her the following day. She offered her thanks to the Lord and the judges and promised to comply with the obligations of the Church. Did her wrists tremble again as she signed her name to the oath she took to live the obligations of a Catholic Christian life? Did her mind stray to the practical concerns of how she would spend the coming Christmas Day? Her signed statement pledged her and her young mulatto servant girl to secrecy about the proceedings. The larger questions remained, however. Had she been cleared of the charges or not? She left the court not really knowing her fate and yet making one more pledge to uphold the Christian faith. This pledge still was not an admission of guilt or answer to any of the charges against her:

> And the said Doña Teresa, after stating that she had heard and understood the decision in her case, with the counsel and consent of her said attorney stated that she would and did give many thanks to Our Lord and to this Holy Tribunal for the favorable conclusion of her case [and for] the just and compassionate examination and decision thereof, and that she has nothing else to reply other than that she intends to live and die as a Catholic Christian, which she is and has been, and is ready to obey what she is commanded. And this is her reply. Thereupon she was admonished in keeping with the said sentence, her said attorney having left, and the said Doña Teresa promised to comply with the obligations of a Catholic Christian and to live in keeping with her obligations.[22]

She was freed after 620 days of imprisonment in the dank Inquisition prison. Yet there was the lingering question of the accusations against her. The judges had deliberated in secret, and their writ seemed to imply that the proceedings were only temporarily suspended. The writ devoted more ink to naming those who presided over the decision than to addressing her fate. Doña Teresa likely found little satisfaction in this decision. Were the accusations still going to be a stain on her character? Did she have to fear returning to prison at some future date? She presented one more appeal to the inquisitors on January 13, 1665, in an attempt to clear her name and to ensure that the stigma of the proceeding did not harm other members of her family.

> I, Doña Teresa de Aguilera y Roche, lawful wife of Governor Don Bernardo López de Mendizábal, state that Your Honor was pleased, by your definitive sentence, to absolve me and set me free, ordering that all my property be returned to me, since, as is well known and I so affirm it, I am the legitimate daughter of the late Colonel Don Melchor de Aguilera, His Majesty's former governor of Cartagena de Indies, and of Doña María de Roche, his lawful wife, whose nobility is likewise well known, so that for her redress and that of my reputation and honor, and so that my innocence may at all times be clear and that two brothers of mine, knights of the military orders, who currently are with my said mother in Madrid, His Majesty's court, may not be adversely affected in their promotions and aspirations, and so that I may benefit from the said decision and request that all the confiscated property be delivered to me, and whatever else may be in my interest, do request and beseech that Your Honor be pleased to order that I be given an exact copy of the said definitive decision in a public form and manner that may serve as certification for the said purposes. I request justice, and in all things necessary, etc.[23]

One month later she received her answer. The judges declined to provide her with the certification of the decision, seeing that no good could come from releasing any of their deliberations. It was enough that she had been released, that the criminal case for heresy had been suspended, and that she had already been given an order for the release of her property. Not one to be deterred, Doña Teresa evidently went to the home of Inquisitor Dr. Don Rodrigo Ruiz on the evening of March 15, 1665, to discuss her request for a certification of the decision. Again, she was told that there was nothing further to discuss in the case and no purpose served by releasing the record of the decision.[24]

Doña Teresa continued to live in Mexico City, close to her husband's family. She arranged for Don Bernardo's body to be moved to the cemetery of the Santo Domingo parish. When she died in Mexico City in 1680, she was still fighting with the Inquisition officials over the release of her personal property. Her heirs continued to press for the release of the property. Fourteen years later, in July 1694, the inquisitors released the last of her property and some six thousand, five hundred pesos to Don Bernardo's niece and her husband, who were listed as Doña Teresa's heirs. They were represented by Don Alonso Alberto de Velasco, then rector of the Cathedral of Mexico City, who also listed himself as her heir.[25]

Doña Teresa refuted the charges of practicing Judaism in several different ways. First, she denied that anything she did was related to Judaism. Second, she asserted that she was ignorant of Judaic practices and was for a long time unaware that some of her actions could be construed as behavior attributed to Jewish households. How much she knew about the reconciliation of Don Bernardo's grandfather is not clear, but it could certainly be argued that there must have been some family history of such a momentous event. Third, she argued that those witnesses who testified against her were ignorant or rancorous. Likewise she strongly professed her own Catholic education and adherence to the principles of the faith. At the same time as she defended herself, she painted a picture of life in the palace and throughout the Province of New Mexico so full of deception, immorality, and conspiracy that no one—not even the friars—was a credible witness.

Governor López de Mendizábal was the architect of many of the conflicts in which his colonial administration was embroiled. López de Mendizábal's abrasive manner and capricious actions were surely disruptive to the elites in the church, to those who formed the fragile colonial political structure, and to the members of the tight economic networks that operated in New Mexico in the 1650s and 1660s. He met his match in Fray Alonso de Posada, a man seemingly as much in the thrall of power as in the grip of faith. There was no surer way to discredit the governor and his wife than to bring them before the Inquisition on charges of claims as elusive as heresy and being judaizantes. Fray Alonso used his power granted by the Holy Office in an uneasy alliance with Governor Diego de Peñalosa's conduct of the residencia to put an end to Don Bernardo's administration. They destroyed his life, but not the discussion of his historical legacy in New Mexico. Both Fray Alonso and Don Diego faced their own Inquisition trials, which suggests that they too had exceeded their authority.

The governor's political enemies tried Doña Teresa in part to further their action against Don Bernardo, but pointedly they tried her for her "haughty and presumptuous" manner. She described her time in New Mexico with characteristic hyperbole as unbearable, dangerous, and rancorous. Don Bernardo's flagrant philandering was the source of household tensions that pushed Doña Teresa to the edge, but her household was already fraught with ethnic and social-class tensions that are observable in the trial record. She discredited many witnesses because of their mixed cultural or racial ancestry. She disdained New Mexicans for their lack of education and for harboring superstitions and following folkways. Those same people testified to their curiosity about and ultimately dislike for Doña Teresa, and then built their case against her from their often distorted perspective.

Why did the inquisitors ultimately fail to uphold the charges against her for practicing Judaism and committing heresy? Why did they suspend the case? Was it because once the governor died and she confessed to the sin of sodomy, there was nothing more to be gained by imposing the sentence of anathema on her? The trial came to no definitive conclusion concerning Doña Teresa's alleged crypto-Jewish behavior, nor is there anything in the record to show that she knew her husband's grandfather had been reconciled through an Inquisition proceeding in Mexico in 1603.

Epilogue

NEW MEXICO IS A PLACE WHERE THE ALLURE of a centuries-old
and lasting crypto-Jewish identity endures. The contemporary expression
of crypto-Jewish identity is still being defined in the light of tolerance and
a more widespread embrace of complexity in identity and social practices.
In our modern times we accept a greater range of actions for the individual
performance of identity. We understand that identity is both situational and
fluid, changing over our lifespan and in response to the context of social
situations and interactions. That was not the case for Doña Teresa in seventeenth-century Santa Fe. Her education and experiences were broad compared to the isolation that defined the life of most New Mexicans. She was
a member of the elite by position, but an outcast because of the conflict that
surrounded her husband's term as well as in response to her own tempestu-
ous manner. At the same time, she seems to have been incapacitated by the
appalling conditions of her marriage and the duty that was expected of her
and other women of her time and place.

With the exception of her personal maids, no one was witness to the practices of her boudoir, and yet many witnesses claimed to know the intimate
details of her life. She pleaded with the inquisitors to hear her defense, noting
that she did not change the linens, fix her hair, or cut her nails on Friday
in preparation for the Jewish Sabbath. She defended her actions as common
hygiene and justified them as something she did as needed, not on a ritually
prescribed schedule. At times, in crafting her defense, Dona Teresa portrays
herself as a woman too inexperienced, and too uncertain of the best course,
to be able to proceed without the inquisitors' assistance and protection. Then
she emerges, as though from behind a demure veil, to strike out with sting-
ing testimony against those who acted out of greed, ambition, and jealousy to
fuel the gossip against her. (Plate 10, a Talavera inkwell, illustrates the power
of Doña Teresa's pen and the legacy of her voice.)

Through nearly two years of imprisonment and dozens of court appearances she maintained her own faith and called for the intercession of the Lord to guide her and her inquisitors to a just resolution. When she finally admitted to her darkest sin, her submission to being sodomized by her husband, the shame of revealing this act and the feeble force of her resistance were almost palpable in her emotional, tear-filled admission. This was her sin and also the only way to be saved from the pain of torture: by revealing the humiliation of her anguish and the embarrassment of her ordeal. Her voice sounds hauntingly familiar, like that of a modern rape-trial victim. She was forced not just to endure the violence of the assault, but also to be humiliated a second time by the inquisitors' insistent search for any hidden acts of reverence to a forbidden faith.

The inexperience and ineptitude of her legal advisors and the dark labyrinth of her path to justice have parallels in our times as well. At the conclusion of the trial, when she was dismissed by the court, she asked for the right to clear her name, not just for herself, but on behalf of her mother, brothers, and future descendants so that they too would be spared the humiliation of the process of cleansing the family tree of so "dreadful" a crime as the suspicion of being Jewish. But even this was beyond her reach. The inquisitor inspector had promised her a just trial, one that would restore the good name of those found innocent, but this too would elude her, and the inquisitors sent her out of prison with neither a conviction nor exoneration.

Reconstructing Sepharad

Jewish culture had and continues to have many expressions depending on geography, history, and political circumstances. No single set of cultural practices defines what it means to be a Jew. Neither the traditional reckoning of Jewish descent through the maternal lineage nor the practice of specific rituals are deciding factors any longer. Appropriation and acceptance, rejection and redefinition of a wide range of practices and beliefs are highly individualized in our postmodern experience. Recollections of practices that differed from those of one's Hispanic neighbors, the deathbed confessions of relatives who revealed long-held family secrets, and the selective incorporation of Jewish rituals into one's own life intertwine in a wide spectrum of crypto-Jewish practices among those who now identify as conversos, anusim, or crypto-Jews. Some people embrace the rituals of the Jewish Sabbath, some women choose to take part in the ritual bath (*mikveh*), some people avoid certain foods, and others incorporate foodways they interpret as Jewish. In this postmodern world, claiming Iberian or Mexican heritage might be the single aspect common to those who claim crypto-Jewish ancestry in northern New Mexico. Genetic testing has certainly defined specific skin diseases and breast cancers that are found aggregated in New Mexico and southern Colorado. But these medical traits are only one part of the confluence of history and identity. What may be most interesting for future generations is the extent to which those who embrace crypto-Jewish identity now form new communities as they perpetuate their identity over time.

Today, those who champion their converso or crypto-Jewish heritage and those who recognize the anusim in their own family lines are the lingering voices of Sepharad. But how many of them would have chosen to remain in Spain or Portugal under the conditions in which their families lived so many generations ago? How many of them will respond to recent invitations to return to the Iberian cities where Sephardic quarters are often marked as tourist attractions? Perhaps it is enough to hear once again the voices of the prophets who cautioned that the glory that Spain sought in 1492 would one day turn against them. Their ancient voices are the voices of poets and writers, the vision of painters and printmakers who recorded the diaspora. Doña Teresa's powerful voice is added to the remembrance of that time and place, when conformity mattered over truth, and when diversity was a threat to order. She was heard, and she will be remembered.

We live in a time when we increasingly hear of the building ethnic tension between Muslims and Jews worldwide, and we listen to the strongly professed assertions of Christian beliefs that often impact the personal freedom and religious practice of others. And while women in this century have gained many rights, privileges, and freedoms, they continue to suffer discrimination, domestic violence, and spousal abuse. With those similarities, it is disconcerting to read the trial transcript of Doña Teresa's case, replete as it is with modern parallels. How deeply moving to read the words of the governor's wife describing the discrimination and violence she witnessed, and in some cases, perpetuated. Her position of privilege did not shield her from abuse. But how much of the case against her was coerced by Fray Alonso and other friars? The final legal brief of her case suggests that the testimony may have been tainted, because it was collected not by the Inquisition tribunal but by Fray Alonso. And one wonders how much of her case was triggered by the climate of opportunity and reprisal that surrounded López de Mendizábal's residencia.

As we listen with growing anguish to news reports from around the world about the rising tide of anger and the terrible acts of terrorism committed in God's name, we pause and look back at the history of genocide and diaspora of previous centuries. Can the ancient horrors of war, the acts of banishment, and the visible and invisible scars borne by victims of discrimination teach us something? What can we learn from the history of the Inquisition, from stories of a time when everyday acts and personal sins motivated widespread investigations of neighbors and friends? Can the stories from the trials and the historical comparisons they invite serve as a vantage point on the intolerance of our own times? *Quizás.* Perhaps.

Appendix A

*Inventory of the Possessions of Doña Teresa Aguilera y Roche,
Arrested in the casas reales, August 27, 1662*

Don Alonso de Posada reports to the Holy Office of the Inquisition in Mexico City his version of the arrest of Doña Teresa in the Palace of the Governors in Santa Fe in the early morning of August 27, 1662. Her husband was already being held in the house of Pedro Lucero de Godoy. Notable is Doña Teresa's instinctive recourse to an image of the Virgin Mary, as well as her captor's description of her proud attitude, which was criticized at her trial as haughtiness. Don Alonso proceeds to inventory the entire remaining contents of the couple's home as he confiscates their chattel, including two slaves, Clara and Diego. This is not a complete inventory of their worldly possessions, for Governor Peñalosa had previously taken other goods from the house in anticipation of the arrest of Don Bernardo and Doña Teresa. The lingering description of the finery Doña Teresa puts on uncannily reenacts for the reader her humiliation at the hands of the four men, at the same time as it provides exquisite details for the modern costume historian and student of the global textile trade. The inventory carefully notes items that were soiled (*sucio*), which perhaps lends us insight into the friar's intent to find something sinful about Doña Teresa's belongings. He evidently ordered the room-by-room inventory primarily to distinguish those items which stood out for their sumptuous materials from those which were incomplete or broken and so less valuable in calculating the value of their goods that could be sold to support them during their imprisonment.

On the twenty-seventh of the month of August of one thousand six hundred sixty-two, in the early morning about four, more or less, I, the Father Custodian and Commissary, Alonso de Posada, in the company of the Alguacil Mayor of the Holy Office, Don Juan Manso, and assisted by Father Nicolás de

---

Source note: From a transcription and translation prepared by Gerald González from "Prisión y embargo de bienes de Doña Teresa de Aguilera y Roche," Santa Fe, August 27, 1662, fols. 396r–397r, Ramo de Concurso de Peñalosa, tomo 1, Archivo General de la Nación. This document was previously published in slightly different form by Gerald González and Frances Levine, "In Her Own Voice," *All Trails Lead to Santa Fe* (Sunstone Press, 2010). Revised by Frances Levine and Tom Ireland.

Freitas, Captain Antonio de Salas, and the Armorer Joseph Jurado, went to the house where Doña Teresa Aguilera y Roche lives and has lived, and having opened the door of the hallway that is there with a passkey, were found in said hallway, Doña Teresa de Aguilera y Roche, seated on her bed. She was half dressed and there, next to her, were two beds. Doña Ana Robledo and Doña Catalina de Zamora were lying in one bed. And in the other was Antonia González, inhabitants of this Villa of Santa Fe who had gone to be companions to Doña Teresa. . . .

And said Alguacil having entered the hallway first, told Doña Teresa de Aguilera that she should surrender as a prisoner of the Holy Office by virtue of a special order which he had concerning her from Your Lordship. To this Doña Teresa, crying and showing her grief, responded by asking why an important person like her was being treated in this way. And saying that she was a Christian Catholic, and she did not know why she was being offended in this way. Turning her face twice toward an image of Our Lady, she asked for justice with pleas to whomever was the cause of outrages like those Our Lady had suffered. And that the Inquisitors would come to know who she was. And if they wanted to make her a martyr, to be done with it.

And then they told Doña Robledo, Doña Catalina, and Antonia González that they should get dressed and go to their homes. And they did this, taking their beds along with them. And with kindness, Doña Teresa de Aguilera was ordered to finish dressing. And she put on a doublet of blue fabric, and beneath that a scarlet damask corset, [and] a blouse of Rouen linen embellished with silk tufts. Then she put on a red petticoat with five tiers of silver tips, and an underskirt of *baieta* [*bayeta*, a coarse-woven wool flannel], or the coarse cloth of this land, bracelets of coral, strings of beads, [and] a thick braid of beads of blue and other colors and false pearls. All of which, along with the shoes she had on, was soiled.

And having put on a red cape, he brought her as a prisoner and put her in custody in a cell of this convento which is immediately after the second door of the convento, and which had a closed window and a single skylight among the beams. After placing the sleeping bed with its two brown linen-covered mattresses, two sheets of linen, pillows of linen, a cotton covering, and a striped tablecloth in the cell, Doña Teresa de Aguilera said that the day before this day of her imprisonment, she had given to . . . Peñalosa a black dress of watered or moiré satin, an outer skirt and doublet, a hooped petticoat and hoop for adornment made of woven flowered cotton manta, a hooped skirt of blue finely woven Holland linen silk, [and] a scarlet cloak with blue point lace and embellished with silver. . . . [She goes on to describe many other items of clothing, jewelry, and personal valuables conveyed to Peñalosa, all of which were later inventoried.]

And during this time the said Governor took out of her house some home-spun clothing that Doña Teresa had hidden, which were shirts of manta, breeches of the same material, buff embroidered jackets, and some chamois—although just a few. And without clearly stating how many such items there were, she did not say more. . . . And she signed this [inventory] along with the said Father Custodian and the Alguacil Mayor. . . .

In said Villa, . . . said year, month, and day, . . . I went to the house and residence of Doña Teresa de Aguilera y Roche, and having shut the doors as the Illustrious Tribunal of the Inquisition ordered and required, I embargoed all of the goods which belonged to Doña Teresa de Aguilera, which are as follows:

1	First a bed made of *granadillo* wood which has four pillars with headboards in two [+]1 parts and five crossboards and fifty-eight balusters—thirty-five small ones and four large ones—all made of red ebony wood, along with eight iron screws, nine posts, and eleven boards, all of which comprise the bed.
2	Also an old bedspread.
3	Also a Chinese porcelain and a jug for chocolate from La Puebla.
4	Also seventeen sandals small and large.
5 [+]	Also two platters and five plates from La Puebla and a cup of the same kind.
6 [+]	Also a very old bed canopy of Chinese silk.
7	Also some red slippers.
8 [+]	Also two wool bedsheets.
9 [+]	Also two bundles, one with rosemary and the other with lavender.
10	Also a bottle case with two or three medium-sized bottles.
[11]	
12	Also a syringe, a spit, and a small caldron.
13	Also a copper chocolate maker.
14	Also a mortar with its pestle.
15	Also a yard of used rose-colored taffeta.
16	Also a handkerchief, half embroidered in purple.

17	Also five towels of local cotton.
18	Also a little less than three yards of old point lace.
19	Also four balls of thread of *coapastle y dos ma* [*más*] *de jue* [cut off].
20	Also an old brass hand warmer.
21 [+]	Also a small pillow with a piece of Rouen linen in which [*enqu* (cut off)].
22	Also another small box for bottles with four small bottles.
23	Also a pouch with three shaving razors.
24 [+]	Also a moth-eaten olive-colored skirt.
25 [+]	Also another skirt of coarse cloth.
26 [+]	Also another purple skirt.
27 [+]	Also some petticoats of green *baieta*.
28 [+]	Also two new doublets of cashmere.
29	Also a *toca* [toque] of watered or moiré satin.
30 [+]	Also a corset of the same.
31 [+]	Also some pieces of black watered or moiré satin, three in all.
32	Also three coconut shell vessels with silver feet.
33	Also two yards of linen and one yard of narrow linen [*b*? (cut off)].
34	Also three linen washcloths embroidered with lace of this land.
35	Also four small pieces of lace-making bobbins for lace making.
36	Also five pieces of white point lace of this land.
37 [+]	An old bonnet of blue embroidered silk.
38 [+]	Also two plain flaxen bonnets.
39	Also a figure of Christ a half vara in size with a canopy of blue linen and two little parchments with their frames.
40	Also, two cloth paintings, one a yard in size and another [*de aq*? (cut off)] two square frames of the same sizes.
41	Also seven wrapped bundles of twisted agave strands.
42	Also a small gilded mirror.
43	Also three sieves of steel and four of silk.
44 [+]	Also a coverlet and [*cortinas de la sierra*].
45	Also a small desk of three drawers with top rail.
46	Also a large desk with eleven drawers in one of which is a gold cylinder set into a stone base with leaf work. Four large net coverings. A pair of pliers. In

another drawer bracelets of coral and abalone, a
crimson ribbon from which is suspended a small
silver medal, [and] three small bracelets of silver. In
another there are thirteen linen roses [cut off] *de
resplandor*. A paper with a few needles and a [cut
off] *bidrio [vidrio] de melancolía*, a beadwork neck
reliquary, and a broken silver scoop. A hand worked
string of two yards of sham lace. In another drawer,
a large bundle of silver point lace, a sash of purple
netting for devotion to Our Lady, and two old bars
of chocolate, [and] three dozen perfumed cakes [?].
A small cup for chocolate with some loose fastening
pins. In another small drawer, a quantity of lacemaking bobbins. Another with liquid amber
balsam and a cross that appears to be made of
squares of manatee hide. A small marble mortar.
One drawer with eighteen colored papers.
Two papers with fastening pins, a small *divano*
[likely a pincushion]. Also nose powders.

[47]   And a small trunk with sewing utensils and a small
pouch with five pesos, two *tomines* in *Reales*, and five
hand-worked door bolts [?]. And a blouse of Rouen
linen needing finishing, [and] seven unsewn slippers.

[48]   Also a small writing desk in which there is about a
half pound of cinnamon and some small cloths,
some powders, and a paper with fastening pins.

[49]   A small writing desk of tortoiseshell which has a
piece of coarse cloth strip. A small silver cover for
a clay pot. A little cross made of jet. A paper of
fastening pins. A small coffer sheathed in dressed
sheepskin with a small silver reliquary of Our Lady
and San Juan. And other paper reliquaries and two
rosaries, one of copal beads and another of glass
beads. And twenty-five ribbon roses of various
colors. Two balls, one black and white, and the
other just white. A pair of gloves with black point
lace. A cloth of blue narrow embroidered linen as
above. Some worthless little blue threads. A fan.

[50]   A medal of Our Lady. And some castanets.
[51]   Also a binding strap made of painted elk hide.
[52]   Also a *rodastrado* of painted elk hide.
[53]   Also a doorway hanging of wool.
[54]   Also a locally made carpet and nine old cushions.

[55]   Also another torn loomed wool tablecloth.

[56]   Also four wrapped bundles of candlewicks.

[57]   Also a small copper coal pan.

[58]   Also an old kitchen hatchet.

[+] [59] Also a small muff of white and black cloth.

[60]   Also two very old barrels, and one small one.

[61]   Also two bowls and less than a half [of another] of lard.

[62]   Also a *metate* with its *mano* from New Spain.

[63]   Also a small copper scoop.

[+] [64] Also two old wool sheets used for the bread.

[65]   Also fourteen cups made by the
          Apaches and [a] large clay jar.

[66]   Also two little chests for storing salt.

[67]   Also a little chest for storing chocolate.

[+] [68] Also three finished blouses and two unfinished.

[+] [69] Also two more small doublets of the manta
          of this land belonging to the mulatilla.

[+] [70] Two wool petticoats; six small blouses.

[+] [71] Also two small blouses; two doublets, one
          embroidered and another of chamois,
          which belongs to the *mulatilla*.

72   Also embargoed was the *mulatilla* named Clara,
          who appeared to be thirty-nine years old.

73   Also the *mulatillo* named Diego, a laborer who
          appeared to be seven or eight years of age,
          both with papers showing they were slaves.

74   Also the large coach, which is very badly abused,
          which has: the coach box, two cushions, two small
          seats, two very old seats no longer serviceable,
          three torn curtains, two green curtains with three
          curtain rods, and four wheels, with some fifteen
          nails but with broken rims, [and] four lynchpins.
          The singletree and the small singletree, the coach
          pole, two main bolts, two old sheepskin harnesses,
          two broken bridles without bridle bits, a trunk
          with its lockplate, a pouch, and the coach box
          lacking the pommels, clamps, and footboards.

75   Also a small belt of gold with thirty-eight equal-sized
          pieces, one with its stones which look like diamonds;
          two of the fastening pieces lack two stones; and
          three large pieces . . . with nine stones each . . . and
          the joining piece with stones, all ill-treated.

76   Also three pieces of point lace, two rose-colored and

white, and the last one black and white, which with
were given up by Doña Ana Robledo through the
Maese de Campo Pedro Luzero de Godoy, saying that
they were given to her for safekeeping by Doña Teresa.

77   [Marginal note: Bestuario (Vestuario, or clothing)]
Also Doña Teresa was dressed as noted in the judicial
proceedings for her imprisonment: with a blue
doublet and a scarlet corset. A blouse of Rouen linen
embroidered with tufted silk, and a red petticoat
with five tiers of silver point lace, a silk underskirt
of *baieta* or the coarse cloth of this land; and some
coral and chestnut-colored bracelets [and] a thick
braid of beads of blue and other colors. And two
strands of misshapen false pearls. All of which
she wore when she went to her imprisonment.
And also covered with the scarlet cloak belonging
to her husband, which she relinquished.

78   [Marginal note: *cama* (bed)] Also the night
bed, which has two used linen mattresses
and two linen sheets and two linen pillows.
A cotton coverlet and a tablecloth.

79   Also there was also placed in her place of
imprisonment for her use and service the following:
some used green petticoats of coarse cotton.

80 [+]   Also two purple skirts of coarse wool cloth of this land.

81   Also an old underskirt of crimson damask.

82   Also a new doublet with gold point lace.

83   Also two old doublets of the same kind.

84 [+]   Also, a bangle and a cap of red cloth.

[+] [85]   Also a corset of scarlet damask.

[+] [86]   Also three pairs of slippers.

[87]   Also some net silk stockings of two colors.

[88]   Also other old flesh-colored socks.

[89]   Also two pairs of old leggings.

[90]   Also a pair of linen sheets.

[91]   Also seven Rouen linen blouses both good and old.

[92]   Also two old linen petticoats.

[93]   Also a pair or two of linen slippers.

[94]   Also three towels.

[95]   Also two new towels and one old one.

[96]   Also a bundle of tablecloths and a napkin.

[97]   Also a chocolate cup from Michoacán.

[98]   Also three cushions and a carpet that serves

	as a floor rug *lla de lana* [of wool?].
[99]	Also a small chest for storing chocolate, with a small cake of chocolate, a loaf of sugar, a pitcher, a gourd cup, [and] a beater with a silver base.
[100]	Also a brass basin.
[101]	Also eleven bars of soap, of which more could not be found.
[102]	Also a small stool.
[103]	Also a small red cloak. All of which fit in a large trunk with its lock and key.
[104]	Also a small dressing table with its mirror, a large hair comb, and cosmetics. Also she was given the small trunk mentioned earlier with all the trinkets it contained, excepting the pouch with the five pesos and two *Reales* and the five pesos. [Also] the unfinished blouse and the day slippers which are not finished, which was all put into a drawer of the large desk.
[105]	Also, Governor Don Diego de Peñalosa provided the following: an outer skirt [and] a short-sleeved doublet of flowered silk.
[106]	Also, another outer skirt, [a] short-sleeved doublet, and a *toca* [toque] of white taffeta covered with black moiré satin.
[107]	Also a hooped skirt of finely woven Holland linen.
[108]	Also a short cloak of silk and gold.
[109]	Also two cloaks of black silk, one with broad point lace and another without.
[110]	Also he gave a red cape with silver point lace mentioned in the middle of this listing.
[111]	Also, another cloak of old gold-threaded silk with three small gold braids.
112	And a piece of coarse cloth in which were wrapped four silver candlesticks and a cup with scalloped edges, which he relinquished.
113	Also six white cotton curtains of [*coapastle?*].
114	Also, a bed canopy with white swag [*manga*] which Don Bernardo also [?].
115	Also a large coverlet of white cotton plush.
116	
117	Also a small crystal perfume bottle trimmed with gold and little emeralds.
118	Also a small crystal charm ornamented with silver.

[*Marginal note:* R°ⁿ] 119   Also a peso, adorned with
                 segoviano [likely a seal or image].

120   Also a wooden tray from China which holds the
        following trifles: two broken coconut cups with
        silver feet for chocolate, four hand mills to make
        vanilla paste, four or five pieces of achiote, five
        pieces of mother of pearl shells and some little
        pieces of tablets of [?], and a book titled *Angeli*
        Custodis.[2] [Also] coarse cotton cloth which the
        said Governor relinquished as is evidenced by his
        declaration accompanying the decree and receipt.

All the preceding goods were inventoried by said Fray Father Commissary with assistance from the aforementioned Alguacil Mayor, Don Juan Manso; and the Recetor [?]res Franᶜᵒ de León and the others who are the Maese de Campo Pedro Luzero de Godoy and the President Secretary. He did so, putting everything in closed boxes, tied and labeled and which say on each one: "Fisco Rˡ." He did this in said house and loaded two wagons and stored them in the convento of Santo Domingo so they would be stored there, and similarly he required said Alguacil to take Doña Teresa de Aguilera her goods. And he put her in a room that is next to the church against the wall of the cemetery. And the clothes in a little office until time to send her to Mexico City as your Lordship ordered. And he said the present inventory is being left open in case some pertinent goods have been left out which the aforesaid will rectify. And as for the chocolate it should be used with his permission so that it will be done without misunderstanding. And I sign this.

said Alguacil Mayor Receptor parte and Notary on the date set forth above

fr Alonso de Posada [rubric]
Comᵒ SSᵒ del Stᵒ Oficio
D Juᵒ Mansso [rubric]
Pᵒ Luzero de Godoy [rubric]
Franᶜᵒ de Leon [rubric]
Passo Antemi de qᵉ doy fee
Fr. Salvʳ de guerra [rubric]

The inventory ended in the usual fashion.

Appendix B

Inventory of Doña Teresa's Items, April 1663

As Doña Teresa de Aguilera and Don Bernardo López de Mendizábal were admitted to the Mexico City prison on April 11, 1663, prison warden Don Fernando Hurtado Merino made a detailed list of their clothing, belongings, and personal papers and an accounting of their servants. Only two of the servants—the children Clara and Diego, who were identified as mixed-race slaves—were allowed to stay with Doña Teresa in the Inquisition prison. Eight other women described as enslaved Indians from Mexican and Southwestern tribes had died on the trail or were sold or placed with other owners. Some of Doña Teresa's things were eventually returned to her in her cell, while others were stored or sold to support her expenses as a prisoner.

No. 1. Copied from the Warden's Register, ff. 63–66v, and the Register of Admissions, ff. 85–87v. [rubric]

In the Holy Office of the Inquisition in Mexico, on April 11, 1663, while conducting his morning hearing, the Inquisitor Inspector Dr. Don Pedro de Medina Rico ordered the appearance of a woman who stated her name to be Doña Teresa de Aguilera y Roche, who was found to be wearing a bodice of satin plush with a flower pattern in brown, black, and white, lined with purple taffeta and with buttons of silver thread;

> 2. a mantelet of scarlet wool, adorned with silver-tipped ribbons and lined in blue taffeta, with buttons of silver thread;
> 3. a petticoat of scarlet wool with five sets of silver-tipped ribbons, lined, or rather, trimmed in yellow damask;

Source note: From María Magdalena Coll, Heather Bamford, Heather McMichael, and John H. R. Polt, translators, *Doña Teresa de Aguilera y Roche ante la Inquisición (1664), 2a parte*, Cíbola Transcription and Translation Project, University of California, Berkeley (2010). The originals are part of Archivo General de la Nación, Mexico City, Ramo Inquisición, vol. 596, pt. 2, fols. 46r–49v.

4. further, some gold earrings;

5. a necklace and bracelets of glass beads, coral, and pearls,
   and the rest was not examined; and she is a woman
   of good build, aquiline visage, rather fair;

6. further, in her pockets were found a complete rosary seemingly
   made of black palm seeds, along with a small chaplet,
   and a small cross, and a bronze medal that she said she
   needed for her use, and that was therefore given to her;

7. further, two silver thimbles;

8. further, two silver reales;

9. further, a receipt from Fray Juan Lobato for
   a donation for seven masses;

10. further, a bag for relics with long strings of gold and purple silk,
    and within it some tied-up pieces of paper, seemingly with
    relics, [fol. 46v] which were replaced within the said bag
    along with the thimbles, the two reales, and the receipt;

11. further, a parcel wrapped in a towel with a white petticoat;

12. an old petticoat of crimson damask with
    11 fine adornments of silver;

13. a white petticoat embroidered with blue thread;

14. further, a bodice of blue and silver cloth, adorned with fine
    silver lace, lined in blue taffeta, somewhat worn;

15. a very old napkin;

16. further, a shawl of multicolored silk, and another old one;

17. an old handkerchief for snuff;[1]

18. a small pillow of dyed linen with a white linen
    pillowcase, [filled] with vicuña wool;

19. further, a book bound in boards, titled *Officium Beatae
    Mariae Virginis*, printed in Antwerp in 1652;

THIS BOOK WAS ORDERED RETURNED TO DOÑA TERESA
ON AUGUST 1, 1663, AS WAS DONE.

[rubric]

20. further, a small chest with a key, inside of
    which were found the following:

21. a girl's cotton chemise, embroidered with black wool;

22. two copper jars for chocolate;

23. further, a mortar with its pestle;

24. further, a bundle wrapped in a towel or napkin,
    in which were found the following:

25. to wit, hazelnuts, Java pepper, tinder, flints, tweezers, a cotton wick,
    and a little sulfur,
    and a spearhead;

26. further, a note whose title is, [fol. 47r] "List

of goods needed for the trade"[2]

27. further, another paper that begins "Jerónimo Fernández, 10
head," and then continues with other names and numbers;

27[*sic*]. further, a brass candlestick;

28. a silver spoon;

29. further, about three pounds of chocolate, one pound
of it in a cake and two pounds in tablets;

30. further, one pound of sugar;

31. further, a black-handled bread knife;

32. further, two pieces of chocolate, one large and the other small;

33. further, three small cups;

34. further, another old napkin;

35. further, a small earthenware vessel with about an ounce of saffron;

36. further, a cloth bundle, and in it two pieces of
unguent, one white, the other green;

37. further, about four ounces of black pepper in a rag;
and nothing else was found in the said chest;

38. further, a small chest of walnut or cedar, and
in it were found the following:

39. an old bodice of silk twill, adorned with black
wool decorations, badly torn;

40. an unfinished chemise of fine linen;

41. another unfinished chemise of semifine linen,
with linen sleeves, also unfinished;

42. a small semifine linen towel;

43. further, a bundle of Flemish lace of medium
quality,[3] with 16 yards of lace;

44. four collars cut from cambric, and another small piece of cambric;

45. an old cambric collar with small lace ornaments;

[fol. 47v]

46. a chemise of ordinary linen embroidered with fine strips of blue
silk, and lace made of linen and blue silk at the cuffs;

47. further, another unfinished linen chemise;

48. further, another chemise, also unfinished, cut
and partially worked,[4] of fine linen;

49. further, a used towel of ordinary linen;

50. further, a semifine linen pillowcase without wool;

51. further, a very old linen petticoat embroidered with red silk;

52. further, two new semifine linen sheets;

53. further, some very old frayed cotton tablecloths;

54. a very old linen chemise with frayed sleeves,
with adornments of silk;[5]

55. further, some two ounces of black silk, and

about half an ounce of agave yarn;

56. some white Toledo understockings;
57. a new pair of sea-green silk stockings;
58. further, a small turtle-shell box, containing a number
    of loose pins and needles, and 16 small rings
    of palm seed and a silver thimble;
59. further, a little *tecomata* in a small cup;[6]
60. further, a paper with seven and a half rows of pins;
61. further, an old face mask of red taffeta with silver-
    rimmed openings for the eyes;
62. further, a small amount of linen and two skeins of thread;
63. further, two pairs of unfinished slippers;
64. further, a small skein of linen ribbon;

[fol. 48r]

65. further, two skeins of agave thread;[7]
66. further, half a pound of storax gum, wrapped in an old rag;
67. further, two small strings of coral and one [of] small
    glass beads, wrapped in a small rag;
68. further, a white bone thimble;
69. further, four small balls of yellow silk and one of blue
    silk and one of white thread, and other small pieces
    of fabric like samples, all wrapped in a cloth;
70. further, a small chest or box of mahogany, in
    which were found the following:
71. a woman's étui, its clasps gilded and tinted with black;[8]
72. further, some papers containing hair;
73. further, a pincushion;
74. material for a coif,[9] with small lace adornments;
75. further, a packet of snuff inside an old silk stocking;
76. further, a bull of the Holy Crusade;
77. two roses made of red ribbon, with silver lace;
78. a leather belt of St. Augustine;[10]
79. further, three yards of buff-colored silk ribbon;
80. further, a mirror with padding, as though for traveling;
81. further, a piece of paper and, wrapped in it, a little storax wood;
82. some white wool gloves;
83. further, a small blue glass vessel with a small amount of wine;
84. further, two curling irons, along with other little things that seem
    to be of no value, [fol. 48v] whereupon the said small chest was
    closed, placing in it the box of powders and the bag of relics;
85. further, a small cambered Michoacán chest, in
    which were found the following:
86. a small book bound in boards titled *El perfecto*

cristiano, printed in Seville in 1642;

87. a coif with blue silk embroidery;
88. a very old and torn napkin;
89. a piece of cotton cloth, about a yard and a half;
90. further, a pair of old stockings of orange-colored wool;
91. further, an old pair of women's shoes;
92. further, four small pieces of red silk ribbon;
93. further, a pair of slippers;
94. further, some very old silk stockings, white and pink;
95. further, a packet with about a pound and a half of rosemary;
96. further, a small pair of scissors for a sewing kit;
97. further, a small box with some white and some blue glass beads;
98. further, a bit of very old gold trim;
99. further, another small string of blue, green, and white glass beads;
100. further, some other small objects such as scraps of linen
    and silk and other trifles of no apparent value;
101. further, some knitting needles, which completed the examination
    of the said small chest, and everything was again placed in it;
102. further, two old mattresses of coarse brown linen, one with [fol.
    49r] vicuña wool, and the other with ordinary wool;
103. further, two old and torn semifine linen sheets;
104. further, a bedspread of worn cotton;
105. further, a pillow filled with vicuña wool, with
    a pillowcase of dyed linen;
106. further, the said Doña Teresa de Aguilera declared that she
    also had with her a large case with some dress fabric
    and other things that she believes to be of little value,
    which had been sent for yesterday and does not at
    present appear among the things she has brought;
107. further, she said that she had also brought two palm-
    leaf baskets with about six pounds of rosemary
    and lavender, and a very old brass basin;
108. further, she declared that she had brought a copper brazier without
    its base, and a small old copper saucepan, and a small spit;
109. and she also brought a small copper saucepan, which the cook
    said had been lost; and she has also brought a quadroon
    girl called Clara, her slave, whom she has with her now;
110. further, a mulatto boy called Diego, who is also a slave;
111. further, four Indian women, two of them Quiviras and two
    Apaches; one of the Quiviras is called María and the
    other Micaela; and one of the Apaches is called Isabel
    and the other Inés; and she has also brought another
    Indian of Mexican nationality, called Cristina;

112. and that she had four other Indian women on the road with
     her, and that they also [*sic*] sold them or placed them
     in deposit as slaves, like the foregoing ones, one called
     Catalina, another Josefa, another Ana, and another María,
     [fol. 49v] all of whom died en route of maltreatment;

113. further, a red bag of dressed sheepskin with adornments of silver
     thread and green silk, and inside it a piece of paper, which
     seems to be an admission by Miguel Vázquez that he has
     received 250 gold pesos, and an additional 100 pesos, or
     rather, 141 pesos, from Don Bernardo López de Mendizábal,
     which was ordered filed with the papers of the sequestration;

114. further, another piece of paper in quarto,[11] containing
     a receipt, or rather, two receipts by the said Don
     Bernardo López, for 300 pesos the one, and another
     300 the other, made out to Simón de Soria;

115. further, another piece of paper, approximately quarto,
     which reads, "List of my ailments";

116. further, a business letter written by Gabriel de Soria to
     the said Don Bernardo López de Mendizábal;

117. further, another piece of paper, which begins, "Jerónimo
     Fernández, 10 head, 1050," and continues with other entries;

118. further, another sheet[12] of paper, titled, "List of goods needed
     for the trade," which papers were ordered filed with the
     first, among the papers of the sequestration, and that the
     said bag be placed with the remainder of the property.

And she declared that at present she does not recall bringing any other property, whereupon she was ordered to be taken to cell No. 17; and before that she signed, and the said warden took her to the said cell No. [fol. 50r] 17.

Doña Teresa de Aguilera y Roche
Fernando Hurtado Merino

And the said Inquisitor Inspector ordered that the mulatto girl she brings with her be placed for now with the said Doña Teresa de Aguilera.

Done before me. Pedro de Arteeta, secretary

Appendix C
Doña Teresa Tenders Her Reply

Doña Teresa de Aguilera y Roche's seven-folio response to the charges against her was read to the inquisitors over three days in January 1664. Not knowing who had denounced her, she adopted a broad-brush approach to discredit any former acquaintances and their kin, as well as known enemies, who might have testified against her. One tactic was to explain why her neighbors held a grudge against her or her husband, which put her in the awkward position of revealing his questionable deeds and wide-ranging philandering. She was not above mudslinging to impugn the character of potential witnesses and their associates. Her candid, yet calculated testimony reveals the tensions between factions backing the three governors living in Santa Fe: her husband, Don Bernardo López de Mendizábal, his predecessor, Don Juan Manso, and his successor, Don Diego de Peñalosa, all competing for access to goods and allies with the potential to enrich them or expand their competing power bases. Not even the friars were spared her tongue-lashing. In its original manuscript form the document captures her intensity—the close-lined spacing and small handwriting, trying to use every scrap of paper the Inquisition afforded her. The corrections she penned and the crossed-out words she marked show how seriously she chose her form of expression and how committed she was to the task of her defense.

[folio 146v]

Hearing Held at Her Request at Which She Tendered the Copy of the Presentation of Evidence That Had Been Furnished To Her and Her Reply Thereto

In the Holy Office of the Inquisition in Mexico, on the 9th of January of the year 1664, while the Inquisitor Inspector Dr. Don Pedro de Medina Rico was

Source note: From María Magdalena Coll, Heather Bamford, Heather McMichael, and John H. R. Polt, translators, *Doña Teresa de Aguilera y Roche ante la Inquisición (1664)*, Cíbola Transcription and Translation Project, University of California, Berkeley (2010). The originals are part of Archivo General de la Nación, Mexico, Ramo Inquisición, vol. 596, pt. 2. Folio numbers refer to the pages in the Spanish transcript.

holding his morning hearing, by his order Doña Teresa de Aguilera y Roche was brought from the cell in which she is held; and once present, she was told that she knows she has sworn to tell the truth at all the hearings that may be held with her until her case is decided, and that the warden has reported that she has requested a hearing, that she is now before it and should state for what purpose she has requested it and should in all things tell the truth under the oath she has taken.

She stated that she has requested it in order to tender the copy of the presentation of evidence that had been furnished to her, along with the reply that she has made to the said evidence, which reply fills seven folios and she likewise returns another blank folio, making up the eight that she has been given to present the said reply; [fol. 147r] and she did in fact tender and deliver the said copy of the said presentation of evidence and the said eight folios, seven of them fully written upon and one blank, with no signature; and since there was no room for her to sign at the end of the last sheet, the inquisitor inspector ordered her to sign it in the margin, which she did, and the said inquisitor inspector ordered the said seven folios with writing to be placed at the conclusion of this hearing so that she might convey their contents to her attorney, who will be summoned as soon as possible, and that the copy of the said presentation of evidence be placed at the conclusion of this transcript, sewn lengthwise so that it may be a permanent part of the record; and the said Doña Teresa de Aguilera stated that for the time being she has nothing else to declare, begging only that her case be dealt with as expeditiously and mercifully as possible, whereupon she was ordered back to her cell; and first she signed.

Doña Teresa de Aguilera y Roche

Done before me. Diego Martínez Hidalgo, secretary [rubric]. Writings presented by Doña Teresa de Aguilera at the above hearing.

[fol. 147v] [blank] [fol. 148r][1] Don Juan Manso, in case he should have testified [Witness 1],[2] is our enemy because Don Bernardo conducted his audit, for which reason he had great differences with him; and apart from that, he always had complaints for various reasons, and also because he arrested him in order to place him under oath because it was always said that he wanted to flee and he was often ready to do so, and finally he did do so from the town hall where he was being held; and he has always had and does have many complaints, and this was seen when, although he was owed nothing, he seized the government provisions that he took there, which is why, because of him and saying it was to replace them, Don Diego [de Peñalosa] took from us a great deal of property, which ought to be returned. And he was also our enemy and very resentful because my husband had dealings with Ana Rodríguez, and because of what had happened or had been done in this city by his nephew Pedro de Valdés, and how they would pick him up off the street, as they told us. For these and many other reasons, which my husband knows better than I and will be able to state, as I do not recall them well, he has always been and is our mortal enemy. Pedro de Valdés, in case he should have testified, is our enemy for all the same reasons as Don Juan Manso, and because like him he [Don Bernardo] held him under arrest in the town hall, and in addition to that because he kept him from entering the house of Juan Griego and I believe ordered him not to do so because of the scandal that he caused with his daughter. And after he returned there with Don Diego, who made him his lieutenant general, he has inflicted so many annoyances and vexations on us that it is impossible to explain them all or recount them except by saying that he is and has been our mortal enemy. And his knowing that he [Don Bernardo] used to say that they often told him in this city that they would pick him up from the street corners was another not insignificant reason [for his enmity]. He feels extreme hostility toward me without my having given him any occasion for it, as he showed in persecuting me to the point of depriving me of all communication, as he did when he sent orders for Juana Mohedana and Josefa to be taken from my house when they were coming from church with me; and having seen them there, he gave orders to Antonio de Salas not to let them come in. And on other occasions when they had been with me he sent orders to drive them out, as was done on Palm Sunday; and it would be an endless task to attempt to recount the persecutions with which he showed his enmity; and if need be they could be ascertained.

Juan Griego, if he should have testified [Witness 18] (who, if I should declare it, is the son of another man with the same name, who, they say, and it is public knowledge there, died with a shoe in his mouth and his face turned to the wall without wanting to be reconciled with the Church or be a Christian even at that hour, because of which they say he was buried in the Santa Ana hills, or elsewhere; I do not know how true it is), has been our enemy since we went there, because Don Bernardo removed him from his position as interpreter, something that he and all his family greatly resented, considering themselves deeply offended. And furthermore he threw his son-in-law out of our house as a thief and said so, and this offended them no less; and also because he asked this man to account for the property he had taken with a dispatch to El Parral, and to this day he has not done so. He scolded his sister Catalina Bernal and her daughters for their loose living and several times threatened to have her whipped, and finally he had her banished. He considered it a grave offense to be ordered out on an expedition at his own expense on a certain occasion that arose. Another time he [Don Bernardo] sent his son-in-law on another expedition, and likewise many of his relatives, which is the general complaint of all the residents against the governors. He imprisoned several of his relatives because of their offenses. He reproached him with his sister's having sold one of her daughters to Don Juan Manso. And he learned that he did the same with regard to the one she gave to Don Diego. He scolded him on account of the visits of Pedro de Valdés and the scandalous behavior of his daughters. He used to tell him that if a man wanted to have defenders there all he had to do was get involved with a woman of some family, whereupon all those of that family would defend him, and this was why they all defended Manso. He imprisoned Diego del Castillo, another son-in-law of his, to have him whipped, and thanks to me he did not do so; and with all this, not only are they and have they been mortal enemies of my husband, as they are, but mine as well, all of them, as they have shown in all things without my having given them any occasion for it, and as the Griegos and the Bernals never fail to show. And I do not know whether Catalina Bernal has filed some claim in the audit; if she should have testified, and likewise her daughters if they should have done so, they are our enemies. She is the sister of Juan Griego and our enemy for all the same reasons as he, and furthermore, since we went there she has joined up with Josefa, because she used to come to my house to prepare some remedies for me, which is why she had occasion to do so, and she was quite ready by her nature to fall in with her wicked ways and habits, and so, to make use of the opportunity, she would come prepared with some empty space under the petticoat or hoopskirt that they wear, with a sack for when chocolate was being ground, and she would pretend to be adjusting her dress and would slip in the tablets; and those who ground it, [fol. 148v] because they had heard me complain about how little there was, informed me and passed me information and complaints so that I should not blame them, in addition to which I saw it myself; and there was nothing she would not deal with in the same way, because of which I scolded her and shamed her a few times, but this only served to make them dislike me more. And this woman also pimped one of her daughters to my husband, and I saw it one night when she came in disguise through the garden gate to look for him, and finding me, who was surprised at her coming that way, and more so because she had left for home only shortly before, I asked her what had happened to her, why was she coming like that; and seeing her agitated I suspected something bad, and she, to deceive me, pretended to ask for sweets and bread, and he quickly ordered it to be given to her; and because I suspected something wrong I looked into it and they told me that the daughter had remained outside, and for this reason among many others they all hate me. And these are the sort of people that in addition to what I have said, in order to deceive a man they pretended that one of them had had a miscarriage, and they developed so many schemes in connection with this, [and] because a relative of theirs said and proclaimed that it was a lie they went to her house and after they had behaved like what they were they came to complain, full of bites and scratches and their hair in disorder, and when those who were there had thrown them out and Don Bernardo had later learned of it he often told her that if he had caught them in the act he would have seized them and flogged them, and this was because he had several times reproached her with their loose living. And on this occasion I treated her very harshly, because I do not know how they got me involved in this. And not only did she do this but in my presence she was murmuring about it one day, although she thought I should not understand her in Tiwa, and by her actions I did understand what she was saying but not of whom she was speaking, and when they were shocked at my understanding them in that language, she said that she would not speak it any more in my presence; and later, when another occasion arose, the other one told me what it was about. And this woman took great offense at the arrest of Juan Polanco because he was her son-in-law, and also at the dismissal of her nephew Gabriel and at Don Bernardo's telling him he was a thief, and because he told her what her brothers and nephews were. She hated him because he banished her, sent her relatives on expeditions and on garrison,[3] tried to have her nephew flogged, demanded an accounting from Francisco Gabriel, who is also her nephew, [and] fired her brother from being an interpreter, and, in short, because she is a Griego and a Bernal, all of whom are our mortal enemies, and especially mine, although I have given them no cause for it and have many for complaints against them. And apart from these reasons, Don

Diego won over this woman and often visited her house; and once during this time she asked me through Josefa for permission to see me, and I gave it to her to see what she would tell me because of all the rumors that had circulated; and on that occasion she told me what I have declared, that the women who talked with me and served me had twisted my words, and when I repeated to her what conversations I had had, because I do not know how often she had heard me say that in my presence there was no gossiping or idle chatter, she replied that that was true, but so was what she was telling me, and that one day I should see that, and I told her that one day everyone would see it and that it did not matter, because one day it would be God's will for the day of truth to come for everything, because sooner or later the truth will come out, and she replied that that was so. And on that occasion she told me that Don Diego had strongly urged and pressed her to sue Don Bernardo, and that he would cover the cost, and that she had refused to do so, and she also told me that to get her to do so he had reminded her of the offenses her family had suffered, but that she had nonetheless wanted only to forgive them. And ultimately Don Diego found out that she had come to my house and I learned that he had summoned her and berated and scolded her severely for it; and so that she would not continue coming and perhaps tell me something that in some way might be to his disadvantage, if she should know it, he banished her to San Marcos; and perhaps if she has testified to anything she must or might be one of those he mentioned to me on the last day when I asked him, so as not to be alone with him, to send for one or two women whom I mentioned to him, and he asked me [fol. 149r] what I wanted them for, that the women there were not good for anything but to bear false witness, did I not know that, to which I replied that I did not, because I had never needed them for that purpose, to which he replied, "Well, I do know it, and that is all they are good for," and I told him that I believed it, and in my opinion he knows very well whether they are.

Francisco de Javier, in case he should have testified, is our enemy, and so is his wife, if she has done so. This man, when Don Juan Manso had sent him from there to this city with his nephew to see to some of his business, and on the day of his arrival he found out that they had appointed Don Bernardo to the office, immediately forgot his business and sent people to plead with us to receive him into our household; and when we did so he engaged in so many swindles that one of my husband's nephews was ready to kill him, and I often scolded him for them. And at the time for the dispatch, Don

Bernardo, although he relied on him because he told him he understood it, falsely telling him that he had done it with others, suffered a good many losses in his property; and when he found it out he berated him, and in many cases he could not get him to settle accounts. And when we got under way and during the voyage, the scoldings were equally frequent, because he had, for his own purposes, taken charge of everything. And as we neared the end of the voyage and it was time to notify Don Juan, in order not to send others who were his enemies, he [Don Bernardo] sent him with the news, as he was his friend,[4] and this served only to send ahead a man who would go to that country to sow endless swindles and discord, and so the first thing Don Juan said to my husband among many other things was, how could he have sent such scoundrels, and he told him, so as not to send him enemies. And finally, when we arrived there he set about managing the property without anyone's having ordered him to do so, until a few days later, when my husband wanted to inspect it all, he found two chests missing, and when he ordered him to settle the account, and he did it so badly that to keep him from doing him further harm he threw him out as a thief, at which all his family took great offense. And on the way he had also much berated him to cure him of a very bad habit he had, which was often to say, like the flatterer he was, that the people up there were so submissive to the governors that they obeyed them as they did God, or even more so, and other nonsense for which Don Bernardo reproved him several times; and finally he grew annoyed and, rightly incensed, threw him out for this behavior and even threatened him, to break him of such a habit. And in short, this man and all of them, being relatives and friends of Manso, are enemies, and because of Pedro de Valdés, who is his brother-in-law and because he let him into his house and opened the side door to let him come in, something for which Don Bernardo often scolded him and severely reproached him, because one time, and even many times, this man had said, because they told him that he wanted to marry her, that he would kill him before he would allow her to marry a man whom he had picked up in the street three times and carried to his house; and he would ask whether it was better to acquiesce in her living in sin, and furthermore that it is false that he wanted to marry her, and for this reason he and they took great offense. And this is the son-in-law of the Juan Griego whom he dismissed as interpreter, and a nephew of Catalina Bernal; and for the way she and her daughters lived he scolded him several times. He was much offended by her banishment, by the occasional arrest of his relatives, by their being sent on expeditions to the great [dis]advantage of his father-in-law, by his wanting to flog Diego del Castillo, his brother-in-law (and he knew that he had threatened his aunt Catalina with the same), by his having reproached him for the loose living of his aunt Inesota and her daughters and many other female relatives. And finally, this man, having been entrusted with a dispatch with so much property, left it, against express orders, in El Paso exposed to be lost, and went to El Parral with only the three carts, which he broke up there, and meeting Don Diego there, who received him into his company and, seeing that he spoke so ill of us, treated him well; and he, to continue his constant schemes and to flatter him, bought a nag[5] from him in exchange for four of our mules from the carts, and Don Diego, pleased with him, entrusted his property to him, which was what he was after, in order to do with it what he had with ours, as has become apparent; and in short, he kept him very close to him and did not want to have him made to account to Don Bernardo, although he requested it before him at the proper time, nor has he given any accounting other than for some of the mules. For all these reasons, both his own and those of his relatives, he has been from the beginning, and is, our mortal enemy and never ceases to speak ill of us, and I have learned [fol. 149v] that he has often and publicly spread slanders about me, and I ask that if necessary they be investigated, for I trust in Our Lord that He will deliver me from them and all others as He did Susanna, for I am equally blameless.

Diego del Castillo, in case he should have testified, and his wife, if she should have done so, is our enemy, the son-in-law of Juan Griego, nephew of Catalina Bernal, brother-in-law of Francisco Javier; and having gone to Senecú to meet us when we went [to New Mexico] and having been cordially received by us, just because of his evil nature he went back to town saying all sorts of bad things about us; and afterwards, because Don Bernardo did not pay him the attention that in his presumptuousness he would have liked, he considered himself gravely offended, and also because he threw Gabriel out of our house for having stolen from him, and because he dismissed his father-in-law from his post as interpreter, which corroborated them all, because they were all partisans of Manso and his relatives and of Valdés, and because of the constant reproofs that Don Bernardo gave and had given to all of them, which were many, and none milder than the rest; because for various reasons he had banished his aunt Catalina, of which, and other things, he frequently complained, as he did of his having threatened her with flogging, and as he did of his having sent his father-in-law on an expedition and other relatives on others, and of the arrest of his nephew Diego González Bernal, and as he pretended to be crazy he said this was due to the three or four days he was jailed, and he also arrested other relatives of his at various times and on various grounds; because he had him under arrest for his resistance and wanted to flog him and was on the point of doing so for being convicted in this case; and because he demanded an accounting from Gabriel. For which reasons and others, all these persons have been and are our mortal enemies, and this man has filed a claim in the audit; and Don Diego made him a magistrate so that in him he would have someone who would aggressively persecute us, as he clearly showed on the many occasions when he sent him to rob us of all we had. Juana, the wife of Juan Griego, and her daughters, if they should have testified, are our enemies for all the same reasons as her husband and her sons and brothers, and likewise her son Nicolás Griego, and if she should have others, if they should have testified. Inesota Bernal, the sister of Juan Griego, and her daughters, his nieces, if they should have testified, are our enemies for all these reasons. Isabel Bernal and her daughters and son, if they should have testified, are our enemies. She is the sister of Juan Griego; and the other relatives and nephews and all of them [are] our enemies for the reasons stated; and I do not know whether she might have some private reasons—Don Bernardo will know that; and Antonio González is her son and is a council clerk; all of them are great partisans of Don Diego and of other persons who hate us. Pedro de la Cruz, in case he should have testified, is the brother of Juana, the wife of Juan Griego, and his daughter [is] her niece; [they are] enemies for all the reasons stated that pertain to them; in addition, he is a claimant in the audit of my husband.

Domingo González the Galician and his wife, in case they should have testified, are relatives of the foregoing and our enemies, whose complaints concern them, and many of them owe us some money on notes.

Miguel de Noriega, in case he should have testified [witnessed twice as 5 and 26], is our enemy, despite my husband's having given him a post in this city when we went [to New Mexico], with full pay en route, corroborated him and, in a word, done for him what he might have done for a brother; and as soon as we reached El Parral he complained of him greatly, and as he is known there because he had lived there with his wife, they took him for what he was worth, because in all that country they call him, because of his behavior, the woe-weeper; and his complaints, even to Don Enrique de Ávila, about being ordered to guard the mules, grew so tiresome that he forced him to ask what offense was done to him, being a soldier, [fol. 150r] by an order to guard the King's property, and did he want the governor to do it, and other things. And nonetheless Don Bernardo later appointed him to be his ensign and then his secretary, which he repaid, despite holding this position and participating in the secret part of the audit of Manso, by going at night, as soon as we had gone to bed, to tell him what the witnesses had testified that day, and in the morning he would jump into our garden covered with a buffalo-hide blanket and come into our house. And beside this, with his intrigues at El Parral, in which he spoke very badly of my husband and even more so of me, who had hardly spoken to him, he got Arteaga and Josefa to run away from my house, as they confessed when they were brought back, and he himself told me not long ago it was so, and all of this for no reason other than his evil disposition and constant quarrelsomeness; and finally, although we always showed him favor, the return he has given us after some days in the town, in connection with whipping a boy of his who had given abundant cause for it, he went to such excess that Don Bernardo threw him out; and what he did was what he always did, and as soon as news of Don Diego's coming arrived, he went out to meet him as far as El Paso, where his cousin had gone, with the intention of seeing whether he could get a job as his secretary; and in order to accomplish this he told great lies, according to what we heard, and to judge by the discord that ensued they must have been quite harmful to us; and Don Diego considered him our great enemy and had him in his house and furthered his career until he sent him as an official guard. And what I had to suffer from him, God knows, to whom I offer it as among the greatest travails I have undergone. His complaints against my husband are countless; but since they are false, I do not know what they are, except that he says that he wanted to flog him and [subject him to] many other punishments. And he is a claimant in the audit. And my husband knows many other evil deeds of this man that I have forgotten. Pedro de Arteaga, in case he should have testified [Witness 12], and Diego Melgarejo, who is [also] our enemy [Witness 13]. The latter is our enemy because on the way to New Mexico Don Bernardo scolded him several times for offenses that he committed, arrested him, and had him in irons for days because he gambled away even his wife's rations.[6] Because of their wicked inclinations, and because of Noriega's lies, they left me at El Parral; and when they were brought back they confessed it and greatly regretted being brought back, and from then on they always hated us greatly, as they showed on all occasions.

And when, on reaching the town [of Santa Fe], we took them into our house for the love of God because we saw them out in the open, this only served so that they might steal from us, at which we caught them many times, with the food that they were sending to the households they were supporting on the outside; and no granary or pantry was safe from them, and they even threw sheep, tied with ropes, over the wall at night, not satisfied with the four that they killed every week and the seven cows, all of which they consumed, and because it was entrusted to them, and several times I was told that they were supporting half the town; and for these reasons we often chastised them severely, without their mending their ways. Apart from this I was informed that they slept outside the house every night; and when I was sick one night and sent my slave to have them bring a woman who used to treat me, she hurried back to say that the servants were running away; and when my husband got up undressed he sent for them and they could not be found, and finally after half an hour they were found and we punished them severely, as we did for the missing items that could not be recovered on this occasion. Likewise they left every day as soon as they had eaten, and when they were wanted great efforts were needed to find them, something that I could not abide and for which I chastised them; and since Josefa was with me we did the same to her, who told them about it, and it all ended with her keeping still and hating me. Beside this I was informed that they went out again at night, and Josefa with them, to revelries and dances in different houses; and when I had proof of this I treated them as they deserved, and more so because to avoid knocking on the door when they came back at night they would leave my front door unlocked; and another time, when they left an opening, my Apache maids escaped through it, and if they had found the door locked, even had they gone into the courtyard they would not have run away if it had not been unlocked; and on this same occasion, when we got up it was no longer possible to find them, nor were they found for a long time, because of which and their failure to amend their ways we chastised and scolded them as was necessary, and then Don Bernardo had them under arrest and told them they would pay for what was missing; and when they were released after a few days and promised to reform, what they did was to start bringing the participants in their revels into our kitchen and keeping them there until we again scolded them when I found out about it, but it did no good; [fol. 150v] and on these occasions, because our slave took part in these things, we had her whipped as an accomplice in them, because she had provided table linens for their banquets and other things. And finally one day Don Bernardo came to tell me during the siesta that I should ask for the key to a storeroom, because when that man had brought a quantity of blankets and he had ordered them to take them into the storeroom as they always did, he went in and it seemed to him that one of them was on lookout and the other one farther inside the room, [and] suspecting trouble and remembering it, he told me about it; and I went out and asked Diego for the key, and as he reached for it he told me that he did not have it but Arteaga did, and when he started to run I went after him [to] the said pantry; and what Don Bernardo had suspected being true, he very promptly picked up a quantity of blankets that they had thrown in there through a window from the storeroom, and while trying to hide them he covered himself in blood because somewhere he injured his head severely in two places; and when I went into a corral not only did I find those blankets, but also numerous others that they had thrown out there from other windows that opened onto it, where they must have thrown out what they were always stealing; and the slave, who was the one who always went to that corral, helped them in this. And when he learned of this, after I had scolded all of them, Don Bernardo slapped Arteaga and arrested them and wanted to flog them as thieves, for which reasons they could not bear us and loathed us because we had been so patient with them. And likewise this man, and all of them with him at their head, procured some women for my husband, because of which I saw myself in such straits that much harm could have come to me; and a person who learned of it, moved to compassion, advised me, and sent me advice through another person, that I should bear it and be patient, lest something should happen to me that would bring on a convulsion and deprive me of my sanity or my life because of the threats that I would sometimes hear they were making against me. And so after endless annoyances I succeeded, almost by violence, to have them expelled from our house, and I greatly wished to have them expelled from town; and even after their expulsion they always did whatever they could against me; and for these and many other reasons all these have been and are my mortal enemies. And this Arteaga is a claimant in the audit. And in addition to this Don Diego attached this man to himself and after giving him other positions made him a mayor, although they say that on his mother's side he is a mulatto or has some such blood. And these men were much devoted to Manso. And so is she and all of them.

Josefa [Witness 17], whose surname I do not know, the wife of Pedro de

Arteaga, in case she should have testified, is our enemy and, like her husband, a leader in all the wickedness committed in my house by my servants and of the hostility they all felt toward us. And this she is for all the reasons stated concerning her husband and Diego, besides which she was herself a woman who spoke badly and had no sense, who was inclined only to whatever was or might be bad, which is why I had constant trouble with her from the first day on; and since their provocations were countless, so also did I scold her countless times, and more so since from the time of our voyage there she could not stand us, both because my husband kept her under arrest for many days, and because one night on the pretext of coming to see me to give me I don't know what treatment, although I had told her that afternoon when she was with me that I did not want to do it, that [night], telling her husband she was coming for that purpose, she went to the tent of a man who was traveling with us, and because she was seen, Don Bernardo found it out and gave her a public dressing down, and if her husband had been a different sort of man things could have gone badly for her, and she so resented it that she complained greatly about it to me. And because of all this she came to hate us intensely. And afterwards, at El Parral, because I found out that when I had her in my house she would go out at night to visit her family and single men and to other places, we most severely rebuked her because she did it and her husband because he permitted it; and since they grumbled against us between themselves and Noriega was giving them [fol. 151r] advice, stirring up the hostility and ill will of them all. And afterwards I learned from them that the bad things he was telling them about me were countless. They decided to run away, as they did, and finally Don Enrique de Ávila rounded them up and put them on the road to catch up with us, writing on their behalf, who, coming now against their will, greatly regretted having returned and felt great hatred and hostility toward us and clearly showed it, for when they were in town in our household she got together with all the white people in it, and then they began doing whatever they wanted there, in order to win them all to their side. Like her, her husband and Diego would go at night to different houses to dance, sing, and put on plays, and on these occasions, and others, they left the front door unlocked so as not to knock when they came back. And when I found out about it, without telling my husband I scolded her severely, and the improvement that this produced was that they did not go out but took to bringing the participants in their carousals to our kitchen, and there they held feasts and great banquets, which caused unbelievable harm to my household, until I got word of it again from outside, as did my husband, and dealt with them as they deserved, and this time with the slave [too], because she had been their accomplice and because knowing it, as she confessed, she had not told me about it; whereupon what they did was that although she did not go, they did and then took to supporting whole households and families, and when we learned of it we caught them with the foodstuffs that they removed from the granaries and pantries wholesale, and though we scolded them and shamed them they never reformed. And one of those nights when they had gone out, something they never gave up, was when I, being sick, had the slave go out to fetch the woman who treated me, and when she came back to say, as I have testified, that my servants were leaving, my husband came out only in his shirt and cape, and I stayed behind getting dressed to go out, and because of my illness I did so slowly, and after a long while I reached the kitchen and there found the slave at the door of a room that had been theirs before, and as soon as she saw me she very quickly turned toward the inside; and as I suspected trouble because she was there, I hastened on and she had already given the alarm, and I found that instead of having looked for the Apaches she seemed to have looked for Josefa, because she rushed out of their room and hurriedly sat down at the door and began to put on her shoes, although they had brought her her clothes much earlier; and when I asked her what she was doing or had done until then, she replied to me very angrily that they had just gone to look for them, that they were not coming back, and while speaking she sneaked out of the room, and to avoid further trouble I kept quiet as best I could and vented my anger when they came back; and when he scolded them he told them they would pay for the servants that might be missing. And on another occasion, when the servants made the opening that I have mentioned and went out into the courtyard, as they found [the door] unlocked they went out through it. And when we got up and went out, they could not be found for a long time, and once they were found we chastised them all, and Don Bernardo was angry and arrested them and told them they would have to pay for the servants that might be missing this time and those missing the previous time, which were altogether seven persons. He kept them jailed many days, and she took great offense at this and at being so sharply reprimanded for allowing her husband and the others to go out to sleep elsewhere and not telling me about it, since she was in charge of all those people. After this she took great offense at what would have made another woman grateful to us, which was that because of the previous revelries that I have mentioned, one of their results, among other disturbances, was that her husband got mixed up with one of the young women they used to bring to them, and because of Lobón, and he came himself to complain to my husband, once the truth was discovered he arrested him and kept him and her stepfather in jail for many days. Another time, at the time of the blankets, he arrested him and slapped him and was on the point of flogging him. And beside this, this was a woman I scolded constantly because she had such a wicked inclination to steal that I did not have anything in chests or desks or anywhere that she did not carry off and that did not disappear. Beside this I learned that she was an accomplice and helped [fol. 151v] in the procuring that her husband carried on for mine and did what she could to further it, for which reason I chastised her countless times, since I did so whenever I had one of the constant fights I had with my husband because of them, because of the great risks to which they exposed me, such that, wicked though she was, she told me aghast one day while I was quarreling with my husband, "Lord, madam, if I weren't seeing this I wouldn't believe it no matter who told me." And I answered her that I owed that to her and her husband and that if he came before me I should stab him with one of the knives with which he used to set the table, and she told him; and they all did what they wished and hated us, until, to avoid greater troubles, I succeeded in having them thrown out of our house, and I greatly wished to throw them out of town, something that they deeply resented, and yet they had to do it because no one who knew them wanted them in his house, until with my consent one of the residents, an enemy of ours, gave them a room in his house, and I permitted it only to get rid of them. And after they were gone, when she sent me word a few days later through my little mulatto girl begging me for God's sake to give her permission to see me because she was dying of hunger and would die without fail if she could not come to avail herself of my charity, I sent her word that for the sake of the God in Whose name she asked me, she should come; and when she did so she was so wretched and thin that she was pitiful to see, and some residents of the town who were there took pity on her and with much weeping she was telling them the great privations she was undergoing, and they, as they knew how hard life was there, pleaded with me that, since I had shown charity toward her until then, I should continue to do so, and I ordered her to come to my house every day, since I was so much alone, and she would eat there; and thus she did until Don Diego came, who, as he used to visit the house where she was living, attached her to himself for various purposes, some of which I learned of from her, and their familiarity reached such a point that I was told that one day they had been seen eating together, although she denied it; and whether this was the time when the persons met her who say that when they asked her where she was going, she said, to that martyrdom and that torment, is something that I request be investigated, in case he, hating us as he did, should have made her say this to make it public so that there might be witnesses who would so testify, determined already to persecute us by this means, as he had already said several times that my husband would be arrested by the Holy Office. And likewise at this time he ordered her husband and her not to come to our house, perhaps because he feared[7] that she might tell. And then when he found out that she had been at our house while he was at Moqui, he was greatly displeased. And during this time, on the occasions when she came unknown to anyone, if Valdés found out about it he had her removed from our house as quickly as possible. And she and her husband also stole two small silver plates from us, although they later turned up in the possession of Noriega; and finally, these two, because of all these arrests, quarrels, thefts, and scoldings, were always so hostile to us that words cannot express the mortal hatred and hostility they felt toward us, and especially toward me; [and] as she constantly had to be scolded because of her husband and Diego and the pimping of them all and her negligence and incompetence and uselessness for anything and because she was nothing but a bad influence on those under her charge, the hatred they felt for me was merciless. And her husband is a claimant in the audit; and furthermore, in case I ought to declare this, I was told several times that she and her husband usually spoke to each other in a language no one understood, and when a woman asked her one day in my presence what language that was and why she was speaking it, another asked her what language she was speaking, and she said it was gibberish.[8] And another woman of my household or who served there on most days told me several times I should have a small box that this couple kept under their bed brought to me, and I, supposing that in it they kept the things they were stealing, and ashamed of how often we had caught them with these things and how neither scolding them nor anything else could make them reform in any way, did not do so; but after considering this and thinking that they might perhaps be keeping something there, just in case, let Ana Carima be asked why she [fol. 152r] told me so often to look at it and why it is[9] that they did not hand the key to it to anyone except the husband to the wife and the wife to the husband. And one time I heard this woman recite a confession that I have never heard from anyone else in my life. I report all this for what it may say about them. And I often scolded her because she did not fast during Lent or on the days of obligation, and said she was sick, and it was not true. And for the great oaths she would utter on the least occasion. And this Diego Melgarejo, besides what I have stated about him in connection with them, is a man whom, since he was a fugitive from this city [Mexico] for I do not know what crime, Don Bernardo used to tell that if he knew his crime he would hang him or burn him or give him the punishment he deserved in keeping with it, and he used to press him with this; which is why, because of his fear, he hated us intensely. Sometimes he slapped him.

The Indian Antonia [Witness 14], who was our cook, in case she should have testified, is our enemy since we arrived there because she was Manso's servant, and when he fled they brought her back under arrest. On this occasion Don Bernardo slapped her for her cheeky replies, because of which, and of her arrest and her hostility toward us, she felt such a hatred toward us that words cannot describe it; and when the cook we had fell ill, we took her out of jail to be our cook, and her behavior always showed she did it against her will, and we were told it was also because she was dissatisfied with not being able to live in the wicked way that she did before [and that] we ordered her not to go out without permission, which she resented to an unbelievable degree; and finally, as soon as Don Diego went there she immediately went to him to complain and ask for permission to leave our house, and he sent her back on that occasion; and when we found out about it we called her and told her we should pay her very well and she should stay, and she complained to me endlessly that I had not cared for her when she was under arrest, because I had the key to the room where she was, and I asked her whether I had not sent blacks and Spanish maids to do it, and if she wanted me to go do it, why had she not informed me; and in short, while she was in my house she always belonged to Josefa's party and group and shared her hatred and ill will, and for all these reasons and because I often scolded her both for shortages that arose and unnecessary expenses and for the great reluctance to do things that I always noted in her, although she was there for all sorts of work, she always has been and is a mortal enemy, as she showed when she fled from my house. Manso sent her a hundred pesos through Father Fletas [Fray Nicolás de Freitas]. Ana, the wife of Juan Joaquín, who is an Indian cook, in case she should have testified, is our enemy, the crony of Josefa and member of her crew and gang, an accomplice in all her wicked deeds and a great friend of hers, for which reasons and many others that she gave me I scolded and severely chastised her several times; and finally, because I learned that my husband had sent to the kitchen for her in my name with the slave in order to take advantage of her, I threw her out; and what she would do is that they hid her in Josefa's room and she stayed there a long time, and although I had scolded her and thrown her out several times, and even though my husband had ordered her to go live with hers and handed her over to him, he would get together with her again; and there was a time when my husband whipped her, at which she and he took great offense, and despite this she always came back to be with Josefa, who kept her hidden from me; and one time, much later, when I found out she was there, I had her brought out and wanted to whip her; and in short she caused me so much trouble and asked that for the sake of a little baby that she had in arms, since it had been born in my house, I should leave her there, and finally I threw her out with stern threats. And for these reasons and many others she is and has been our mortal enemy, and especially mine, and she is a claimant in my husband's audit, she and her husband. And he is the servant of Juan Lucero. Juana, the wife of Alonso, one of the Jémez Indians, in case they should have testified, is our enemy, because when she was our cook I scolded her [for the] many reasons she gave me, and because having been brought from her town because of troubles that she had had there, she was there unwillingly. She formed part of Josefa's gang and helped her as best she could, both in covering up what they were constantly [stealing] and in the other wicked deeds that they carried out in that kitchen. I used to tell them that that room and all who lived in it should be burned because I no longer knew how to keep them in check, and they loathed me and hated me; and finally I threw her out because I learned she was having relations with my husband; and because we caught them stealing they are our enemies, and especially mine for these stated reasons and many others, and I do not recall whether they are claimants in the audit. The Indian María Zuñi, former wife of the late Juan Zuñi, in case she should have testified: this is a savage and completely inept woman, but because she depends on someone it may be that she was made innocently to do what they wanted, and in case this is so I say only that she has no basis for any testimony.

[fol. 152v] My black woman, in case she should have testified, is our enemy because she is a slave, as they all are enemies of their masters; and besides I punished her frequently for her insolence and idle chatter, carelessness and negligence and also gluttony, and because ever since we were on the way there she allied herself with Josefa and they were great friends, so much so that we even saw them [plead] to go together in one cart and kiss each other, for which reason we scolded them severely, and also for their inattentiveness, not to put it another way; and because of this great friendship, as soon as we reached town she began to help in everything that she did and covered up for her; and when I found something out I would have her whipped for it, and then the two of them got together to grumble about us, something they never stopped. And this slave's cleverness allowed her to practice such deceit that she pretended to be pregnant, wrapping herself in rags to create a belly, and she would pretend to faint, affecting to fall and sometimes holding on to the walls; and one day, among others, when I saw it I said or asked Josefa what was the matter with her, and she told me, "Since she's pregnant," which she had told me some days before, "and is fasting, she has these fainting spells and she keeps falling down"; and that is when I told her for the said reason, and I have heard that I told her, that she should not do it; and she thought up so many deceptions about this pregnancy that these women deceived not only me but everyone, and I had even prepared what was needed for her and the baby, as those who made the clothes, and others, know; and this is the way they acted in everything. She used to go out in the morning, if she went out a little before we got up, and went to this house and the other to grouse about us, and sometimes we whipped her for it, and other times after dinner if we lay down; and I also whipped her a few times when I got up and caught her outside the house; and perhaps Josefa was the cause of this because she took her along when she went out. And she was so sloppy that she burned everything, and I remember Josefa telling me that one night when she wanted to [go out] after [her] going to bed, because she had set up a pot or brazier next to her bed when she went to bed and had fallen asleep, her clothes had caught fire, and on this occasion a skirt adorned with silver lace that she was wearing, and part of a bodice, among other things, were burned, as was the scapular or part of the scapular of Our Lady of Carmel concerning which they accuse me that when I scolded her because of the skirt when I saw her, and I had already done so because of the scapular, and Josefa had told me that it had torn, and I have recalled that on this occasion she told me that it had only burned. To find out the facts she should be pressed to tell the truth, since she knows it. I also chastised this slave for covering up the procuring of the others and her own, and several times on account of Josefa in particular and because of what she was stealing from me in chests and desks and cupboards, and she helped her. And because Josefa had so many secrets with this woman that, not content with their talk in the kitchen, if they came in at about nightfall to make my bed they would stay there half an hour or an hour or more talking with such secretiveness that sometimes I tried very hard to hear them and I had some of my girls do so, and neither they nor I were able to hear those things, which, after I have seen this [indictment], has caused me more concern as to whether this woman, who perverted her in other matters, had done so in some evil thing. I scolded her for covering up for Petrona, when she was in our house and afterwards. In short, this woman, as a slave with the hostility of a slave and because of her quarrels and Josefa's and those of the others, and covering up all I have mentioned and her deceptions, always felt mortal hatred for us, and because of her master's great hatred for her and the punishments I inflicted on her and many other reasons is and has been our enemy. Petrona de Gamboa and her parents and brothers, in case they should have testified, are our enemies. This woman and her parents were brought to my house under arrest because of a girl whom her mother had beaten to death; and when, because she said she was a virgin, I ordered her to sleep in a room farther inside the house than mine, where my maids slept, what she did was to pry loose a board from one of the windows and go out that way and go to sleep with whomever she wished, although I did not learn of this until later; and they also told me that the slave accompanied her, because they were great friends, and it is a fact that she could not have done this without her consent because she slept there; and in the morning they came back through the same garden [fol. 153r] and window. I scolded this woman on different occasions and chastised her and her mother because she vehemently denied having committed the murder, and because of my pity for the poor victim I could not stand her. Another [time I scolded her] because, when Noriega was standing there talking to Don Bernardo, she pretended to be passing by and tried to take hold of his hand; and after they left I spoke to her as her brazenness deserved. And later I did so because I was advised not to let her go out in the morning because she had often been brought back from his door. And because of her quarrels and squabbles with other women on various occasions. And because of other shameless actions that I saw and learned of, because she was of the type to go after anyone. After the trial of her parents Don Bernardo ordered her to go with them. I afterwards learned that while she was in our house, and outside the house, she had had relations with him; and when I was informed of this I learned that he would bring her to a room to see her, and when I had asked for the key to get rid of this difficulty and ordered Ana Carima, who was her aunt, that she should not come to my house because I should skin her alive with whippings, because when she came on the pretext of seeing me she would see him there before or afterwards, and when I had asked my husband whether this was right, and other things that as his own wife I had to say, and he [was] blinded by the deceit and felt it as they all do, and for this reason I came to have more quarrels with him than I can say; and when she learned of them because her go-betweens and Josefa told her about them, because she was one of her gang[10] and party, as one for whom her husband pimped and she covered up, she came to be so insolent that often, when he and I were standing at the parlor door toward nightfall like two silent statues, with him resenting my watching over him, and as I did so I heard this woman come to the front door where the servants were, and especially after Arteaga had been thrown out by Diego Melgarejo, who, as he was there, tried to drive her out, even shoving her, but he could not do it, but like a weaver's shuttle or a mad dog she would constantly rush in and out furiously as though giving him to understand with those actions that why was it that he did not drive me out and allowed me to keep her from seeing him; and when he saw that I was weeping because of the threats that he had made to me on account of her and others and I dared not speak a word lest they grow even more insolent toward me, I went out to shout at Diego, what did he want, some armor, and pretending not to recognize her, and for all they both did, she paid no heed, because of which I used to speak of her as she deserved, and it was all reported to her, and she hated me intensely. And this woman and her mother, who, once she knew about it, served as her go-between as best she could, used to send one of her sons so brazenly that in my presence he came to ask him for something, and I scolded him several times, speaking ill of them, and he told them about it and for these reasons they hated me no end. And one time I took off after him calling my servants to beat him and others with a stick.

This woman seemed like a shadow or goblin, and there was no place I could be but she would show up, in the garden and everywhere; and since I had to resent this, they brought upon me every day countless very tiresome and dangerous conflicts with my husband, which was what she provoked him to because of their great hatred of me. After Peñalosa, or Don Diego, came there he attached this woman to himself, and through her all her family, because after countless incidents she and her family came to hate my husband; and although she spoke ill of him she got him to marry her to his coachman, and she sued him on account of her honor, and her father [sued] for his having condemned him, if I remember correctly, for the death of his wife; and for these and other reasons all of these are and have been our mortal enemies, and especially mine.

The late Álvaro de Paredes, who was killed by lightning, in case he should have testified, was our enemy because, having gone there when we did, he had some quarrels on the way, especially with the commander of the soldiers, and Don Bernardo reproached him for these several times, and I do not recall whether for one of them he had him under arrest for a while. And once there, because he had married and because of his bad character, both his father-in-law and his wife [fol. 153v] had various complaints against him, for which reason he frequently reproached him; and at last, because he did not reform in any of his affairs, he sent him on escort duty [*escoltas*] as a punishment. On other occasions he ordered him to go on expeditions [*jornadas*]. On still others he sent him to town under arrest; but nothing was of any use, because of which and of great quarrels that he had with various of her relatives, even wounding some of them, and all of them complaining, he punished him. When Don Diego came and everything was in turmoil with his machinations against us, he was called to testify in the audit, and he came to our house to pay endless homage to my husband, and they say that afterwards he boasted of having deceived him and having testified against him ruthlessly; and he is also [our enemy] because of the great enmity of his brother-in-law Tomé Domínguez, and because they and Bartolomé Romero and Bartolomé de Ledesma, provoked to it by Don Diego or on his orders, submitted a petition or complaint against Don Bernardo on behalf of different persons or in the name of the council, and when he was informed of it he submitted a contrary one, according to the information he had been given concerning it, with the full truth of that matter; and when he took it to Don Diego he had very serious encounters with him, even challenging him to a duel, of which he later complained to me very bitterly. And he was so sorry that the said complaint or petition was discovered that he removed Bartolomé de Ledesma from his post as attorney for the council, saying that the men there did not know how to keep a secret, and he made great efforts to find out who had told Don Bernardo about it. In short, this man, for all these reasons of his own and of his brother-in-law and other relatives, was a great enemy of ours. And we were also told that to get revenge he had given damaging testimony before the custodian, and to judge by his shamelessness and lack of judgment, that would not be surprising, although I do not know what truth there is in this, as I do know the great enmity he felt toward me and my husband.

Tomé Domínguez de Mendoza, in case he should have testified [Witness 4], is our enemy because ever since we went there, as he was very loyal to Manso and was his lieutenant general, Don Bernardo removed him, and he greatly resented it. He sent him on expeditions. He sent some of his relatives on escort duty, which is what they all complain about. On one occasion, because of his arrogance, having put up with a great deal from him, he grew angry with him for good reasons that he had given him, and he knocked him down and even shoved him and kept him under arrest in town, and they considered themselves much offended, saying that he had punched him in the face. He complained of his relatives, the Granillos, on account of the dispatch to Sonora.[11] And likewise for all these reasons and many others and because of the matter of the petition or complaint and of many of his relatives, he is and has been our special enemy. And apart from this, this man, both during the audit and thereafter, would come to our front door at night and call for his brother Juan Domínguez, who was living in our house, and they would be there talking for a long time; and when the brother came back we used to ask him who had sent for him, and when he told us, as he did, about the great warnings and urgings that he employed to get him to leave my husband, he said that he did this because the friars were threatening him, saying that if he did not do so he would find himself in the worst travails in which any man had ever found himself, and many other things in this vein, and he said this because he was much devoted [to the friars] and especially to Father Fray Salvador Guerra, secretary to the custodian, who is the worst enemy we have, and a great friend of his. And finally, after all these threats, and in fact making many more against him later, they did not do anything to this Juan Domínguez, and he worked for some friars. I do not know the reason for their not inflicting on him the harm with which they had threatened him, other than that they had succeeded in doing to us what they wished.

May the truth about this become known and valued as such. [fol. 154r][12] The Chaveses, in case they should have testified, are our enemies, because one of them is the son-in-law of Tomé Domínguez [Witness 4],[13] and the other, the father-in-law of Juan, and for all the reasons stated [concerning them], and also on their own, they have many complaints of having been sent both on escort duty and on expeditions, and because he reproved them for sowing discord and other things, for which reasons they are and have been our mortal enemies. The Granillos, in case they should have testified, are our enemies, both as cousins of Tomé's wife, who is our enemy and proved it by speaking very ill of us, and because of the reasons stated concerning them, and because when one of them was taking the dispatch that my husband sent to Sonora, we know for sure that two weeks after he left the kingdom a Theatin friar gave him 7,000 pesos for it, effectively buying it all, and he, to suit himself, wanted only to go to Sonora, and after more than a year he returned to us the men who had driven the pack animals and some of the beasts, without sending silver [*plata*, payment in silver] or anything; and after Don Diego came, because from El Parral he ordered him to bring him the silver as though it were his property, he came with part of it, and although it should have been the said 7,000 pesos, they say he only brought 2,952 pesos, which Don Diego took, like everything else; and he did not want to settle accounts before, because he asked my husband for the account book, which he had sent to El Parral and therefore could not deliver even had he wanted to, after great urgings and demands he fined him 200 pesos because he did not hand it over, despite his having told him that he did not have it there. And in addition to this, they lodged a claim against him then, although the audit had long been over, for the carrying charges of the mules that had brought the silver that Don Diego seized; and for all these reasons and many others they have been and are our mortal enemies.

Francisco de Trujillo, his wife, his son, and daughter-in-law, Andrés Hurtado and his wife, who is the son of Vaca, who is also his son-in-law, and his wife, in case they should have testified, all are and from the first day have been our mortal enemies.[14] The father, because when we went there he removed him from his post as mayor of Moqui, where he was from, and they all took offense at that. He also sent them on escort duty and expeditions and had them under arrest on various grounds. In addition he sequestered and rebuked the women several times as the most scandalous women in the place. And after countless occasions like these he sent them word to come to town; and having notified them, and they having said that they would obey, the old man and his son took the latter's wife and dressed her in men's clothes, and when they had walked past two or three houses in this way, and people saw her like that in a big leather jacket and all of them dressed for travel, they asked them where they were going, and they said that in order not to come to town they were running off to El Parral; and afterwards it was said that they had hidden her in a monastery, and others said in a house, and leaving her hidden they went to El Parral; and when Don Diego got there a little later he brought them back, very much attached to him, and after some dealings he reappointed the old man mayor of Moqui, and he had great authority with them and later even had relations with one of the women, for which reasons and many others they have been and are merciless mortal enemies not only of my husband but also, as I have learned, of mine, even though I hardly know them. And Alonso Vaca and his wife, in case they should have testified, are also part of this, in case he has some complaints, which also makes them our enemies. And Trujillo and some of his sons-in-law are claimants in the audit. A mulatto called Ortega, whose first name I do not know, in case he should have testified, is one of these and our mortal enemy, in case he complains of escort duty and expeditions like all of them, and of other things.

Francisco de Valencia, in case he should have testified, is our enemy because he is the enemy of every governor. He has the usual complaint about escort duty and expeditions, and others that Don Bernardo will know better than I, as with many others that I do not know. Alonso García, in case he should have testified, has been our enemy since we went there because he is much devoted to Manso, and was the one who eventually brought him to this city when he fled. And for this reason he has many complaints against my husband, because of which he is [our enemy]. Ana Rodríguez, her mother, grandmother, and aunt, in case they should have testified: [fol. 154v] This woman, with Arteaga as go-between, had relations with my husband, for which reason, after I found it out, I publicly spoke about them as they deserved, and my resentment almost made me tell her husband, which they found out through Josefa and her husband and considered themselves much offended by it as though they were in the right; and when Don Bernardo, who had been away, came back and I had the opportunity to let him know I was informed of it, there was such unpleasantness and grief that words cannot express it; and as they kept it up and I found out that he brought her to my house several times and that her wicked mother, who covered up for her with her husband, would accompany her, and I was affected by it as his lawful wife, they eventually put me in so bad a state, unable to find a remedy or to remain unaffected by it, and seeing that every day brought more and more grief on account of these women and I had no remedy but always to speak ill of them, I did so constantly; and when they found out about it, as they did through the aforesaid, they hated me no end.

And despite all this I learned that one Easter, to dissimulate, they wanted to come to see me with their husbands, who told them to come, and I said they should do so, for I should have my Apaches whip them one by one until they were skinned alive. Apart from this I made them feel ashamed so that they might not show themselves before me, and to their aunt Ana, for reasons that she gave me, I sent word several times telling her what she deserved on their account. And also because I found out that some of the times that they were brought to my house they were shut up in the storeroom to hide them from me, and on these occasions carried off whatever they wanted and afterwards sold what they wished, I called them thieves, and they were not unaware of this, because that is what they were called in town. And in short, all these women, for these reasons and many others impossible to recount, are and have been my mortal enemies, and so much so that on account of them I was sometimes threatened even with the loss of my life, so vexed was I because of these women. And when Almazán, who was their grandfather, and his sons and sons-in-law found out about it they hated Don Bernardo for it more than one can say, and even me, although they knew I was in the right, for because of those women I hated them, and when they came to the house I spoke to them as unkindly as may be imagined, and for this reason and because they knew what I was saying about them, they hated me to an incredible degree. And Don Diego attached these women to himself, so much so that he called them his relatives, and there would be no end to it if one tried to tell all that happened with this; and he made Almazán a clerk for my husband's audit because he knew of his enmity. Colonel Pedro Lucero de Godoy, in case he should have testified, and his sons, who are many, in case they should have done so, and the people of his household: Since we went there this man has harbored the greatest ill will toward my husband because he told him I do not know what on the day he rode out to meet us because he had learned some things about him. To suit his purposes he kept these feelings to himself while my husband was governor, and he is in the habit of saying, "Keep quiet and move on, for another [day] will come." And on every occasion they all say, "To the rising sun, not the setting sun," and this they say because of the governors who come and the one whose term is over, indicating that the latter can no longer do them any good, and the new one can, and this is very common there and I heard it said several times. This man and all of them were much devoted to Manso. And sometimes he grows angry with the governors and withdraws from them and then pretends to be sick, and since my husband realized this and said so to his relatives, they resented it. They also resented the fact that on receiving some news he sent Bartolomé Romero on escort duty when he had gone only recently, because others were about to set out on an expedition, and then he fell ill and they said it was because of going, despite having treated him very kindly on that occasion, which they repaid as they repay everything, and they lodged various complaints about it and they resented their sons and brothers having to go on other such expeditions. And if they had not had other reasons to be angry, as they are at their judge about everything, there would have been sufficient reason with the return of their brother and son with the dispatches that they were taking to the tribunals of this city, and they came back with them and did the other things that are known about this matter. And Don Diego, because they came back with him, and in order to attach them to the others because of what had happened, made Juan Lucero, the son, his secretary, who tried to attach all the others, and for various reasons they were finally all attached, like the relatives they were. And Don Diego caused no little trouble [fol. 155r] to help achieve this by telling them countless slanders against Don Bernardo, and one was that shortly after he had gone there, when Doña Catalina de Zamora, this man's daughter, had come to see me, he had her go about asking who had heard what I had said to her, and when some people asked her what it was, she said that I had fought with her and among other things had called her a so-and-so, all of which was false; and when we tried to find out where this story had come from, she herself told me that Don Diego had invented it and that she could find no other reason for it than that he had done it to separate her from me and so that it should come to the notice of her family in order to put them on bad terms with us. And he did many things like this, and I also found out from a sister of this woman about the great trouble he stirred up with Francisco Gómez, saying, why did he not kill my husband; and to incite him to do this he told him that he had said many bad things about him and his father, which was false. I heard and she told me many other things, and among them also that he told him that his mother[15] was overly fond of friars, all of which is false, because it was one of his lies. And I also learned that just now or a little before we were arrested he had called Doña Ana Robledo and her daughter Doña Francisca, who are the mother and stepmother of Francisco Gómez and of Juan Lucero, and for an unknown purpose had told them that having received orders—I do not know whether he said from the royal audiencia—to cut off the heads of these two because of the return,[16] he had not done so, and that for all that he could not content them, and I do not know why he would have told them this, nor did they know. They are our enemies also because of the [enmity] that Antonio de Salas feels toward us, and because he was jailed for a few days because of things that he did, and because he reprimanded María de Vera and her daughters, because sometimes we would laugh at how Salas's daughter was pulled out of the chimney, and they found out about it. And in short, even if this family had no reason other than the mortal enmity of Juan Lucero, that would suffice for them to hate us without mercy or limits, because being, as Don Diego's secretary, so fierce an enemy, and the depositary of all his secrets and deeds, what would he and his family not do for their preservation and to please him, as we have seen and experienced whenever an occasion arose. To try to recount all of these would be an endless task, but for [the reasons] mentioned and many others all of them are and have been our mortal enemies.

Diego Romero and his wife [Catalina de Zamora, Witness 23], in case they should have testified: She is this man's daughter, and he, his son-in-law, and so they are our enemies because these complaints affect them. They also considered themselves wronged by our complaints that they had testified falsely at the audit, although he always said and insisted very emphatically that what the charges of the audit said had been his testimony was untrue, and he sent us word to this effect through various persons; but they nonetheless declared themselves our enemies on this occasion and took the side of his brother Juan Lucero and his cousin Francisco Gómez, who were on that of Don Diego, as I have stated, who I suppose told them, among other things that he told, if not to Diego Romero himself, to his relatives, so that they should tell him, what Father Villar was said to have said a few days earlier, that my husband had had something to do with Doña Catalina in a bean field; and I was told that they were furious about it, although the truth is that what the friar had said was not that, as we later learned, and this was false witness against him, and what he was saying had happened with another friar; and she complained to me about it at the time; and she felt affronted by me because, with good intentions and without believing it to be true, I told her about her niece, Salas's daughter, so that they might remedy it, and she took offense at

it. She was greatly disturbed by the arrest of her brother and his being made
to pay what he owed. They resented the matter of the sheep that he gave my
husband in lieu of what he owed him, and afterwards they considered themselves deeply offended on that account; and in short, these two, for all these
reasons of their own and those of their relatives, which it would be an endless
task to try to recount, have been and shown themselves to be our enemies.
And in addition, if she should have testified, Don Diego will know very well
why, because she was one of those whom I asked him to call for me and he
asked me what I wanted her for, that the women there were only good for
giving false witness, and the other things that I have stated he said to me on
that occasion. Antonio de Salas, his wife and sons and daughters, in case they
should have testified: These are our enemies. He is the brother of this Doña
Catalina and Juan Lucero. He declared himself [our enemy] shortly after we
went there, because at the request and on the complaints of the Indians of
[fol. 155v] Puaque on account of the great vexations that they all inflicted
on the Indians and of those that his sons inflicted on the Indians and other
offenses, he [Don Bernardo] ordered him to demolish a small adobe house
he had in the town; and he took great offense because the Indians asked for
the land that was theirs.

He jailed his sons for their misdeeds. He sent them on escort duty and
expeditions, which is the general complaint and cannot be avoided. He had
him under arrest for a day or a day and a half for having gone as an absolute ruler to take from an Indian the few supplies he had, for no reason and
without his owing him anything; and after he came to complain of him he
was ordered to make restitution, and since in his arrogance he would not do
so he placed him under arrest until he paid.[17] He complains that on another
occasion he made him pay another man, and pretending that he had nothing
to give him, he gave him a jacket or cape, intending that it be returned to
him; and because he received it as payment and went off with it, he complained loudly. And he did the same because of some sheep that my husband
received, and although he gave them to him as payment for what he owed
him, he later repented and complained constantly, saying that he had taken
them from him. He complains about his son-in-law's having asked him for
what he owed him, which he has not paid, and he has given a note for it. And
besides this he has given many an occasion for punishment, and although he
did not receive it as he deserved, he and his family have been such enemies
of ours that even after Juan Lucero attached him to himself, and Don Diego,

too, despite his having carried off his virgin daughter through the chimney, instead of feeling offended with the man who had done this he was offended with us who sometimes witnessed it. And because he is our great enemy, and for his own reasons, Don Diego, as soon as he arrested my husband, made him the chief guard, in which position, giving vent to his own hatred and to Don Diego's, he inflicted so many vexations and annoyances on us that they cannot be told. And he is a claimant in the audit. And when this man was at our house, if someone came in without his seeing them and he saw them as they were leaving, he stripped them to see whether they were carrying dispatches from my husband, as he did with Francisco Jiménez; and when we asked him why he did that, he said it was by order of Don Diego, and in this respect he did things impossible to describe. And on other occasions he would search the persons who entered the house, even my own Indians, and especially at nightfall; and when we asked him several times why he did that, sometimes he said it was by order of Don Diego, who strongly urged him to take care lest some disguised friar should come in to kill my husband, and at other times he would say that he did it on his own for that same reason; and there was an occasion, among the few when my husband spoke to him while he was at the house and told him that one day he would be called to account for the many things he was doing, when he answered him that as for searching those who went in and out, he did not want a disguised friar to come in and kill him; and when Don Bernardo answered him, "Go on, what friars? Because the others do not get involved in such things or think of it," he answered him that he was inside there and did not know anything, and many things were going on outside and everything was topsy-turvy, and that his bed was very well made, and many other things, so many that to tell them all is impossible.

María de Vera and her daughters, in case they should have testified: This woman is the stepdaughter of this Salas, and as such all his complaints affect her, and she has many on behalf of herself and her daughters, and not the least of them is that Don Bernardo sent them reprimands several times because of the scandals that they occasion with their loose living, and also because he collected what she owed him, and I believe she is still in debt to him. And beside this he took away from her the estate [*encomienda*] that belonged to her stepson Pedro de Montoya, and since it belonged to him he assigned it to him, and it is unbelievable how much offense she took at this and how many complaints she lodged. And he also had some other business with her, which Don Bernardo knows and can explain better than I, for what I know in general is the great enmity that for this and other reasons she has always felt and feels [toward him] and toward me, speaking ill of me without my knowing her and showing herself to be the mortal enemy of both of us. In addition she is a claimant in the audit. And furthermore she is the mother-in-law of Trujillo's son, and all of their complaints affect her. And beside this she is very much attached to Don Diego and very close to him because one of her daughters has an illicit relationship with him. Another [daughter], whom I have mentioned, belongs to Fray Nicolás de Fletas [Freitas], who is one of our greatest enemies. Inés de Zamora and her son, in case they should have testified: She is our enemy, and her son more so, and his hatred reached such a point that once he met my little mulatto girl in some houses that he frequented, and as though the girl had reached the age of reason he [fol. 156r] threatened her, telling her, with reference to my husband, "Now your daddy will see, he'll see"; and when she told me that he kept telling her this, and when I looked into who it was that was telling her this, I learned it was he, who I believe is called Domingo López; and although, if he has some complaints, I do not know for sure what they are, except for an argument about a petty estate, and I know of no other reason whatsoever other than his being part of the conspiracy mounted against us by them all. The mother was a strong adherent of Don Diego and I do not [know] whether he is, and she is considered to be one of the most wicked tongues there are there, and I have some experience of that. She is a dependent of the Luceros and even related to some of them, and they are our enemies, like all of them. Bartolomé Romero [Witness 15] and his wife, in case they should have testified: He declared himself our enemy, and so did she, on the occasion when they all conspired, without there having previously been any reason for it; but as they never lack reasons as long as they are against the judge, that is how it turned out, for at the time of the petition or complaint that I have mentioned, either on behalf of private citizens or prepared, they said, on behalf of the council by order of Don Diego, and it appeared that it was drawn up at his house, and they said he said that in it they should say that my husband had tried to scale his house to get to his wife, when the fact is that no scaling was needed to get at her, besides the report being false, and it is a fact that Don Bernardo did not leave his house except to go to church. But as long as he could malign him he had no concern for his own repute, and finally, it was said, those who were drawing it up refused to put down such a thing and blamed him for it. And this man, only because of the escort duty on which he sent him shortly after we arrived because there was no one else to send, always considered himself our enemy. And he is a cousin of Francisco Gómez and Diego Romero, related to Juan Lucero, and all of them and she are [relatives?] of those they call "the many,"[18] which is enough for them all to be our enemies, and I know they are also mine, without my having given them any cause for it, unless she is my enemy because she was a friend of Josefa's, because she was the sort of woman who does not miss the chance to make trouble with whomever she can. And I believe he is a claimant in the audit.

And concerning Miguel de Noriega [Witness 5 and 26], in addition to what I have stated, I now remember that when he had joined with Don Diego and was at his house, it was said he had the council summoned for I do not know what documents, and he sent him for them, and what I found out is that when he would not comply with what some of the residents seemingly wanted, the mayor, who was Bartolomé Gómez Robledo, had some differences with him about them and after exchanging some words they drew their swords or partly drew them or were about to do so in the council; and when Don Diego learned of it he had the mayor arrested and brought him to his house, and when we found out what was going on and investigated what it was about, we were told it was about some letters or I do not know what documents that Don Diego was making the council prepare against Don Bernardo, but we could not find out for certain what they were or what they contained or about what, and we only learned that the quarrel had been about the mayor's having said that that was the greatest and most obvious unfairness, and we were also told that he had said other things that I do not now recall, nor do I know whether the documents were drawn up or not. So that it may be known, in case it is important, Manuel Jorge, the smith, and his wife, in case they should have testified: He is our enemy and has various complaints against my husband and has on every occasion shown his hatred for us. And he is a claimant in the audit. And he is at all times truly our mortal enemy, and his wife along with him.

Francisco de Madrid and his wife and sons and daughters, in case they should have testified: This man has been our enemy since we went there, in the first place because he is very devoted to Manso, and because after he had told my husband that he is a mestizo, he asked I don't know whom whether it was true, and he answered him that it was, and he told him, and since he is so conceited he took great offense at this.[19] He was also offended because when he was on the expedition to the Rio Grande, he sent him as a soldier and not as a commander; and Manso, it was seen, had no small part in this trouble, as on their return, when it became known that they were on the way, he came to tell Don Bernardo before they arrived that he should be aware of the fact that many of the men who were coming would desert and that Madrid was their leader; and when finally they all came back he asked him or told him what he had been told, and he replied that it was true, he had been about to desert, that on the way he had been given a letter that he had shown to some of the men and in which he was told that when he reached town Don Bernardo would do him much harm, [fol. 156v] and that some of the men had counseled him not to worry and he would see that the warning was false, to which Don Bernardo replied that no such thought had occurred to him; and finally, when he asked him from whom the letter had come, he insinuated, if I remember correctly, that it was from Manso. I do not know whether this was true, yet nonetheless he always harbored enmity and complaints.

Several times he rebuked his sister. Because of complaints he several times arrested his nephews, sometimes obliged them to go on escort duty and expeditions, and also his brother Lorenzo, who is also our enemy for different reasons. He pointed out how little attention they paid to their mother while she was perishing. This man is related to the little mulatto girl whom Don Diego has in his house and is very much attached to him, as is Lorenzo, and for all these reasons and many that my husband knows better than I, he and all of them have been no end hostile to us; and he and, I understand, his brother are claimants in the audit. Mariaca and her daughters, in case they should have testified: She has always been our enemy and is a sister of the Madrids, and she clearly showed her hatred toward us, because her vengeance did not stop until she saw me taken away under arrest on the night they did that, and I know this because when we got to the corner of the square Fray Nicolás de Fletas said, "Listen, who is that woman over there?," and the others answered him, "Where?," and he said, "Over there next to the poplars," and when they all looked they said, "Mariaca," and they also said, "I would have sworn it had to be she," and this was without my knowing her or ever having spoken to or of her in my life. Her complaint stems from the rebukes that my husband used to send her because of her loose living, and from his arresting her sons on some complaints and making them pay for some things that they were stealing in the towns and other places. And he sent them on escort duty when it was necessary, and they went out on some expeditions.

And finally she is related to the one they call the woman of many, who is the mother of the little mulatto whom Don Diego has in his house, and they are all mortal enemies of mine and speak and have spoken about me like the sort of people they are. Miguel de Hinojos, in case he should have testified, and his wife and sons and sister and daughter: He is our enemy because Don Bernardo removed him from the chieftainship of the Jémez on account of illness and incapacity, and he had a complaint about his collecting what he owed him, and also about the rebukes to his sister and niece, which they all complain about bitterly, even though they live as they do, and also for many other reasons that my husband knows better than I; and he is a claimant in the audit. I do not know that this man has any reason [for complaint] other than his having told him often to rebuke his daughters, because of which he and they are our enemies, because that is all the reason one needs there. He clearly showed his hatred when Don Diego had made him chief bailiff and sent him to our house on various errands and he took his revenge as best he could. Don Bernardo must know whether he has other complaints; I do not, since I hardly know these people. I do not know whether he has lodged some claim in the audit. José Téllez Girón and his mother-in-law, wife, and sisters-in-law, in case they should have testified: This man is our enemy because, on account of his lack of judgment and things that he did, he removed him from his post as adjutant, [and] because he told him to hand over some lands to a brother-in-law of his because they were rightfully his, because he was obliged to send him on escort duty, and he jailed him for a day or two; for which reasons, and others of his mother-in-law and brothers-in-law, he and they are our mortal enemies. And he is the brother-in-law of Juan Lucero, and a claimant in the audit.

The Cerrillos, Doña Bernardina, her daughters and sons, in case they should have testified, all of whom are our enemies, because Manso is the godfather of Doña Margarita's child,[20] and Agustín de Carabajal, who is her brother-in-law, is the son-in-law of Madrid; and they all have many reasons, which I do not know and Don Bernardo does, and he will explain them. And I know only that they are all mortal enemies not only of my husband but also mine. And some of them are claimants in the audit. Elena Gómez and her daughters, in case they should have testified, are our enemies, and one of her sons more than any of them, because, if I am not mistaken, when he was guarding Don Juan Manso at the time he fled, he fled with him, and I think his name is Domingo López. They also have other complaints, which are never lacking against a judge, and they have the usual one about escort duty and expeditions. And my husband probably knows other things that I, since I hardly know them, do not; and some of them are claimants in the audit. And I know that some of them owe my husband money, and he must have notes signed by them.

Diego González Lobón and Margarita, his wife, in case they should have testified: [fol. 157r] This man, when Don Bernardo sent him to El Parral with a dispatch shortly after we arrived, gave some persons some of the bulls or oxen that he was taking and did other things like that; and after he came back he failed to give a proper account of what he had taken, and some things were missing, and when he was asked about it he had countless excuses, and one of those who had gone with him told him and reported to him all he had done, and when he was told this he replied that he had done it with the intention of paying for it if it were found out; and when Don Bernardo ordered some persons to settle the accounts there, they did so, and he said he would pay within a time limit that he requested and that was granted to him, and a few days later he asked for permission to go to the salt pits to collect I do not know what things, and he came to this city and stayed here until he became strongly attached to Don Diego when he went [to New Mexico], and he kept him with him there, too, and would not make him pay my husband what he owed him. And he sent him with Father Fray Nicolás de Chávez to this city to deliver the audit he had made of him and the dispatches that the friars were sending to this Holy Office, according to what people said there; and afterwards, because Fray Nicolás died as soon as he arrived in this city, he took the replies back to Don Diego and the friars, as was seen by their effect, and it was said that Don Diego rewarded him for the good news, and his own sister told me that. And his wife and he are our enemies because at the outset she was one of Josefa's gang and her close friend, and she covered up for the girl with whom Arteaga was involved, who became pregnant; and on the day he quarreled with her, Arteaga said the quarrel was about her wanting to give her a potion that would make her miscarry, and because he did not want this they were finally on the point of killing each other. And Don Bernardo had her under arrest for a few days because of this, and he also rebuked her several times for her loose living and about other women for whom she covered up both within and without her house. And for these reasons and others these two have been and are our mortal enemies. And he is a claimant in the audit. Antonia González, in case she should have testified, and Pedro de Montoya, her nephew, in case he should have done so: She is the sister of Diego González Lobón, and he is his nephew, and they have the same complaints as they and in addition, that he rebuked her for her loose living, for that is all the reason you need there to make them your enemies. The nephew is much attached to Don Diego; he has made him his adjutant and brought him from Zacatecas in his immediate circle and almost always has him in his house. And he serves him in other ways that are not good. And for these reasons he is our enemy.

Juan Durán and his father, in case they should have testified: These are a couple of wretched Indians. The son is warden of the jail, very devoted to Arteaga and his wife and so must share their wiles. He is our enemy, and a claimant in the audit. Nicolás Durán and his wife and sons—he is Don Diego's adjutant—in case they should have testified, it must have been to follow in the path of all the others. I do not know of any reasons. He was our enemy.

Hernando Martín and his sons and daughter-in-law, in case they should have testified: This man adapts himself to every change in the weather and acts in keeping with it. And as long as he can play his tricks, as he says, he is satisfied. If he has done anything it must be so as not to do without them, and he would be our enemy. And his daughter-in-law is very much our enemy.

Bartolomé de Ledesma, in case he should have testified, and his wife: This is the man Don Diego made attorney for the council and the one who prepared the aforesaid petition or complaint. He is our enemy because he rebuked him for allowing his wife to live as she does. He has the usual [complaint] about escort duty and expeditions and other things that Don Bernardo will know better than I; as he did not tell me about them, I do not know them. And if she has done anything it would be because of Noriega, because of the relations she maintained with him. And as soon as we were arrested, this man fled to Sonora, I do not know why. An Indian of the Apache nation, married to an Indian muleteer whose name I believe must be Alonso, and hers, Antonia [Antonia Isabel, Witness 14], in case they should have testified: [fol. 157v] This woman was brought from the Río Abajo area from the house of a Spaniard in which she was employed, because it was known that she maintained unlawful relations with him; and she had I do not know how many children by him despite being married. We hired her as a cook, and she lived there as though under compulsion and against her wishes, and she joined up with Josefa like all the others and helped her in all she did, for which reason, and others, I sometimes chastised her, and also for being there so grudgingly even though she was being paid; and finally, after I do not know how long, for reasons that I do not remember and for being unskilled, I threw her out, and Don Bernardo ordered her under various threats not to return to the house where she had been; and because of her regret at losing the comforts she had there, and for other reasons, she and her husband have been our enemies. A young Indian called Alonso, in case someone should have made him testify: He was brought to our house and flogged for thefts that he was committing in the towns and ranches. And when he was at our house he was flogged several times for this bad habit and we often scolded him, and as that was his nature there was no reforming him. And finally, because he gambled away some stirrups and buffalo hides, he ran away, and Peñalosa, or Don Diego, took him along in his service when he went to Moqui. And because we scolded and punished him he is our enemy, and because he goes along with all the others. A certain Francisco, whom they call Calavés, in case he should have testified: This man is our enemy and always has been. He has some complaints, because people will always complain against judges. Toward the end I scolded him and grew very angry because of a rug that he was making for me and that was almost finished, and he replied that Don Diego had taken it away from him and ordered him to finish it for him. And I have paid him for the work and have given him full deposit for it, and despite this, at the end of our time there he sent for a deposit and I gave it to him and he gave us a note for [the rug] and for what I had given him for it, because that was the truth, despite his being angry at us; and if he has done anything it must have been in order to go along with all the others and because Don Diego brought him to his house to make rugs and kept him there. A certain Apodaca, whose first name I do not know, in case he should have testified: Don Bernardo kept this man in jail for many days, and although I do not know the reason in detail, in general it was this, that on complaint from his wife or report that [Don Bernardo] received that he had illicit relations with two or three of his stepdaughters, and some of them had children or had had them by him, and finally some or all of them confessed, and he banished him and punished him in other ways. And when Don Diego found him at El Parral he brought him along attached to him, as he did others, and later he examined the case and arrested him and was so stern with him that he sentenced him to be hanged, although afterwards he did not do it; and if he has done anything it might be to support his denial, and for this reason he is our enemy, [and] for the same reason, his wife and stepdaughters and their husbands, because both of them are married now, and also the other one and the daughter who had been placed under the protection of the court, and I do not know whether this one had relations with him, or I do not remember what I heard about her, although I do recall that she has a baby, and I do not know whose they told me it was. And I believe he is a claimant in the audit.

Juan Muñoz Polanco [Witness 7], in case he should have testified, has been our enemy almost since our arrival there, and he went with us as a soldier, and stayed there, and we did a great deal for him. Because [Don Bernardo] had learned that he had had relations with one of the daughters of Catalina Bernal and had scolded him for it, both because he was offending against God and because he was spending on her what he had taken with him and what his wife would need here, and after other things Don Bernardo had told him several times he should come here to live with her, because he had no business there, one of those times when he so ordered him he replied with I do not know what impertinence that obliged him to arrest him, and he indicted him and held him for punishment for the lack of respect, and finally I interceded for him and he did him no harm; and despite this he has been one of our worst enemies, and as our enemy, and as a countryman of Valdés and Noriega, he joined up with Don Diego as soon as he arrived; and as he spoke so badly of us, he kept him very close to him and made him one of the captains whom he appointed; and he lodged a complaint against Don Bernardo in the audit. And afterwards he made him a guard at our house and he served as such for a few days; and on one of them, when he came in for some reason, they spoke of the complaint, and at last he told him that he [fol. 158r] was not avoiding payment of his debts, but so that he should see that he was mistaken in the accounts and that he owed him nothing he should go over them himself right there, and finally between the two of them they did it, and even when he forgave him many things and dealt with them as he wished, he came to see how mistaken he was, and as my husband went along with everything he wanted, what he owed him came to very few pesos, and he told him to pay, and he answered that he would do so forthwith, but that he should file a petition and reduce the amount for a note he would give him immediately, and he said he would do it but that he did not dare because of Don Diego, but since he needed it badly he would go to ask for his approval; and after he went and did not come back, someone who lived in our house, I do not remember who, came from his house, I do not know whether it was

Toribio or Juan Domínguez, and when he was told what had happened he said that he was coming from there and had heard Don Diego reply when he was asked for permission for the aforesaid, "Hold fast, Captain Polanco, and I'll make him pay you all of it." And that was why he did not come back then. And I mention this here because if anyone is owed some small amount—because it all came to little—he interferes and he would not allow them to be paid, as happened in the case I am speaking of. And the same thing in some others. And a poor Indian shoemaker whose need made him come, and he paid him some five or six pesos that he owed him. He persecuted him in such a fashion that whenever something had to be sent somewhere he would say, "Call the cobbler," and the cobbler would go at once, and he wound up owing us some pesos that he gave him in addition to what he was asking for paying the boys in kind.[21] When Polanco came back the next day or the one after, he finally said that he did not dare and [gave] other excuses until at last he said it clearly that time and many others; and despite what had happened, his enmity was such that although he now almost hated Don Diego, although without saying so, he took part in almost every attachment carried out and was the first to trouble us in every act of persecution against us, and on the road he did a good deal, nor was there any occasion on which he failed to show his lack of respect for my husband and me with harsh persecutions to which, if I were to recount them in detail, there would be no end, as there is none to his enmity.

Jusepe Jurado, the armorer, in case he should have testified: Ever since we went there and he went with us, and even before we left here, this man took offense for no reason whatsoever, even though we favored him. And once there, he always displayed the ill will he bore us. And he caused trouble, but I do not now recall the reasons, and my husband knows them better than I. And at the end he even witnessed my arrest, coming there with the friars, I do not know what for. He is a bitter enemy, and I do not know whether he is a claimant in the audit. The carters, in case they or some of them should have testified: On our voyage there, Don Bernardo rebuked many of them and punished some, although few, for offenses that they committed; and although this is no reason and they do not have to testify, in case they should have done so I can find no reason for it other than the one that Don Diego told me, that they might have done it because Fray Juan Ramírez was so great an enemy of ours, or that he, for this reason, might have made them do it, because those whom he mentioned to me were so devoted to him. I do not know what truth there is in this, other than that he told it to me. And this Fray Juan Ramírez is and has been our bitter enemy for reasons that arose before we left this city, when we went there, which are known; and apart from that he deceived my husband in some things, not keeping his word and the promises that he would make and then regret and not keep; and during the voyage, although he dissimulated to suit his interests, he always, although discreetly, showed his ill will toward us; and although now he spoke to us [fol. 158v] a few times, this was not because of any love or good will that he felt toward us, but only because he was on bad terms with the other friars and he knew how hostile they were to us. He wanted to do this because he thought he would thereby cause them chagrin, and he even told me this a few times and told me they were very upset by it because they believed that as our enemy he would help to have us burned, and they saw that he had become our friend and were very upset by it. And I know that the feelings he had toward us were to speak quite badly of us where they might not hear it, and my girls told me the things he used to say when the father commissary of this Holy Office had them returned to me in Zacatecas at the request of Juan, something he resented to an incredible degree; and if he had disliked me up to then, he did so far more afterwards because on that day, when they had been brought and while they were being entrusted to Francisco de León, he begged me repeatedly to ask that they be entrusted to him, and I would not do it because I had heard people there shout aloud what he wanted them for, something I had not known until then, but later they told me all about it; and in short, for this reason and the aforesaid and many others he is a great enemy of my husband and mine. Father Custodian Fray Alonso de Posadas [*sic*], in case he should have testified: He has been our enemy since before we left this city, because when he came to our house in the afternoon of Corpus Christi Day to see Don Bernardo and was told that he was not there, he said that he wanted to see me, and when he was told to come right in he did so, and after we had greeted each other he said he was coming to see my husband to tell him that if he thought that he was going to govern men, he was mistaken, because he was going only to govern riff-raff, and since he had not found him at home he was telling me so that I might tell him. And I, scandalized at what he was telling me, said, "Good Lord, Father, don't say that!" But he, as a man who knew them, began to tell me so many things, both of men and of women, that I was astonished at them; and while he was talking and I defending them all, he came to tell me among other things that if Pacheco had cut off the heads of Colonel Pedro Lucero de Godoy and Sergeant Major Francisco Gómez Robledo, his father, they would have richly deserved it. To which I replied, "Well, Father, if they deserved it and were accomplices as you say, how is it that he cut off other [heads] and not theirs? Because it seems to me that if they were as guilty as your reverence says, he would have cut them off as he did the others." And he replied to me that he would tell me the reason, and it was that Lucero deceived him with some tamales or a pie or something like that, and apart from that, out of fear and to flatter him, he would get up early and have his house and kitchen swept, and that is how he deceived him, and he had pardoned him and not beheaded him. And that Francisco Gómez came every morning to curry his mule, and that is how he deceived him so that he would not do it. And the things he told me about this matter and others were so many that they make a long story, as he told me countless bad things about everyone and I defended them vigorously; and he eventually left, and, scandalized, I said to my husband's mother, who was present—although, not knowing any of them, as she hardly knew any of those who were in this city, she had remained silent during the conversation because she did not have the information that I did about people there or my knowledge of those here—"Madam, if we were to go to confession and said that we had said these things, would this friar not order us to ask those involved for their forgiveness?" And, crossing herself, she answered me, "Yes indeed." And I asked this about the women there who carried on illicit [fol. 159r] relations, and although I did not know them I did so on behalf of their husbands who were here. And sometimes she would ask me afterwards whether that father had come back, who later saw my husband and told him the same things or others more or less. And, finally, since then he bears me ill will; and after he went back there as custodian Don Bernardo had some differences with him that he will be able to explain better than I, because I do not remember them well, and for this reason he has been and is the enemy of both of us. This is apart from his carousing and feasting with Don Diego; and other things could be said about this, and as I do not know how to do so I shall not do it, to avoid error. And I shall only say that I heard some residents say in general that some friars were complaining that he was plundering, or I do not know how they put it, the monasteries in order to get presents for himself, because I also heard that he sent orders or word that from each monastery they should send him a present of what he asked for. I do not know what truth there is in this, and I know only that it is true that he received presents every day and that sometimes I saw what they were taking him pass by my house, and also the mule trains of wheat and corn they brought him even from Taos.

Fray Salvador Guerra [Witness 25], in case he should have testified: Almost since we went there he has been our most mortal enemy possible. I have already mentioned his reasons for this, and if there are others, Don Bernardo will know and [tell] them, as he is better informed of these matters than I; I only know what I chanced to hear there at times, that although I had not offended against him in any way, he would speak about me as he wished and has on all occasions shown his hatred for me. Fray Nicolás de Fletas [Freitas, Witness 3], in case he should have testified: He has been our mortal enemy since the time of our journey there, firstly, because he is one of the favorites of Fray Juan Ramírez and [because] of his [enmity?]. He showed this on one occasion, when one afternoon a soldier and one of the carters were fighting with knives, and when Don Bernardo saw it, he went there and got out of the cart in which he was riding and began to argue about their being arrested, in order to defend the carter, although Don Bernardo told him that he had judicial authority over them; and finally I went there and said to two more sensible friars that were there that they should go and take him away, and they answered me that they were keeping quiet because they had no reason to get involved in something that did not concern them, what did they have to do with the stabbings, and that the father was doing it because of the custodian's indulgence toward him; and from that point on his ill will was even greater. Later, in New Mexico, because of whippings with a leather whip, which they say is a severe punishment, and shearing [tusar] the Indians and other things of which the poor natives complained several times, and for other reasons that my husband will also know and explain better than I, he is and always has been our fierce enemy, and mine, too, although I have done nothing to him or given him any reason whatsoever. He came back from this city traveling from Zacatecas on in the company of Don Diego, who is his close friend. And he was not satisfied until he could arrest me without having any warrant. And afterwards he insulted me as stated and asked me about papers and other things. The vice custodian Fray García de San Francisco [Witness 2], in case he should have testified: He is our enemy and has always shown it, and he took offense at being told to attend to the complaints that he received from the friars, of which he was informed so that he might do so. There are many reasons and I do not know them either; Don Bernardo will specify them; I only know that his enmity is great. Fray Diego de Santander, who was his secretary, in case he should have testified: This is one of our greatest enemies and has revealed himself as such on every occasion. When we went there he was the secretary of Fray Juan Ramírez, in which position he also showed his ill will toward us on every occasion; and his great complaint is that when he was guardian of Jumanos—I believe that is the name of the town—he told him to take the monastery's cattle to where the guardians have always kept it, near the town, and not in it, as he had done. And this [fol. 159v] was because there is no water in that town, and the little that it has often dries up, and the inhabitants go very far off to fetch their drinking water, at great risk of [attack from] Apaches, and they say he had taken a great number of cattle and sheep there. They used to draw their water by hand with ropes from very deep wells, and since it was as scarce as I have said, in addition to the great effort it required, they needed it badly. And, finally, this is a town that the governors never go to visit because of the lack of water, so that the horses in their train may not drink up the natives' water. And the father complained about this a great deal. He also occasionally spoke ill of my husband and of me without our having done anything to him or given him any reason, and neither do I know what reasons for complaint he has, and my husband knows them and will explain them, for I know only that he is our great enemy. Fray Fernando de Monroy, in case he should have testified: This friar says himself that I have given him no reason for the enmity that he admits to feeling toward me, but that as he is my husband's enemy he is mine, too, and that his enmity toward my husband stems only from a petty annoyance that he says he caused him; and although it is a thing of no consequence, his rancor toward us is so great. God will give him his reward, and he is our enemy.

Fray Benito [Benito de la Navidad, Witness 6], in case he should have testified: He has felt offended since we went there because, as a result of his discourtesy and inattention toward us, we did not go to lodge at his monastery, and when he found out he went to plead with us to go there, excusing himself with his absentmindedness; and finally we went, to do him a favor, and he asked Don Bernardo that we should not go that day or the following one, and as a favor he did that, too; and despite all this he had complaints, and I have heard that he circulated some false rumor about the visit to the monastery or I do not quite know what. He also complains that once during an inspection an Indian woman publicly asked him for a blanket that Father Hore owed her and had not paid her, and Don Bernardo, scolding her, said that if there

was any soldier there who had a blanket or deerskin, he should give it to her
and throw her out, and since there was no blanket, one man gave her a deerskin that he had, and she said she did not want it, that he had promised her a
blanket. And when she was again scolded and told to take it, they say that
Fray Nicolás de Chávez, who was there, said, "No, no, give it to her, that's my
order," and going inside, he brought it out and gave it to her, and they threw
her out, because of which, although my husband was not to blame and had
scolded her, he felt deeply offended. And he is our enemy and has always
shown it, and so are they all. Fray Fernando de Velasco, Fray Antonio de
Ibergaray [Witness 20], Fray Felipe Rodríguez, Fray Juan de la Chica, who is
a little demented because of an illness he had, Fray Juan de la Ascensión, Fray
Nicolás del Villar [Witness 9], Fray Josué [José?] de Paredes, Fray "Something" de Monpián, and many others whose names I do not know, are all our
enemies and have all shown it, because all they need is for one of them to
have some petty complaint, and then they will all have it, and they need little
reason for one, and among these are Fray Pedro Moreno, who is not one of
the least ill-disposed toward us, Fray "Something" de Alvarado [Witness 21],
Fray Blas, and these and all the others that were there are our enemies for
different reasons and have always demonstrated it. And likewise all the friars
who were in town when the edicts of the faith were read. From the day they
were read they began, one by one and two by two, and sometimes more, to
go from house to house, constantly visiting the residents, in which Don
Diego was of no little assistance to them, and sometimes he went with them.
And he and they did not cease to do this, and sometimes, where they were,
there would be dances and parties and gossip of all sorts; and apart from this,
they and Don Diego, and Don Diego and they, lived in constant banquets
and festivities, so that they and the residents were in such turmoil that I cannot describe it. And they would say various things against us unfortunates,
and when they saw my little Apaches in town they would even set to saying,
"There go that heretic's boys," as Toribio de la Huerta then sometimes told
me they called them; [fol. 160r] and some of the friars were with Don Diego,
playing cards till the small hours of the night, and on other occasions he did
the same at the monastery until very late. And besides this, in order to intim-
idate the residents, Don Diego had a gallows set up and a gibbet and a pulley
and had two or three poles put up in the jail for garroting, and he would
threaten punishments for the least thing, as he sometimes imposed [on some
persons], although I do not recall on what occasions; and there was one resi-

dent who once told me a little before the audit, or during it, that it was not because he did not want to that he had not come to our house, but that they were telling him that he came to report on what was going on, and when Don Bernardo came out of one of the rooms as he was telling me that—and if I remember correctly he had gone there to get I do not know what document that he had come to ask him for, I do not know whether on behalf of Don Diego—and he asked him what he was saying, he repeated it to him, saying that he had had a very disagreeable incident with him and that among the threats he had made against him he had told him that that was why he had set up that gallows and that he knew how to hang and quarter many people and was very eager to do so, and many other things, and that for this reason he did not dare to visit us, lest some slander be spread about him to his disadvantage; and this is what he constantly did with many people. On other occasions he would say that his enemy's friend was not his friend, and that anyone who came to our house should not go to his. And at other times he would send for Juan Domínguez late at night when he was at our house, and when he went he told him, putting his sword up against him, that he knew how to fight and fence; and this was because he was at our house, and he ordered him and Toribio de la Huerta to leave our house, and Toribio, feeling sorry for our abandonment and because we had only him to do anything for us on the outside, explained this to him and asked him for permission to serve us at least during the day to meet our needs as best he could; and in short, so much could be said about this matter that it is no exaggeration to say that no human tongue could explain it, because none could do it justice. And I shall say only that these disturbances and threats, together with the docility of the local population, finally sufficed to make everyone turn against us; and all of them joining and conspiring to persecute us in every way, they shamelessly spread so many and such great slanders against us as in so many ways they have done. And all the friars who were in that country during the time that my husband was governor are also claimants in the audit on account of their cattle that they say died because of the severe winter, which also caused the loss of many of ours. And concerning the cattle they are demanding, I heard Juan Domínguez de Mendoza say that some of the friars who were asking for cattle had used them to marry off some girls and given them to them as dowries, and they would tell the custodian they were dead, and he also named the friars who had done this, whose names I do not at present recall except for a certain Alvarado, and he also named the houses where the girls and their husbands and the cattle were. And he said that others had done other things with them, and that Don Bernardo should not reply to their petition except in his presence, so that he might tell him individually what many of them had done with them and where they were and under what conditions, and that he would go and show them to the custodian if he wished. And I heard him say this many times. And besides this, only God can control the weather. And as soon as the news of Don Diego's coming arrived, many friars came to town to say a mass of thanksgiving, which I heard they had promised to do on receipt of news of a new governor. Juan Luján the Elder, in case he should have testified: what with the disturbances, this man followed the behavior of the crowd, and so if he did anything it would be because he was one of those threatened. I do not doubt that he would probably do anything to avoid trouble, [fol. 160v] especially since they always keep a close watch on him because of something they say he plans to do; and apart from this he is related to Lucero and is the brother-in-law of Francisco Gómez, and so he was of his party, which was that of Don Diego, and for this reason he must be our enemy. Pedro de Leiva [Witness 16], in case he should have testified, and his wife: This man also followed the course of all the others; and as he told me himself, Don Diego threatened him repeatedly, as a result of which he followed him out of fear and became our enemy. And on his own behalf, or perhaps on Apodaca's, he is a claimant in the audit, in which, because of some accounts that he examined, or for some reason I do not quite understand, I believe he has been shown to be a false witness, it seems to me I do not remember in what way. May the truth of whatever it was prevail.

The late Luis Martín and his sons and wife and daughters, in case they should have testified: These are all our enemies. As he was about to die, or, once dead, in his name, they filed a claim in the audit, and I do not doubt that Don Diego had a hand in it, because, as he was such an enemy of ours, he wanted him to be mayor even after he was dead, only because that was a hostile act toward us. And if he and his family did anything it would have been because they went along with all the others and because they were our enemies. Francisco de León, in case he should have testified: When this man was coming in the carts as a soldier, Don Diego attached him to himself and regaled him in his house, lodging him there, because Don Bernardo recused him and rejected all his appeals. In short, after many incidents, and others with a man who only to give himself importance sought to be accompanied, and not wanting to do so he finally chose him to accompany him;[22] and the said Francisco de León, puffed up with being a judge, did what Don Diego wanted, and since in all this he was only a figurehead I do not blame him much. Afterwards Don Diego appointed him chief guard over all and over my poor husband, so that, prejudiced as he was, he [and] I would have in him a man who would truly persecute us like an enemy, as he demonstrated on every occasion during our voyage, missing no chance to persecute us as much as he could, and constantly treating him and me with disrespect, and some of the other guards said he did this because he was also much attached to the friars, who, the guards said, had persuaded him that if he brought us here in the way he was doing, this Tribunal of the Holy Office would send him back for the witnesses who had testified against us, and I do not know to whom they were referring, or how to find it out; and with what they say they told him he was so puffed up that what I know to be true is what he told me many times, which was that he was convinced that as soon as we arrived he would be sent back there, and that he would be very sorry to do so because he would not want to return to a country where such slander was spread and people behaved as sinfully as they did there. And after he had often told me this and other things, perhaps unable to bear his vanity, I once asked him to tell me for heaven's sake why they would send him and the others back as they said, because who were they that anyone would entrust anything to them, or did they think there were no men in the world, and only if there were none could what they were saying be true, at which he took great offense, and so did some of the other guards, to whom for the same reason I sometimes said the same thing. And concerning this man, Polanco sometimes told me, and Arteaga, and I think Noriega, too, that he had given his word to the friars that within I do not know what time of his going there he would bring them lots of work, concerning which I do not know the truth [fol. 161r] except that it is true that they said that. And this was because of the bad terms on which they were with him because he sometimes threatened them with writing down how utterly they failed to fulfill the obligations they had undertaken, in order to testify to it before this Holy Office. But after we drew near this city they all joined in making submissive declarations to him so that he might not accuse them and might help them in all things, and I believe he promised to do so. And of all of them and him in particular, all I know for sure is that for these reasons and many others he is and has been the most bitter enemy of my husband and myself, and he has demonstrated this as much as can be, and he would always threaten us that he might testify against us whatever he pleased, perhaps because he really had nothing to say. And he was also extremely resentful of my telling, as one so hurt by them, the things that Don Diego had done with us, and he defended him most vigorously, on account of which we sometimes had some squabbles, which he deeply resented. Francisco de Anaya and his wife, in case they should have testified: He is the son of Almazán, who was Don Diego's secretary in the audit, and he has his own cause for complaint because Don Bernardo scolded him for the troubles he caused because a mulatto attacked him with his sword on account of his wife. And he is our enemy because he is the uncle of Ana Rodríguez, and Don Diego called them his relatives. He has the usual complaints about escort duty and expeditions, and he is a great troublemaker, and she is the sister of Miguel de Hinojos. And for these reasons and others they are our enemies. Francisco Jiménez, in case he should have testified, and his wife: It seems to me she is one of the Griegos, and if they should have done so, they will be following all the rest. And she was very close to Josefa, and they were our enemies. The Indian Antonia, the cook: in addition to what I have said, I have remembered that after serving us, she would go at night to sleep in her house, [and] that one of the causes of her enmity was our not allowing [it and], when we could do so, ordering her not to do it because we had learned that it was in bad condition; and I found out that some of those nights she would go to see Don Diego and they would hold long conversations, I did not find out about what subjects. And this woman also would constantly carry on with Pedro de Valdés during the daytime, and she did the same at night, and during this time there would be great conclaves with him at Josefa's house. I could not learn the purpose of this either, but because they were all enemies of ours they were great friends, and Valdés being such a fierce enemy, it is obvious that they would not have been consulting with each other to our benefit. A little Indian of the Humana nation, who was our coachman, in case he should have testified: This fellow belonged to Noriega and shared all his tricks and complaints.

He was flogged as a thief many times, and we often chastised and scolded him for various reasons. And finally after various incidents we sheared him and flogged him for an outrage and impertinence that he committed in our house, which was why we threw out his master. And for this reason, and because of him, he is our enemy, and if he should have done anything they must have made him do it.

Juan González Bernal and his wife Polonia and his daughter, in case they should have testified: These are allied with the Griegos [and] are our enemies for the same reasons as they, and also because the daughter was the one who had relations with Pedro de Arteaga. We had them scolded several times, because they were stealing from us to maintain their household, and Don Bernardo had the father jailed because he did not control his daughter; and for these reasons and others having to do with commotions that they caused and quarrels, all of them, as Griegos, have been and are our enemies. Cristóbal de Anaya and his wife, in case they should have testified: They are our enemies because they followed the path of all the others. And when he was summoned to testify [fol. 161v] in the audit and was about to do so, we found out one holiday when Don Diego was coming out of mass that he had only gone in and left right away and gone home, and he sent us word that he had already testified. And it was said that they had prepared his testimony and all he had done was to sign it, wherein one can see what they probably did in everything, because he himself probably did not know what they had written. And on the voyage this man would say to me, "Now we're all going there, and the truth will come out, because we'll be able to speak it freely," and he often shouted this at me. And he did speak it, as well as what he did or was made to do in this matter or another. This man is the uncle of Ana Rodríguez and the brother of Inés and Ana de Anaya, and I often chastised all of these and their mother. And his wife is the sister of the Domínguezes, and all of them are our enemies.

Nicolás de Aguilar and his wife, in case they should have testified, it must have been to do like all the others. And he told how Don Diego, as soon as he went there, had prepared the written testimony against Don Bernardo that I have reported him as saying that they made him give. And they say the friars made this public, and for this reason he must be our enemy. And as for what they say about not seeing me pray or knowing me to have any special devotion, and so that this may be seen clearly, and as a Christian, which by the grace of Our Lord I have been, am, and shall be, a member of the following confraternities: first, in that of St. Peter and St. Paul; in that of Jesus, Mary, and Joseph, and I had its bull, and likewise in that of St. John Lateran, and I had its bull; and that of St. Anthony; and that of St. Roch; and that of St. Augustine, and I had its bull and wear its girdle and am inscribed in its register of members; and with the Dominicans as a slave of the Blessed Virgin of the Rosary, and I had the certificate as a slave and an assigned time for the rosary, and the truth of this can be seen in the books of these confraternities; and wherever I have been, I have tried as best I could to comply with all of these devotions and say their prayers in keeping with the places where I was, and in addition I have always prayed the ten-bead rosary of the Passion of Our Lord Jesus Christ, for which so many blessings are granted, and I had a list of them and of the great ones that are granted for a thousand beads.

And likewise when Fray Diego de Santander read the first edicts I handed him the liturgy of the pure and immaculate conception of Our Lady and that of the glorious patriarch St. Joseph, and some litanies of the sweet and adored Mother of God and the list of the five greatest sorrows of the Blessed Virgin, all of which were among the things that the edict said this Holy Tribunal had ordered collected, and as a faithful and Catholic Christian and as such obedient to its commands, although these were among my favorite devotions, I was the first to turn them in. And I have always said these prayers and others and also the lesser office of the Blessed Virgin, and in it I have long recited the penitential psalms and the graduals and other devotions, and by their means, by the mercy of Our Lord and His Blessed Mother, I trust that His holy mercy will deliver me from my false accusers and for His sake bring me to a safe harbor out of so many torments, for His greater service.

Magdalena, an Apache, in case she should have testified: When she was making lace at our house I threw her out for good cause that she gave me, and I chastised her severely on that occasion. She greatly resented being thrown out, and Josefa more so, as she was very close to her. Another one, Jacinta, belonged to me, and I also threw her out for many reasons, and she was with Josefa and her group, and they are our enemies.

Signed: Doña Teresa Aguilera y Roche

Notes

Introduction

Epigraph. This and all translations of trial proceedings were taken from the extensive work prepared by María Magdalena Coll, Heather Bamford, Heather McMichael, and John H. R. Polt for the University of California, Berkeley, Cíbola Transcription and Translation Project. The originals are part of the Archivo General de la Nación (hereinafter AGN), Mexico City, Ramo Inquisición, vol. 596. Thanks to María Magdalena Coll and project director Jerry Craddock for undertaking this monumental work and for permission to use the transcript.

1. Population estimates for Santa Fe in the pre-Revolt period (before 1680). Governor López de Mendizábal described Santa Fe as a settlement of thirty-eight adobe houses. It is not clear if he excluded the soldiers and priests in this graphic description of its limited size. José Antonio Esquibel, "Thirty-eight Adobe Houses—The Villa de Santa Fe in the 17th Century," in *All Trails Lead to Santa Fe* (Santa Fe: Sunstone Press, 2010), 109–28.

2. Stanley M. Hordes, To the End of the Earth: A History of the Crypto-Jews of New Mexico (New York: Columbia University Press, 2005), briefly summarizes on pp. 148–65 the events that unfolded between May 2 and August 27, 1662, the period in which all six defendants were arrested. Gómez Robledo faced the most invasive physical investigation, as several surgeons focused on whether the marks on his penis were in fact evidence of circumcision. The evidence against Gómez Robledo even included claims of his family's alleged Jewish ritual practices that were said to have taken place years earlier in Portugal (Hordes, To the End, 157–61). At the conclusion of all the hearings, despite the lengthy procedures and the many claims examined, not one of the six defendants was ever convicted of the charges.

3. Marc Simmons, Witchcraft in the Southwest: Spanish and Indian Supernaturalism on the Rio Grande (Lincoln: University of Nebraska Press, 1974), 28.

4. Ramón A. Gutiérrez, When Jesus Came, the Corn Mothers Went Away: Marriage, Sexuality, and Power in New Mexico, 1500–1846 (Stanford: Stanford University Press, 1991), 115–27. Carroll L. Riley, "Bernardo López de Mendizábal: Could He Have Prevented the Pueblo Revolt?" El Palacio 112, no. 3 (2007): 38–46.

5. Yitzhak Baer, *A History of the Jews in Christian Spain* (Philadelphia: Jewish Publication Society of America, 1971); Jane S. Gerber, *The Jews of Spain: A History of the Sephardic Experience* (New York: Free Press, 1992); María Rosa Menocal, *The Ornament of the World: How Muslims, Jews and Christians Created a Culture of Tolerance*

in Medieval Spain (Boston: Little, Brown, 2002).

6. Américo Castro and Willard F. King, *The Spaniards: An Introduction to Their History.* (Berkeley: University of California Press, 1985), 205n57.

7. Henry Kamen, *The Spanish Inquisition: A Historical Revision* (New Haven, Conn.: Yale University Press, 1997), provides a renewed analysis of the broad social powers and processes that were encompassed by the Inquisition. It was, in many ways, as much an institution for controlling political and social power in the newly unified Spain as it was an instrument of the Catholic Church seeking control over the practices of conversos or new Christians.

8. Bartolomé de Las Casas, *A Short Account of the Destruction of the Indies*, ed. and trans. Nigel Griffin (London: Penguin Classics, 1992). Las Casas transcribed and edited logs and diaries kept by Christopher Columbus and used them in his own 1542 account to argue for more humane treatment of native peoples. Las Casas's account was published in 1552 and still reads as an eloquent plea for social justice, albeit too late for many native peoples of the Americas. Las Casas wrote of his fervent belief that Columbus was chosen by God to bring the Gospel to the New World, and he contrasted Columbus's expedition with the destructive force of later explorers.

9. J. M. Cohen, ed. and trans., *The Four Voyages of Christopher Columbus* (London: Penguin Classics, 1969), 37–38.

10. Isidro G. Bango, *Remembering Sepharad: Jewish Culture in Medieval Spain* (Madrid: State Corporation for Spanish Cultural Action Abroad, 2003); "1492 / Granada: Unifying the Body Politic," *Lapham's Quarterly* (September 2012): 109–110.

11. Bango, *Remembering Sepharad*, 195–98; Decree of Expulsion of the Jews, Granada, March 31, 1492, translation of the manuscript from the Archivo General de Simancas (PR 28–6).

12. Bango, *Remembering Sepharad*, 200–202; Isaac Abravanel's [sic] Response, www.jrbooksonline.com/edict_resp_by_isaac_abravanel.htm.

13. Cohen, *Four Voyages*, 20. Hordes, *To the End*, 25–26, reviews the evidence—historical, literary, and allegorical—and judiciously concludes that much genealogical and historical research is needed before any conclusion about Columbus's religious background can be known with certainty. Edward Kritzler, *Jewish Pirates of the Caribbean* (New York: Doubleday, 2008), seems to accept as proof of Columbus's religious leanings the timing of the expedition and the presence of several Jewish sailors.

1. Becoming New Mexico

1. Linda S. Cordell and Maxine E. McBrinn, *Archaeology of the Southwest* (Walnut Creek, Calif.: Left Coast Press, 2012), 247–77, succinctly review the arguments that archaeologists have advanced to account for the massive settlement shifts of the period.

2. A fascinating study of Spanish explorations of Florida, Mississippi, Louisiana, Texas, New Mexico, Arizona, and California is found in the catalog of an exhibi-

tion of first-contact documents from the Archivo General de Indias in Seville, Spain (hereinafter AGI). The catalog, *The Threads of Memory / El Hilo de la Memoria* (Albuquerque: Fresco Fine Art Publications, 2010) contains reproductions of first contact accounts, maps, navigational charts, and illustrations from Spanish expeditions and explorations of North America.

3. The many translations of the *Relación* include that by Cleve Hallenbeck, *The Journey of Fray Marcos* (Dallas: Southern Methodist University Press, 1949); Cyclone Covey, ed., *Cabeza de Vaca's Adventures in the Unknown Interior of America* (Albuquerque: University of New Mexico Press, 1961 (6th ed., 1992); and a more recent annotated volume of the *Relación* by Martin A. Favata and José B. Fernández (Houston: Arte Público Press, 1993), which includes a chronology of the published editions and translations. More recent comprehensive translations and annotations are those of Rolena Adorno and Patrick Charles Pautz. See particularly Rolena Adorno and Patrick Charles Pautz, eds. and trans., *The Narrative of Cabeza de Vaca* (Lincoln: University of Nebraska Press, 2003); and Rolena Adorno and Patrick Charles Pautz, eds. and trans., *Álvar Núñez Cabeza de Vaca: His Account, His Life, and the Expedition of Pánfilo de Narváez*, 3 vols. (Lincoln: University of Nebraska Press, 1999).

4. David Weber, *Myth and the History of the Hispanic Southwest* (Albuquerque: University of New Mexico Press, 1988), 2–4, discusses the powerful motivation that medieval legends and myths played in the Spanish explorations of the New World. The search for El Dorado—the gilded man—and the land of Amazon women was in some ways a search for Utopia or an earthly paradise, and their shimmering visions were at least part of the fuel for many expeditions. But the real power of myth lies in the realm of the possible, as the riches of Mexico and Peru proved for Cortés and Pizarro. In many instances, myths are a combination of histories shared in archetypes spelling out our own cultural ideals and contrasting them with our perception of other cultures. Myths can embody the retelling of oral histories and recollections within the family or in our broader culture, as can be seen in the modern identities built around converso and crypto-Jewish family histories told in New Mexico and elsewhere.

5. The famous ethnographer Frank Hamilton Cushing received a lesson in Zuni history when, in the summer of 1880, a group of Zuni elders recounted for him their version of Esteban's entry into the village of Kia-ki-me. Counting out 350 grains of corn, their nuggets of golden grain, the elders counted back the years and centuries to tell Cushing about the coming of the "Black Mexican" who came from the land they called "Everlasting Summer." Esteban had come with the Indians of Sónō-li (perhaps "Sonora") to battle with war clubs, bows, and arrows. In that battle the "Black Mexican" was killed. This story is related in Jesse Green, *Selected Writings of Frank Hamilton Cushing* (Lincoln: University of Nebraska Press, 1979), 172–75. See also Jesse Green, ed., *Cushing at Zuni: The Correspondence and Journals of Frank Hamilton Cushing, 1879–1884* (Albuquerque: University of New Mexico Press, 1990), 110.

6. Richard Flint and Shirley Cushing Flint, *Documents of the Coronado Expedition,*

1539–1541 (Dallas: Southern Methodist University Press, 2005), 388–493, reproduce Pedro de Castañeda de Nájera's narrative of the 1560s, "The Relación de la Jornada de Cíbola," which contains some fascinating myths of its own. Castañeda attributes Esteban's death at Zuni in part because they did not believe his stories and because of his request for more turquoise and women. Castañeda also repeats the gossip of the day that Viceroy Mendoza favored Coronado because he was known to be the illegitimate son of King Ferdinand. *Documents of the Coronado Expedition*, 387.

7. Weber, *Myth and the History*, 22.

8. Coronado's investors included his wife, whose ancestry was said to include conversos. José Antonio Esquibel explores the genealogy of Coronado's wife in his article "The Jewish-Converso Ancestry of Doña Beatriz de Estrada," *Genealogical Society of Hispanic America Journal* 9 (Winter 1997): 134–43. Esquibel finds three generations of her maternal line were associated with converso families and more particularly were practicing Jewish cultural traditions in the community of Villa de Almagro in the fifteenth century.

9. Surely the most comprehensive reexamination of the documents of the Coronado expedition is that of Richard Flint and Shirley Cushing Flint (*Documents of the Coronado Expedition*), which includes their newly edited, translated, and annotated versions of the core documents of the expedition. In their earlier work, *Great Cruelties Have Been Reported: The 1544 Investigation of the Coronado Expedition* (Dallas: Southern Methodist University Press, 2002), they review the charges leveled against Coronado for his conduct and management of the expedition. And in their edited work *The Latest Word from 1540: People, Places, and Portrayals of the Coronado Expedition* (Albuquerque: University of New Mexico Press, 2011), they compile a selection of recent archaeological, genealogical, and historical reinterpretations of the continuing scholarship on the expedition. They have shown that the Coronado expedition is far from dried up as a research topic but is instead an example of the ever-unfolding nature of evidence and revisions that fuel historical scholarship.

10. George P. Hammond and Agapito Rey, *The Rediscovery of New Mexico, 1580–1594* (Albuquerque: University of New Mexico Press, 1966), 77, 128, 134, contains the depositions of Hernán Gallegos, chronicler of the Chamuscado-Rodríguez Expedition, and Pedro de Bustamante, a participant in the expedition. Both testified that they were influenced to take part in the 1580 expedition by the descriptions in Cabeza de Vaca's publication. Neither mentions the chronicles of the Coronado expedition.

11. Hammond and Rey, *Rediscovery*, 7–8.

12. Hernán Gallegos and Baltasar Obregón each wrote accounts of the Fray Agustín Rodríguez expedition. Hammond and Rey, *Rediscovery*, 67–150.

13. Albert H. Schroeder, "Pueblos Abandoned in Historic Times," in *Handbook of North American Indians*, vol. 10, *Southwest*, edited by Alfonso Ortiz (Washington, D.C.: Smithsonian Institution, 1983), 236–54.

14. Hammond and Rey, *Rediscovery*, 127–40.

15. Ibid., 147–50.

16. Espejo assumed leadership, but who appointed him and why are less clear.

Hammond and Rey point to several inconsistencies as to when and under what circumstances Espejo assumed command of the party (*Rediscovery*, 17–21). Hordes casually mentions that Espejo was an agent of the Inquisition and an underling of Luis de Carvajal, the embattled governor of Nuevo León, who was later tried by the Inquisition for practicing Judaism (*To the End*, 84). Carvajal's family certainly had converso roots, and his namesake nephew was rather flagrantly Jewish in his dress, demeanor, and public professions of the faith and suffered for his practice of mysticism and the Jewish faith. Samuel Temkin, *Luis de Carvajal: The Origins of Nuevo Reino de León* (Santa Fe: Sunstone Press, 2011), 121–23, summarizes the inconsistencies in Carvajal's testimony before the Inquisition in 1587, in which he claims to have sent Espejo to New Mexico. Temkin suggests that Carvajal and Espejo may have been vying for the governorship of the new lands. That may explain why Espejo did not mention Carvajal.

17. Hammond and Rey, *Rediscovery*, 15–28, 153–234.

18. Hordes, *To the End*, 79–81.

19. Temkin, *Luis de Carvajal*, 164–70; Hordes, *To the End*, 77–81; Hammond and Rey, *Rediscovery*, 28–30.

20. Albert H. Schroeder and Dan S. Matson, *A Colony on the Move: Gaspar Castaño de Sosa's Journal, 1590–1591* (Santa Fe: School of American Research Press, 1965), 6, suggest that Castaño "bypassed" official authorization because of personal ambition and the depletion of the mines. Hammond and Rey attribute his haste in organizing the expedition to recklessness, disillusionment with the mineral resources of Nuevo León, and the powerful "mirage" of Gran Quivira to the north (*Rediscovery*, 28–30). Hordes makes a strong case that several among the settlers were descendants of converso families, such as Alonso Jaimes from the Canary Islands. In other cases he makes this association primarily on the basis of surnames, linking Juan de Victoria Carvajal to the governor's own "stained" family history. Another member of the expedition, Melchior de Paiba, may have been related to a well-documented Jewish family from Pachuca, Mexico. And Juan Nieto Rodríguez, he surmises, was likely related to a Jewish family in Mexico City of the same family name (Hordes, *To the End*, 85–92). Hordes, "The Participation of Crypto-Jews in the Settlement of the Far Northern Frontier of New Spain, 1589–1663," *Chronicles of the Trail: Quarterly Journal of El Camino Real de Tierra Adentro Trail Association* 6, no. 1 (Winter 2010]), 17, notes that this was the only colonial expedition without a priest, adding to the suspicion that Castaño was fleeing with people seeking a safer haven than Nuevo León for their religious practices.

21. The viceroy evidently not only forbade Castaño from undertaking the colonizing expedition, he also included a cédula from King Felipe II. The wording of the cédula seems to forbid any colonist recruited by Carvajal from settling the frontier, but it is a little unclear whether this applied to Nuevo León or to New Mexico. From the context, Hordes reads the edict as enjoining the settlers from traveling to New Mexico (*To the End*, 81, 102).

22. Hammond and Rey, *Rediscovery*, 298–303.

23. Ibid., 46–48, 305–20. Hordes argues that Castaño's rhetorical style shows Jewish identity. Hordes notes that scholar David Gitlitz, *Secrecy and Deceit: The Religion of the Crypto-Jews* (Philadelphia: Jewish Publication Society of America), 1996; reprinted, Albuquerque: University of New Mexico Press, 2002) considers this linguistic nuance to be particular to the crypto-Jews of Spain and Portugal (Hordes, *To the End*, 94–96).

24. George P. Hammond, "Don Juan de Oñate and the Founding of New Mexico," *New Mexico Historical Review* 1, no. 1 (1926): 54–77; reprinted, Santa Fe: El Palacio Press, 1927. See also the biography of Oñate by Marc Simmons, *The Last Conquistador: Juan de Oñate and the Settling of the Far Southwest* (Norman: University of Oklahoma Press, 1991). The Cibola Project, under the direction of Dr. Jerry Craddock, has prepared and published translations of many documents from Oñate's administration of New Mexico. They provide perspectives on the exploration reports, inspections, and in-depth examinations of several key investigations of that critical time in the Reconquest of New Mexico. A complete list of the documents is found on the California Digital Library, eScholarship index: www.https://escholarship.org/uc/rcrs_ias_ucb_cibola.

25. George P. Hammond and Agapito Rey, *Don Juan de Oñate, Colonizer of New Mexico 1595–1628* (Albuquerque: University of New Mexico Press, 1953), is the standard translation of the documents covering Oñate's selection, the inspection reports during the years he struggled to assemble colonists and the materials required to sustain the colony, his correspondence, and ultimately the defense of his failures.

26. Donald T. Garate, "Juan de Oñate's *Prueba de Caballero*, 1625: A Look at His Ancestral Heritage," *Colonial Latin American Historical Review* 7 (1998): 132–33, 144. A more exhaustive genealogical analysis of Oñate's maternal line comes from José Antonio Esquibel, "New Light on the Jewish-Converso Ancestry of Don Juan de Oñate: A Research Note," *Colonial Latin American Historical Review* 7 (1998): 182–83. Hordes argues passionately that the Spanish emphasis on family history and genealogy makes it likely that even the new Christians who might have fully embraced their new identity had some knowledge of their Judaic roots, no matter how far back they extended (*To the End*, 108–109). The vast body of fourteenth through eighteenth century *ejecutorias, hijuelas,* and *pruebas*, all forms of portable dossiers of one's ancestry, is one of the great bases of Hispanic genealogical research. As much as these dossiers contain, they also can be highly selective tracings of lineage, leaving some branches of the family tree blank, and including only those men and women with illustrious or spotless Christian backgrounds. The books were often contracted by conversos to "prove" their limpieza de sangre.

27. Hammond and Rey include the reports of inspections of the colonists made by Lope de Ulloa from June 1596 to February 1597 (*Don Juan de Oñate*, 94–168) and then again by Juan de Frías Salazar from September 1597 to February 1598 (199–308), and the one made by Juan de Gordejuela and Juan de Sotelo when additional recruits were sent to the colony in August 1600 (514–79), each containing fascinating information about the recruits' origins, households, and possessions and in some cases

details of their physical appearance. Hordes compares the names of participants in the three inventories and finds several men who were descended from new Christians in Spain, or who were later themselves accused of being judaizante in Mexico (*To the End*, 110–17).

28. Joseph P. Sánchez, *The Río Abajo Frontier, 1540–1692* (Albuquerque: Albuquerque Museum, 1996), 48; John L. Kessell, *Spain in the Southwest: A Narrative History of Colonial New Mexico, Arizona, Texas, and California* (Norman: University of Oklahoma Press, 2002), 73, 391).

29. Gaspar Pérez de Villagrá, *A History of New Mexico*, trans. Gilberto Espínosa (Los Angeles: Quivira Society, 1933).

30. Jorge Cañizares-Esguerra, *Puritan Conquistadors: Iberianizing the Atlantic, 1550–1700* (Stanford: Stanford University Press, 2006) contrasts the personification of the Spanish conquerors as effeminate conversos with the Puritan New World conquerors, using the work of Gaspar Pérez de Villagrá as a counterpoint to the works of English chroniclers. See also the characterization of the base and untrustworthy settlers of the Indies in the newer translation of Villagrá's epic poem by Miguel Encinias, Alfred Rodríguez, and Joseph P. Sánchez, *Gaspar Pérez de Villagrá, Historia de la Nueva México, 1610* (Albuquerque: University of New Mexico Press, 1992). Additional analysis of the Villagrá poem is found in the work of Manuel M. Martín Rodríguez, *Manuel M. Gaspar de Villagrá: Legista, soldado y poeta* (León: Universidad de León, 2009) and Manuel M. Martín Rodríguez, ed. *Gaspar de Villagrá, Historia de la Nueva Mexico* (Alcalá de Henares: Instituto Franklin, Universidad de Alcalá de Henares, 2010).

31. John L. Kessell argues poignantly for the contenders to lay aside their strident defense of differing interpretations of the past and to learn from the atrocities, giving voice and memory to the participants in his highly readable account of the seventeenth-century meeting of Pueblo Indians and Spaniards. John L. Kessell, *Pueblos, Spaniards, and the Kingdom of New Mexico* (Norman: University of Oklahoma Press, 2008).

32. Hordes, *To the End*, 111–12.

33. Ibid., 112.

34. José Antonio Esquibel, "The Romero Family of Seventeenth-Century New Mexico, part 2," *Herencia: Journal of the Hispanic Genealogical Research Center of New Mexico* 11, no. 3 (2003), examines the extensive connections within the Romero family throughout the seventeenth century.

35. Hordes, *To the End*, 117–23.

36. Seth D. Kunin, *Juggling Identities: Identity and Authenticity among the Crypto-Jews* (New York: Columbia University Press, 2009).

37. Janet Liebman Jacobs, *Hidden Heritage: The Legacy of the Crypto-Jews* (Berkeley: University of California Press, 2002).

38. Cary Herz, *New Mexico's Crypto-Jews: Image and Memory* (Albuquerque: University of New Mexico Press, 2009).

39. Judith Neulander offered several critiques in the mid-1990s of Hordes's work,

including her "The New Mexican Crypto-Jewish Canon: Choosing to be 'Chosen' in Millennial Tradition," *Jewish Folklore and Ethnology Review* 18 (1996): 19–58. And earlier, "Crypto-Jews of the Southwest: An Imagined Community," *Jewish Folklore and Ethnology Review* 16 (1994): 64–68. Barbara Ferry and Debbie Nathan followed with a more popular piece, but one that embraces the larger point made by Kunin, that identity is a form of bricolage: "Mistaken Identity? The Case of New Mexico's Hidden Jews," *Atlantic Monthly* 283, no. 6 (December 2000): 85–96.

40. Hordes, *To the End*, 271–72.

41. Jeff Wheelwright, *The Wandering Gene and the Indian Princess: Race, Religion and DNA* (New York: Norton, 2012).

2. Intrigue in the Royal Palace

1. We know a great deal about Don Bernardo's character from primary and secondary sources, but not much about his physical appearance. He was born in Chietla, Mexico, near Puebla, in 1620. Scholes, "Troublous Times in New Mexico, 1659–1670," chaps. 3–4, *New Mexico Historical Review* 12, no. 4 (1937): 152, described him as "belligerent, self-confident, and contentious . . . with an unfortunate talent for biting, scathing speech."

2. Maria Magdalena Coll, Heather Bamford, Heather McMichael, and John H. R. Polt, *The Trial before the Tribunal of the Holy Office in Mexico City of Doña Teresa de Aguilera y Roche* (hereinafter Coll. et al.), pt. 2, 291.

3. The inventory of items she carried with her into prison on April 11, 1663, shows that she kept several lists that the guards did not describe in detail, including a list of goods for trade, a list of names and numbers, and a receipt for masses she had paid for (Coll et al., pt. 2, 222–27).

4. The inventory includes several items associated with coiffure and mentions a style known as *toca de reina*, perhaps referring to a cloth toque, a style common in paintings of the era (Coll et al., pt. 2, 222–27).

5. Two curling irons were in the inventory of possessions taken during her entry into Inquisition custody on April 11, 1663 (Coll et al., pt. 2, 222–27), and another inventory dated April 21, 1663, included a small box containing items relating to the coiffure and adornment of the head (Coll et al., pt. 2, 228–29).

6. Coll et al., pt. 2, 167–68.

7. Ibid., pt. 2, 168.

8. Terms for race and ancestry have precise, but mutable, meanings in colonial Mexico and New Mexico. A series of colonial paintings called *pinturas de casta*, or caste paintings, illustrated the social class and household property of various levels of society in the New World colonies. Although no specific set of casta paintings for New Mexico is known from the colonial period, several sets from Mexico and Spain help us to illustrate the concepts of race and social class. See, for example, "La Pintura de Castas," *Artes de México* (Mexico City), n.s., no. 8, (Summer 1990). At a later point in the trial, Doña Teresa seems to have been attended in prison by a child of ten or

eleven, also named Clara. This young girl was hauled before the tribunal and asked to testify in secrecy about Doña Teresa's behavior while in prison.

9. Her reference to her grandfather's fears reflect the major movements and displacements in Europe during the Thirty Years' War (1618–48). Coll et al., pt. 2, 232. This must be a reference to the second Marqués de Santa Cruz, Álvaro de Barzán, based on his lifespan (1571–1646) and his military, naval, and diplomatic service in England and then Italy at the end of the sixteenth and the early seventeenth centuries. His valiant service in Genoa is depicted in Antonio de Pareda's 1634 baroque painting, *The Relief of Genoa by the Marquis de Santa Cruz*, held by the Museo del Prado, Madrid.

10. Coll et al., pt. 2, 232–36, contains Doña Teresa's lengthy testimony about her genealogy and education on May 2, 1663.

11. Doña Teresa is not always clear about the dates or sequence of events, but her father must have been in service to Don Carlos of Coloma de Saa before 1630, when Don Carlos left Milan, where he had been the commander, to take up residence in London, where he was tasked with restoring peace between Spain and England. Don Carlos had served in this post before; he was in England in the 1620s and was recalled to Spain, where he served in the Battle of Breda in 1624 and 1625. He is supposedly among the men depicted in Diego Velázquez's painting *Las Lanzas*, or *La Rendición de Breda*, held by the Museo del Prado, Madrid. He was military commander in Flanders from 1631 to 1634, and then spent the rest of his career serving the court of Felipe IV. Don Carlos of Coloma died in Madrid in 1637.

12. Coll et al., pt. 2, 234–36, and AGI, Pasajeros, L. 11, E. 3561 and L. 11, E. 3560. Melchor de Aguilera had not served as governor for very long before he was involved in a lawsuit that took him back to Spain in 1642. He apparently won the lawsuit but was then imprisoned along with Lieutenant Rodrigo de Ovieto for bringing back unregistered gems and gold. Coll et al., pt. 2, 232, folio 56v, and AGI, Indiferente, 435, L. 11, f. 151v–154v, f. 162r–162v, and f. 176r–176v.

13. Ron Duncan-Hart, "World Politics, Illegal Jews and the Inquisition of Cartagena," *HaLapid* (Society for Crypto-Judaic Studies, University of Colorado–Colorado Springs, Fall 2006); Rodolfo Segovia, *Las Fortificaciones de Cartagena de Indias: Estrategia e Historia* (Bogota, Colombia: El Áncora Editores, 2009); Jaime Borja Gómez and Pablo Rodríguez Jiménez, eds., *Historia de la vida privada en Colombia*, vol. 1, *Las tronteras difusas del siglo XVI a 1880* (Bogota, Colombia: Aguilar, Altea, Taurus, Alfaguara, 2011, reprinted 2013).

14. Coll et al., pt. 2, 234.

15. Prisión y embargo de bienes de Doña Teresa de Aguilera y Roche, Santa Fe, August 27, 1662, fols. 397r–400v, Ramo de Concurso de Peñalosa, tomo 1, AGN. Appendix A describes the event and items confiscated from the governor's residence in the Palace of the Governors in Santa Fe in August 1662, and appendix B contains the list of items in her possession at the time of her entry into the Inquisition prison in Mexico City in April 1663.

16. The description of Doña Teresa's garments is according to the inventory taken

during her entry into Inquisition custody in Mexico City on April 11, 1663 (Coll et al., pt. 2, 222–27).

17. The governor's inventory was transcribed in part by Adolph Bandelier in 1912, and a short extract was published in Charles Wilson Hackett, *Historical Documents Relating to New Mexico, Nueva Vizcaya, and Approaches Thereto, to 1773* (Washington, D.C.: Carnegie Institution of Washington, 1937), 3:175. A much more complete inventory of a man's possessions is included elsewhere in Hackett's work (pp. 139–40); it is the inventory of possessions of Nicolás de Aguilar when he made his first appearance in the Inquisition prison on April 12, 1663. He was one of the men arrested with the governor on suspicion of Jewish practices in New Mexico and who were later acquitted. His clothing and personal effects were in a wooden trunk and included few items of imported fabrics—only cordovan leather shoes and a Rouen linen shirt. His clothing was primarily woolen and cotton, which were likely locally produced in New Mexico or at least were not as high-quality as the fabrics and wardrobe of Doña Teresa.

18. Jan Pietersz Coen, director general of a Dutch trading company, writing in 1619 and quoted in John Guy, "'One Thing Leads to Another': Indian Textiles and the Early Globalization of Style," in Amelia Peck, ed., *Interwoven Globe: The Worldwide Textile Trade, 1500–1800* (New York: Metropolitan Museum of Art, 2013), 17.

19. Elena Phipps, "The Iberian Globe; Textile Traditions and Trade in Latin America," in Amelia Peck, ed., *Interwoven Globe*, 34.

20. A delightful popular history of cochineal and the centuries-long search for a deep and lasting color that befitted European kings and painters is that by Amy Butler Greenfield, *A Perfect Red: Empire, Espionage, and the Quest for the Color of Desire* (New York: Harper Perennial, 2006, 1st ed. 2005). Indigo is produced in many countries; it was produced in Mexico as an export known as *añil*.

21. José Antonio Esquibel, "The Palace of the Governors in the Seventeenth Century," *El Palacio* 111, no. 3 (2006): 24–29, and Esquibel, "Parientes: Founders of the Villa of Santa Fe #10," *La Herencia* (Winter 2009), 32.

22. Esquibel, "Parientes," *La Herencia*, 33. Chamiso traveled to New Mexico in 1659 and must have been part of the same convoy in which the governor and Doña Teresa traveled. Perhaps he was brought by them to work on the palace grounds. Pecos Pueblo carpenters were noted for their skill and artistry in woodworking, which not only adorned their own village but also was used in building the casas reales and in making furniture for the Spanish settlers of Santa Fe. For brief overviews of Pecos woodworking, see John L. Kessell, *Kiva, Cross, and Crown: The Pecos Indians and New Mexico, 1540–1840* (Washington, D.C.: National Park Service, 1979) and Genevieve N. Head and Janet D. Orcutt, *From Folsom to Fogelson: The Cultural Resources Inventory Survey of Pecos National Historical Park*, 2 vols., Intermountain Cultural Resources Report, no. 66 (Santa Fe: National Park Service, 2002).

23. Robin Farwell Gavin, "La Sala de Estrado: Women's Place in the Palace," *El Palacio* 115, no. 4 (2010): 49–55. Jorge F. Rivas Pérez, "Domestic Display in the Spanish Overseas Territories," in Richard Aste, ed., *Behind Closed Doors: Art in the Span-*

ish American Home, 1492–1898 (New York: Monacelli Press and Brooklyn Museum, 2013), 49–104. María del Pilar López Pérez, "La vida en casa en Santa Fe en los siglos XVII y XVIII," in Jaime Borja Gómez and Pablo Rodríguez Jiménez, *Historia de la vida privada en Colombia*, vol. 1, *Las fronteras difusas del siglo XVI a 1880* (Bogota, Colombia: Aguilar, Altea, Taurus, Alfaguara, 2011, reprinted 2013), 80–107, describes the function of the estrado and other special rooms in seventeenth- and eighteenth-century Colombia in a study of *la vida cotidiana*, or domestic life, an important research topic in colonial studies.

24. The rooms that Esquibel identified may hew too closely to the later, nineteenth-century interior plan for the building, based on our understanding of the many remodels that the building has undergone over the centuries. Nevertheless it is still a useful plan to envision how the space and the objects recovered from the governor's residence might have been used.

25. Josefa de Sandoval was witness 17 (Coll et al., pt. 1, 107). She had testified in Santa Fe before Fray Posada on October 31, 1661. She was about twenty years old at the time and was a native of Mexico, married to Ensign Pedro de Arteaga, who was also a witness against the governor and his wife. As a servant in the governor's residence, she was present at critical moments and appeared to be one of the principal witnesses.

26. Seventeenth-century majolica characteristically had blue-on-white patterns, sometimes with just a simple edge decoration on plates; chocolateros often had more elaborate patterns such as the Puebla blue-on-white style that included birds, flowers, and pagodas that were copied from Chinese designs. Robin Farwell Gavin, Donna Pierce, and Alfonso Pleguezuelo, *Céramica y Cultura: The Story of Spanish and Mexican Majolica* (Albuquerque: University of New Mexico Press, 2003). The Talavera style of the inkwell shown in plate 10 is distinguished by the creamy color of the slip.

27. Translated by Gerald González as red ebony, but more likely a fragrant red wood such as a species of cedar or of *Dalbergia*, which grows in Mexico and Central America. Rivas Pérez ("Domestic Display," 82–88) describes and illustrates a similar style of bed that was painted with gold and made, he suggests, of cedar from Peru. I have used the original term *granadillo* rather than red ebony in appendix A.

28. González transcribed this from folio 398r, Ramo de Concurso de Peñalosa, tomo 1, AGN, as *moquina de lana*, which he took to mean that it was a woolen cloth woven at one of the Hopi Pueblo villages, but more likely this was *maquina de lana*, meaning a loomed cloth. I have made this change to the translation in appendix A.

29. Several extensive excavations in the Palace of the Governors and on the grounds surrounding the building have shed light on the colonial diet, economy, and trade networks. See, for example, Cordelia Thomas Snow, "A Brief History of the Palace of the Governors and a Preliminary Report on the 1974 Excavation, " *El Palacio* 80, no. 3 (1974): 6–21; Heather B. Trigg, *From Household to Empire: Society and Economy in Early Colonial New Mexico* (Tucson: University of Arizona Press, 2005); Stephen S. Post, "Excavations for the New Mexico History Museum (LA 111322): 350 Years of Occupation and Changing Land Use behind the Palace of the Governors, Santa Fe, New Mexico." Manuscript in author's possession. Office of Archaeological

Studies, Santa Fe, New Mexico, in preparation.

30. *Orlando Furioso* is an epic poem by Ludovico Ariosto published in 1516, that became the inspiration for music and paintings beginning in the sixteenth century and was widely known by educated people throughout Europe. William Stewart Rose, *The Orlando Furioso: Translated in English Verse from the Italian of Ludovico Ariosto, with Notes* (London: John Murray, Albermarle Street, 1823).

31. Coll et al., pt. 1, 108.

32. Ibid., pt. 2, 229.

3. A Gathering Storm

1. A portion of this discussion of the Inquisition proceedings was published by Frances Levine and Gerald González in "Doña Teresa in the Palace," *El Palacio* 116, no. 3, (2011): 40–47. See also Hordes, *To the End*, 57–59. Seymour B. Liebman, *Los Judíos en México y América Central: Fe, Llamas e Inquisición* (Mexico City: Siglo Veintiuno Editores, 1971), 113–20, 122–25.

2. Asunción Lavrin, Foreword to John F. Chuchiak, ed., *The Inquisition in New Spain, 1536–1820: A Documentary History* (Baltimore, Md.: Johns Hopkins Press, 2012), xv.

3. John F. Chuchiak, "The Holy Office of the Inquisition in New Spain (Mexico): An Introductory Study," in *The Inquisition in New Spain*, 1–12. Chuchiak's brilliant, comprehensive study of the Holy Office in New Spain is an encyclopedic treatment of the procedures and several specific cases that came before the tribunal in the New World. It is an indispensable reference that at the same time makes for fascinating reading . My quick summary here is intended to capture a complex and highly variable process that depended on time, place, and participants, but operated within the system that Chuchiak details so skillfully.

4. Sanchez (*Río Abajo*, 74) notes that during the seventeenth century the *Memorial* of Fray Alonso de Benavides was so widely read that it was translated into German, French, Latin, and Dutch. There have been several editions since that time, including a translation prepared by Mrs. Edward E. Ayer with annotations by Frederick Webb Hodge and Charles Lummis, published in 1916, and reprinted by Horn and Wallace, 1965. Frederick Webb Hodge, George P. Hammond, and Agapito Rey wrote another translation and annotated version of the *Memorial* published by the University of New Mexico in 1945. A recent translation and annotated edition is that of Baker H. Morrow, *A Harvest of Reluctant Souls* (Niwot,: University Press of Colorado, 1996).

5. Benavides writes of the "miraculous conversion of the Humana Nation" in the 1630 edition of the *Memorial* (Morrow, *Harvest of Reluctant Souls*, 79–83), but he also had the opportunity to interview the nun, then twenty-nine years old, at her abbey in Ágreda, Spain, in April 1631. For a biography of María Coronel de Arana, or as she was known in her abbey, María de Jesús de Ágreda, see Marilyn Fedewa, *María of Ágreda: Mystical Lady in Blue* (Albuquerque: University of New Mexico Press, 2009).

6. A portion of the discussion of Sor María de Ágreda was prepared for publication

in the exhibition catalog for "*Fractured Faiths: Spanish Judaism, The Inquisition, and New World Identities*" at the New Mexico History Museum, Santa Fe, planned for 2016. The catalog has been edited by Roger L. Martinez-Davila, Ron Duncan-Hart, and Josef Díaz (Albuquerque: Fresco Books / SF Design, 2016).

7. Nancy Parrott Hickerson, *The Jumanos: Hunters and Traders of the Southern Plains* (Austin: University of Texas Press, 1994); Hickerson is also the author of the entry on the Jumano Indians in *The Handbook of Texas Online* (www.tshaonline.org/ handbook/online), where she traces the interaction between the Plains-based Jumanos and the Pueblos of New Mexico. Although this relationship is well documented historically, as was their interaction with the Spanish from the earliest contact period, their linguistic and cultural affiliations are still not precisely known. Jumano may have been a reference to people described by the Spanish as having stripe-tattooed faces, rather than to a specific or singular cultural identity.

8. Scholars differ on the links between the Coronel family and Abraham Senior, who changed his name and identity to Fernández Pérez Coronel after the 1492 writ of expulsion, and who served as financier of Columbus's expedition; see discussion in Fedewa, *María of Ágreda*, 12–16.

9. Clark Colahan, in his brief 1999 biography of Sor María, takes a more jaundiced view of this event, arguing that it was her spiritual relationship as confidante to King Felipe IV, maintained through letters between the two, which protected her from being investigated as a heretic. For an English translation of some of the voluminous correspondence between the king and Sor María, see Clark A. Colahan, *Writing Knowledge and Power: The Visions of María de Ágreda* (Tucson: University of Arizona Press, 1994).

Colahan makes the case that the Inquisition proceedings were not immune from political manipulation. He raises the question of whether Benavides led María de Jesús to conclusions that he would find useful as he argued, ultimately unsuccessfully, for New Mexico to have a bishop of its own. María de Jesús, for her part, also seems to have known how to give her confessors what they were seeking, when later in life she skillfully dismissed her youthful embrace of mysticism without falling afoul of the Holy Office. Another explanation for her knowledge of New Mexico is offered by Sánchez (*Río Abajo*, 82), who suggests that Sor María might have gleaned some details from the account of a 1629 expedition of friars from the Taos Pueblo convento who ministered to the Apaches and Jumanos in western Texas.

10. Hordes, *To the End*, 142–43. While there was no reference to Perea's ancestry in the New Mexico records of the period, it is curious that knowledge of his maternal line did not impede his ascent as a well-regarded priest.

11. The Cíbola Project has produced outstanding transcripts and translations of the file of documents relating the anguish of friars who served in New Mexico during the tyrannical reign of Governor Rosas. See Martha Hidalgo Strolle, Jerry R. Craddock, and John H. R. Polt, *Dossier Concerning the Abuses of Luis de Rosas, Governor of New Mexico (1637–1641), his murder in 1641, and the extrajudicial execution of the alleged conspirators in the murder by Alonso Pacheco de Heredia, governor of New Mexico*

(1642–1644), Berkeley: University of California, Cíbola Project (2010), http://eschol-arship.org/uc/item/ofr37213.

12. Hordes, *To the End*, 146–48. Hordes argues that there were clear-cut endoga-mous marriage patterns in the converso families in New Mexico. The overall popula-tion was so small that the endogamous patterns may have been preserved because of other social and historical factors, such as ancestral ties to specific regions of Spain and Mexico, inheritance, land use and land tenure, and political factions, without necessarily involving the persistence of crypto-Jewish or converso identity.

13. Scholes, "Troublous Times," chap. 2, sect. 2, 153–55.

14. Scholes, "Troublous Times," chap. 4, 157–60.

15. Scholes, "Troublous Times," chap. 3, 390–91.

16. Scholes, "Troublous Times," chap. 1, sect. 5, 162

17. Ibid., 163–64.

18. AGN, Inq. 596, Proceso de Mendizábal, 1660, Document for the History of New Mexico, BANC-MSS-M-A-1, Bancroft Library, University of California, Berke-ley. Summarized by Scholes, "Troublous Times," chap. 3, 407–409.

19. Scholes, "Troublous Times," chap. 5, sect. 2, 64–65.

20. Scholes, "Troublous Times," chap. 3, 381–85.

21. Juan Manso was the younger brother of Fray Tomás Manso, a trusted admin-istrator of the New Mexico mission supply service and former custodian of the New Mexico Franciscans, giving him special standing and long-term relationships in New Mexico. Fray Juan de Ramírez was the successor to Fray Tomás. Scholes, "Troublous Times," chap. 1, sect. 2, 143.

22. Scholes, "Troublous Times," chap. 3, 386–87.

23. Scholes, "Troublous Times," chap. 4, sect. 1, 436.

24. Scholes, "Troublous Times," chap. 3, sect. 4, 426. A longer discussion of the conflict between the governors and the inquisitor appears in Kessell, *Kiva, Cross, and Crown*, chap. 5.

25. Scholes, "Troublous Times," chap. 1, sect. 3, 139–40.

26. Scholes, "Troublous Times," chap. 4, sect. 3, 445–47.

27. Witness testimony is found in Coll et al. The originals are part of AGN, Ramo Inquisición, vol. 596, 81–120. Page numbers in Coll et al. citations refer to the transla-tions in the pdf format of Coll et al. I have retained the capitalizations used for honorific or official titles (e.g., Don, Doña, and Fray) contained in their transla-tions. Notes in brackets are mine. A partial translation relating to Inquisition proceedings in New Mexico between 1629 and 1671 is found in Hackett, *Historical Documents*, vol. 3.

28. Isabel de Pedraza was the wife of Matías Romero and the daughter-in-law of Captain Bartolomé Romero, who was the Santa Fe magistrate and witness number 15 (*New Mexican Roots:* www.cybergata.com). Although several witnesses pointed to Isabel de Pedraza as the source of their knowledge, it is not clear why she was not questioned by Posada.

29. New Mexico Genealogical Society, preface to the compilation of the baptismal

records of the Church of Nuestra Señora de la Inmaculada Concepcíon, Tomé, New Mexico, www.nmgs.org/bksA11–12.php. From the introduction prepared by Margaret Espinosa McDonald, November 1998. The Domínguez de Mendoza family was forced to flee their substantial hacienda during the Pueblo Revolt of 1680 and received formal permission to abandon this land in favor of a new grant near El Paso del Norte in the year following the revolt, according to the genealogical research by José Antonio Esquibel, "The People of the Camino Real: A Genealogical Approach," in Douglas Preston and José Antonio Esquibel, *The Royal Road: El Camino Real from Mexico City to Santa Fe*, (Albuquerque: University of New Mexico Press, 1998). Hackett, *Historical Documents*, 177–80, provides portions of Domínguez de Mendoza's testimony relating primarily to the governor's permitting kachina dances, and his disrespect for the friars.

30. France V. Scholes, Marc Simmons, and José Antonio Esquibel, eds., *Juan Domínguez de Mendoza: Soldier and Frontiersman of the Spanish Southwest* (Albuquerque: University of New Mexico Press, 2012), 19.

31. Coll et al., pt. 1, 86–87.

32. Ibid., 92.

33. Ibid., 97.

34. Ibid.

35. Ibid., 100.

36. Ibid.

37. Ibid., 101.

38. Ibid., 105.

39. Ibid., 106–107.

40. Ibid., 106.

41. Ibid., 105.

42. Ibid., 106–107.

43. Ibid., 111.

44. Ibid., 113–14.

45. Ibid., 116.

46. Ibid., .117.

47. Ibid., 117.

48. Coll et al., pt. 2, 221–22. The document is a printed form, with the names and specifics filled in by hand. Nonetheless, the scope of Manso's authority was broad and absolute.

49. Scholes, "Troublous Times," chap. 6, sect. 3, 255–60, and for Don Bernardo's outbursts against the friars, 264–65. Hackett, *Historical Documents*, 233, 240.

50. Translation by Gerald González. Prisión y embargo de bienes de Doña Teresa de Aguilera y Roche, Santa Fe, August 27, 1662, fols. 396r–397r, Ramo de Concurso de Peñalosa, tomo 1, AGN.

51. Coll et al., pt. 1, 118.

52. Ibid.

4. Charged with a "Haughty and Presumptuous Spirit"

1. Coll et al., pt. 2, 260.

2. Chuchiak, *The Inquisition in New Spain*, 128–29.

3. Ibid., 122–23.

4. Coll et al., pt. 4, 193–96.

5. The transcript from which this translation was made was produced by Adolph F. Bandelier in 1912 during his research in the Archivo General de la Nación in Mexico City. This description was taken from a new partial translation of the Bandelier document by Thomas Merlan. The transcript is not always clear in its spacing or punctuation, or even in its word choice. Here Bandelier uses terms (*calcon destameña fraileses* and *acano* or "*a cano*") that might mean that the governor's trousers were of the style of a friar, and might mean striped, or gray, or simply old. He was permitted to retain the gabardine, the breeches, and the reliquary. The mustache form was bound with scarlet that was dyed with grana, or cochineal.

6. Coll et al., pt. 2, 229, from the hearing of April 21, 1663.

7. Coll et al., pt. 2, 228–29.

8. Juan de Leyva de la Cerda, the Conde de Baños, was viceroy of New Spain from September 1660 until June 1664. His term of service parallels the span of the troubles of Doña Teresa and Governor López de Mendizábal with the Inquisition. The governor would have been appointed by a previous viceroy but recalled by Leyva de la Cerda.

9. Coll et al., pt. 2, 229.

10. Ibid., 236.

11. Ibid., 236–37.

12. Ibid., 225, 230.

13. Ibid., 231.

14. Ibid., 238.

15. Ibid., 238.

16. Ibid., 240.

17. Ibid., 242.

18. Ibid., 243. Gutiérrez claims the friar poured burning turpentine over the wounds, killing the man (*When Jesus Came*, 127–28). More of Fray Salvador's misdeeds were reported to the Holy Office when Cristóbal de Anaya Almázan, an ally of Governor López de Mendizábal, was tried before the Inquisition in 1663. Anaya revealed that the friar had had a flagrant affair with Juana Rueda, the wife of Captain Francisco Domínguez de Mendoza, when the friar was in service at the church in the Sandia province. Scholes, Simmons, and Esquibel, eds., *Juan Domínguez de Mendoza*, 369–70.

19. Coll et al., pt. 2, 244.

20. Ibid., 244–45.

21. Ibid., 246.

22. Ibid., 248.

23. Ibid., 249. The thread she requested was transcribed as *hilo de clema* or *hilo de*

clemen. It refers to fine thread manufactured in Crema, Italy. There were several types of thread in her embargoed possessions—agave thread, silk thread, and thin linen thread, as well as several items of clothing trimmed with lace or ribbons. She also requested linen for her maid.

24. Coll et al., pt. 2, 249.
25. Ibid., 250–51.
26. Ibid., 260.
27. Ibid., 253.
28. Ibid., 255.
29. Ibid., 256.
30. Ibid., 259.
31. Ibid., 262.
32. Ibid., 261–63
33. Ibid., 262.
34. Counts 1 to 3 are translated by Coll et al., pt. 2, 263.
35. Counts 4 and 5 are translated by Coll et al., pt. 2, 264.
36. Coll et al., pt. 2, 266.
37. Ibid.
38. Coll et al., pt. 2, 269.
39. Ibid., 270.
40. Ibid., 269–70
41. Ibid., 271.
42. Ibid., 272.
43. Ibid., 273.
44. Ibid., 273–74.
45. Chuchiak, *Inquisition in New Spain*, 64.
46. Coll et al., pt. 2, 274

5. Taking Matters into Her Own Hands

1. Coll et al., pt. 2, 275.
2. Chuchiak, *Inquisition in New Spain*, 122.
3. Coll et al., pt. 2, 275.
4. Ibid., 276.
5. Ibid., 276.
6. Guido Waldman provides a wonderfully detailed translation and annotation to the prose version of *Orlando Furioso*, the classic epic poem by Ludovico Ariosto (New York: Oxford University Press, 1983, reprinted 2008). Ludovico Ariosto (1474–1533), an Italian nobleman and poet, was an envoy in the employment of Cardinal Hippolytus (Ippolito d'Este). In 1516 Ariosto published his first version of *Orlando Furioso* when he served as court poet in Ferrera, Italy, located on a branch of the Po River. Ferrera had a large Jewish ghetto, though Ariosto makes little reference to it in his work. He was something of a rogue in matters of the heart. In 1532, nearing

the end of his life, he was recommended as poet to Emperor Charles V, a post he did not take. The third edition of his masterwork was published just before his death. *Orlando Furioso* is considered a major triumph of Italian poetry for its length and beautiful writing, which inspired writers and artists over the centuries.

7. Coll et al., pt. 2, 276–77.

8. Ibid., 278.

9. Ibid., 280.

10. Ibid., 280.

11. Ibid., 282.

12. A longer discussion of the place of chocolate among colonists in the Americas is found in Frances Levine, "So Dreadful a Crime," *El Palacio* 117, no. 4 (Winter 2012): 52–59.

13. Sophie D. Coe and Michael D. Coe, *The True History of Chocolate*, 2nd ed. (London: Thames and Hudson, 2007).

14. Manuel Aguilar-Moreno, "The Good and Evil of Chocolate in Colonial Mexico," in Cameron L. McNeil, ed., *Chocolate in Mesoamerica* (Gainesville: University of Florida Press, 2009), 273–28.

15. Martha Few, "Chocolate, Sex, and Disorderly Women in Late-Seventeenth and Early-Eighteenth-Century Guatemala," *Ethnohistory* 52, no. 4 (Fall 2005): 673–88.

16. Coll et al., pt. 2, 283.

17. Peñalosa's fall from grace and from his alliance with Fray Alonso de Posada came about in 1663 when he too was arrested by the Holy Office for his conduct of the López de Mendizábal residencia. When the Inquisition issued its findings in 1665, Peñalosa was barred from public service, faced a public denunciation and confiscation of his property, and was banished from New Spain. He journeyed to England and France, where he tried, unsuccessfully, to proffer his knowledge of New Spain to both governments. The French considered adding Peñalosa, with his ideas for exploration and conquest, to the LaSalle expedition in 1684, but did not. David Weber, *The Spanish Frontier in North America*, 148–49; Richard Flint and Shirley Cushing Flint, "Diego Dionisio de Peñalosa Briceño y Berdugo" (Santa Fe: Office of the State Historian), http://newmexicohistory.org/people/diego-dionisio-de-penalosa-briceno-y-berdugo.

18. Coll et al., pt. 2, 286–87.

19. Ibid., 287.

20. Alonso de Alavés Pinelo may be the same person as the author of a legal treatise on the powers and responsibilities of the office of the viceroy, *Astro mitológico político que en la entrada y recibimiento del conde de Alba de Aliste*, published in Mexico in 1650.

21. Chuchiak, *Inquisition in New Spain*, 68.

22. Coll et al., pt. 2, 290.

23. Ibid., 291.

24. Ibid.

25. Ibid., 292–93.

26. Ibid., 294.

27. Ibid., 295.

28. Ibid., 296.

29. Ibid., 297.

30. Ibid., 298.

31. She offered the excerpts from Peñalosa's letter to refute what she identifies as count 31. See Coll et al., pt. 2, 298. That count, however, is a specific count against her use of love magic. She really meant counts 35 and 36.

32. Coll et al., pt. 2, 298–99.

33. Ibid., 299–300.

34. She returned eight "folds" or folios to the court, seven of which had been written on, and each was duly accounted for by the inquisitors. Coll et al., pt. 2, 327.

35. José Antonio Esquibel, "Thirty-eight Adobe Houses," 124.

36. Manso's testimony of January 13, 1661, is found in Coll et al., pt. 1, 82, folios 2r–2v. Doña Teresa's written statement and suspicions about Manso are found in Coll et al., pt. 2, 328.

37. Coll et al., pt. 2, 328.

38. González and Levine, "In Her Own Voice," 198, suggest that she was informing the court of other heretics, perhaps even suggesting that Griego's father was a crypto-Jew. An alternative is that he was turning back to his Tiwa upbringing and traditional beliefs at the moment of his death.

39. Coll et al., pt. 2, 329.

40. Ibid., pt. 3, 105–107.

41. Coll et al., pt. 2, 151n108, define *panocha* as Mexican brown sugar, or a kind of cornbread, and suggest that it is the solid chocolate that is being ground. I read this passage to mean that the sugar, maize, and chocolate may have been mixed into tablets for storage and then used to make the drink.

42. "*que le dieran una cageta i pan*: *cajeta* is a small box, especially for sweets. It can also mean *dulce de leche* 'caramel spread.' It is of course also possible that the woman was merely asking for a box, but it seems unlikely that such a request would be coupled with one for bread." Coll et al., pt. 2, 152n109.

43. Coll et al., pt. 2, 329–31.

44. "*i ella i todo*: translators guess that 'she' is probably Arteaga's wife, Josefa de Sandoval." Coll et al., pt. 2, 157n116.

45. Ibid., pt. 2, 334–35.

46. Ibid., pt. 2, 337.

47. Ibid., 338–39.

48. Ibid., 339–40.

49. Coll et al., pt. 2, 162n125, note that the term *hermanos* could also be translated as "brothers and sisters" since in Spanish the plural for brothers and sisters takes the masculine form.

50. Coll et al., pt. 3, 115.

51. Leonor de Pastrana, Don Bernardo's mother, was the widow of Cristóbal López

de Mendizábal, a man of Basque origin from the town of Oñate. Her father, Pablo de Pastrana, was descended through his maternal line from Juan Núñez de León, who had been tried and reconciled for practicing Judaism by the Holy Office in Mexico in 1603. Further, there may be a connection between Doña Leonor's father to the Pastrana family who had been investigated as judaizantes in Toledo, Spain, in the 1530s according to Hordes, *To the End*, 154. After the failure of a sugar plantation that Doña Leonor and Don Cristóbal operated in Chietla, Mexico, she was apparently dependent on the support of her son and was evidently living with them while they were in New Mexico. She died in Mexico City in April 1666, three years after Don Bernardo, and was buried under one of the altars in the church of Santa Catalina de Sena. Scholes, Simmons, and Esquibel, *Juan Domínguez de Mendoza*, 95n2.

52. Coll et al., pt. 3, 115.

53. Ibid., 116.

54. Ibid., 121–22.

6. Reaching Conclusions

1. Coll et al., pt. 3, 123–24.

2. Ibid., 125.

3. Ibid., 128.

4. Ibid., 129–30.

5. Ibid., 130–31.

6. Ibid., 137.

7. Coll et al., pt. 3, 140.

8. Ibid., 151–52.

9. Ibid., 157.

10. Ibid., 159.

11. Ibid.

12. Coll et al., pt. 4, 154.

13. Ibid., 156–57.

14. Ibid., 157–58.

15. Chuchiak, *Inquisition in New Spain*, 6. Mary E Giles., ed., *Women in the Inquisition: Spain and the New World* (Baltimore, Md.: Johns Hopkins Press, 1999), explores several cases of women who stood before inquisitors in Spain or the New World to defend themselves for their visions, their sexuality, or the mitote, or gossip, spread by jealous neighbors or spouses who had earlier deserted them. Bigamy was not uncommon in the colonial period. Years might elapse between the time a man set out for the Indies and when, or if, he ever came back to the peninsula and his wife. Some women who were tried for bigamy in Spain and New Spain were these deserted wives, who occupied an ambiguous place—they were neither virgin nor widow. Other women, who professed an understanding of the divine, were tried for heresy. Women who experienced visions were called *alumbradas*,

and they too could face an Inquisition panel to justify their claims of enlightenment, ecstasy, or in some cases, sexual attraction to the saints.

16. Coll et al., pt. 4, 159.

17. Ibid., 160–61.

18. Scholes, "Troublous Times," chap. 7, sect. 1, 377.

19. Coll et al., pt. 4, 168.

20. Ibid., 188–89.

21. Ibid., 190–91.

22. Ibid., 191.

23. Ibid., 193.

24. Ibid.

25. Hordes, *To the End*, 164 and note 125.

Appendix A

1. Throughout the document, a cross with dots in each corner was used in several places. We have preserved this in translation with the sign +. —Trans.

2. Likely a book dealing with the concept of the guardian angel, a topic of importance in seventeenth-century theological and poetic writings and art. —Trans.

Appendix B

The notes that follow are those of translators María Magdalena Coll, Heather Bamford, Heather McMichael, and John H. R. Polt for the Cíbola Project. Though the notes begin with 33 in this excerpt of the translation, I have renumbered them from 1 here. My additional comments appear in brackets with my initials, "FL."

1. *un paño de tauaco viejo:* possibly, "an old tobacco-colored handkerchief."

2. *memoria de los generos que son menester para el officio:* The last word can mean a trade, but I do not know what trade that might be. It can also mean divine offices or prayers, or the office of a scribe.

3. Or size.

4. *començada abanicar:* I have not discovered the meaning of what seems to be a technical term of the seamstress's trade. [FL: a piece of fabric partially pleated or folded like a fan.]

5. *de seda agujada:* my conjecture is that one should read *agujada* in the sense of "pierced." The adornment would consist of silk with piercings to produce an effect similar to lace. [FL: This might be a type of "cut-work" lace with appliqued edges.]

6. *un poco de tecomata en una xicarilla pequeña:* As far as I can tell, *tecomate* (with an *e*) is a gourd, a vessel made of a gourd, or an earthenware vessel of the same general shape. Here it is the contents of the small cup, but I am at a loss as to what it consists of. [FL: Maybe *poço de tecomate*, i.e., *pocillo*, "vasija pequeña de loza, como la del chocolate."]

7. *pita de niñas: pita* is the agave plant and also thread made from it, but I do not know what it has to do with girls (*de niñas*).

8. *con la remienta dorada y pabonada de negro:* I find no such word as *remienta*, but *la remienta* could be a scribal error for *la herramienta*, referring to the metal parts of the small case.

9. *toca de reina:* I do not know what style of coif this is. [FL: This might mean a queen's toque, or a similar head wrap in a style found in seventeenth- and eighteenth-century paintings.]

10. Seemingly a token of devotion to this saint.

11. *quarto de medio:* I do not know how this differs from plain quarto.

12. *medio pliego: Pliego*, as will become evident when Doña Teresa submits her own writings, is used in the sense of a fold, that is, a piece of paper folded in two, thus forming two sheets or leaves and four pages. Half a *pliego*, then, is one sheet.

Appendix C

1. Coll et al. point out that Doña Teresa's remarkable testimony is often a little confusing to follow, as she likely wrote the same way she spoke, and the rambling text can make it difficult to determine exactly who she is talking about. The translators "refrained from 'regularizing' all of Doña Teresa's prose, in part in order to preserve its flavor, and at times because its precise meaning is unclear." pt. 2, 150n105.

2. The witness numbers, identified in brackets, were not known by Doña Teresa; these people testified before Fray Alonso de Posada and other Inquisition officials. The witness numbers were originally given by Coll et al. as endnotes, but I have inserted them in the transcript itself. Doña Teresa names many more people than actually testified against her. I have shortened some of the original footnotes in which Coll et al. give further linguistic analysis of Doña Teresa's writing and patterns of speech. In those cases, I have referred to the original footnote number so that readers can consult the originals as well.

3. "*a escoltas i predio: Predio* is a piece of real estate. I take it to be a scribal error for presidio." Coll et al., pt. 2, 152n110.

4. Coll et al. translate the term *compadre* as "friend." But more precisely, it denotes something closer in a fictive kinship relationship, since one's *compadre* is the godfather of one's child, or the father of one's godchild.

5. "*un rocin de bracos:* A *rocín* is a nag, but [the translators] have found no meaning for *de bracos* (more likely, *de braços*)." Coll et al., pt. 2, 154n112.

6. "*le gubaba a la muger asta la comida:* [the translators] read *gubaba* as *jugaba*. Doña Teresa habitually uses a 'g' instead of a 'j.'" Coll et al., pt. 2, 156n115.

7. "*tenia* in the ms., which [the translators] believe to be a *lapsus calami* for *temia* 'feared.'" Coll et al., pt. 2, 159n118.

8. "*algarabia:* colloquially used to mean 'gibberish,' but originally signifying 'Arabic,' a meaning that Doña Teresa may have had in mind as incriminating the witness against her." Coll et al., pt. 2, 160n119.

9. "Doña Teresa writes *se*, but [the translators] suspect this is a *lapsus calami* for *es*." Coll et al., pt. 2, 160n120.

10. "*camarada:* 'comrade,' probably *camada* 'gang.'" Coll et al., pt. 2, 163n126.

11. "*por auerle echado por alli el despacho de sonora*: The meaning of *echado* in this context is not clear to the translators, though clearly the dispatch was the cause of the problems." Coll et al., pt. 2, 163n128.

12. Coll et al. in pt. 3.

13. There are no Chaveses among the witnesses. Catalina de Zamora, who offered testimony about the events of Good Friday on March 9, 1662, at the mission at Sandia, later recanted her testimony and asked it to be stricken, saying that she did not know if the scene described to her by Fernando Durán de Chaves had actually taken place. Zamora's testimony was offered voluntarily and seems to have been dubious information that was little more than gossip. Tomé Domínguez, witness 4, testified at San Antonio de Isleta about the events of Good Friday based on what he had been told by Bartolomé Romero about the alleged incident of Don Bernardo and Doña Teresa exchanging caps and drinking from cups as though taking part in a secret ceremony. Coll et al., pt. 1, pp. 86–87.

14. None of these people testified. Although Coll et al., pt. 3, 103n134, note that Diego de Trujillo was witness 8, his relationship to this list of people is not established.

15. Coll et al., pt. 3, 105n136, analyze this passage as *le decia que su madre* because it is not clear whether the subject is masculine or feminine and to whom *su* refers. They suggest that what is being reported is an unflattering remark by Don Bernardo to Francisco Gómez. Doña Teresa clearly says that the report is one of Peñalosa's lies, a charge she often makes against him.

16. Crossed out after *buelta* is *de los despachos*, without which Doña Teresa's meaning is unclear to the translators. Coll et al., pt. 3, 106n137.

17. Coll et al., pt. 3, 107n139, consider "this sentence a good example of how, in Doña Teresa's prose, the masculine singular subject pronoun can shift meaning. The 'he' of the sentence refers at different points to Antonio de Salas, to the anonymous Indian, and to Don Bernardo López de Mendizábal."

18. Coll et al., pt. 3, 108n142, note several difficulties in translating this sentence. "The discrepancy of gender (*las que llaman los muchos*) could also be read 'she is one of those [women] whom many [men] call.'"

19. Coll et al., pt. 3, 109n143, write, "One possible interpretation of this rather confusing passage is that Francisco de Madrid told Don Bernardo that he (F. de M.) was a mestizo, that Don Bernardo asked someone whether this was true, that this person said that it was and mentioned it to F. de M., who then took offense, although why he should do so if it was he who first raised the matter is not clear to me. Another possibility is that . . . Don Bernardo told F. de M. that he (F. de M.) was a mestizo, that F. de M. then asked someone about it and that this person said that it was true and also told Don Bernardo about it."

20. Coll et al., pt. 3, 110n146, offer an alternative explanation: "that *la doña margarita es la comadre de mans*." This can mean that Manso is the godfather of her child, or

that she is the godmother of Manso's child, or simply that she is Manso's good friend."

21. Coll et al., pt. 3, 114n149, note that the reference here is not clear but might mean that Don Bernardo is being accused of not paying the cobbler's apprentices.

22. Coll et al., pt. 3, 119n166, note that there is some confusion in this passage, but think that it means that it is Don Diego who wants to be accompanied, and he chooses Francisco de León to accompany him.

Bibliography

Archival Materials

Archivo General de Indias (AGI), Seville

Indiferente, 435, L. 11, f. 151v–154v, f. 162r–162v, and f. 176r–176v.

Pasajeros, L. 11, E. 3561 and L. 11, E. 3560.

Archivo General de la Nación (AGN), Mexico City

"Prisión y embargo de bienes de Doña Teresa de Aguilera y Roche, Santa Fe," August 27, 1662. AGN, Ramo de Concurso de Peñalosa, tomo 1, fols. 396r–397r.

"Segundo cuaderno del proceso contra Don Bernardo Lopez De Mendizabal, gobernador de Nuevo Mexico, por proposiciones hereticas," 1660. AGN, tomo 587, expediente 1, fols. 1–281.

"El señor fiscal del Santo Oficio contra doña Theresa de Aguilera y Roche, muger de don Bernardo López de Mendizábal, por sospechosa de delictos de judaísmo," 1664. AGN, Ramo Inquisición, vol. 596, expediente 1, fols. 1–277.

Bancroft Library, University of California, Berkeley

Tomo 596, Proceso de Mendizábal, 1660, Document for the History of New Mexico, BANC-MSS-M-A-1.

Books, Articles, and Dissertations

Adorno, Rolena, and Patrick Charles Pautz, eds. and trans. *The Narrative of Cabeza de Vaca*. Lincoln: University of Nebraska Press, 2003.

———, eds. and trans. *Álvar Núñez Cabeza de Vaca: His Account, His Life, and the Expedition of Pánfilo de Narváez*. 3 vols. Lincoln: University of Nebraska Press, 1999.

Aguilar-Moreno, Manuel. "The Good and Evil of Chocolate in Colonial Mexico." In *Chocolate in Mesoamerica*, edited by Cameron L. McNeil, 273–88. Gainesville: University of Florida Press, 2009.

Aste, Richard, ed. *Behind Closed Doors: Art in the Spanish American Home, 1492–1898*. New York: Monacelli Press and Brooklyn Museum, 2013.

Ayer, Mrs. Edward E., trans. *The Memorial of Fray Alonso de Benavides, 1630*, edited by Frederick Webb Hodge and Charles F. Lummis. Chicago: privately printed, 1916. Reprint, Albuquerque: Horn and Wallace, 1965.

Baer, Yitzhak. *A History of the Jews in Christian Spain*. Philadelphia: Jewish

Publication Society of America, 1971.

Bango, Isidro G. *Remembering Sepharad: Jewish Culture in Medieval Spain*. Madrid: State Corporation for Spanish Cultural Action Abroad, 2003.

Borja Gómez, Jaime, and Pablo Rodríguez Jiménez. *Historia de la vida privada en Colombia*. Vol. 1, *Las fronteras difusas del siglo XVI a 1880*. Bogota, Colombia: Aguilar, Altea, Taurus, Alfaguara, 2011. Reprint, 2013.

Cañizares-Esguerra, Jorge. *Puritan Conquistadors: Iberianizing the Atlantic, 1550–1700*. Stanford: Stanford University Press, 2006.

Casas, Bartolomé de Las. *A Short Account of the Destruction of the Indies*, edited and translated by Nigel Griffin. London: Penguin Classics, 1992.

Castro, Américo, and Willard F. King. *The Spaniards: An Introduction to Their History*. Berkeley: University of California Press, 1985.

Chuchiak, John F. "The Holy Office of the Inquisition in New Spain (Mexico): An Introductory Study." In *The Inquisition in New Spain, 1536–1820: A Documentary History*, 1–12. Baltimore, Md.: Johns Hopkins Press, 2012.

———, ed. *The Inquisition in New Spain, 1536–1820: A Documentary History*, Baltimore, Md.: Johns Hopkins Press, 2012.

Coe, Sophie D., and Michael D. Coe. *The True History of Chocolate*. 2nd ed. London: Thames and Hudson, 2007.

Cohen, J. M., ed. and trans. *The Four Voyages of Christopher Columbus*. London: Penguin Classics, 1969.

Colahan, Clark. "María de Jesús de Ágreda: The Sweetheart of the Holy Office." In *Women in the Inquisition: Spain and the New World*, 155–70. Baltimore, Md.: Johns Hopkins Press, 1999.

———. *Writing Knowledge and Power: The Visions of María de Ágreda*. Tucson: University of Arizona Press, 1994.

Coll, María Magdalena, Heather Bamford, Heather McMichael, and John H. R. Polt. *The Trial Before the Tribunal of the Holy Office in Mexico City of Doña Teresa Aguilera y Roche. Archivo General de la Nación, México. Ramo Inquisición, vol. 596*. Berkeley: University of California, Cíbola Transcription and Translation Project, 2012.

Coll-More, María Magdalena. "Un estudio lingüístico-histórico del español en Nuevo México en la época de la colonia: Análisis de las cartas de Doña Teresa de Aguilera y Roche al Tribunal de la Inquisición en 1664." Ph.D. diss., University of California, Berkeley, 1999.

———. "'Fio me a de librar Dios Nuestro Señor de mis falsos acusadores': Doña Teresa de Aguilera y Roche al Tribunal de la Inquisición (1664, Mexico)." *Romance Philology* 53. Special issue, pt. 2 (1999–2000).

Colligan, John B. *The Juan Páez Hurtado Expedition of 1695*. Albuquerque: University of New Mexico Press, 1995.

Cordell, Linda S., and Maxine E. McBrinn. *Archaeology of the Southwest*. Walnut Creek, Calif.: Left Coast Press, 2012.

Covey, Cyclone. *Cabeza de Vaca's Adventures in the Unknown Interior of America*.

Albuquerque: University of New Mexico Press, 1961. 6th ed., 1992.

Dodge, Meredith D., and Rick Hendricks. *Two Hearts, One Soul: The Correspondence of the Condesa de Galve, 1688–1696.* Albuquerque: University of New Mexico Press, 1993.

Duncan-Hart, Ron. "World Politics, Illegal Jews and the Inquisition of Cartagena." *HaLapid* (Society for Crypto-Judaic Studies, University of Colorado–Colorado Springs, Fall 2006).

Encinias, Miguel, Alfred Rodríguez, and Joseph P. Sánchez. *Gaspar Pérez de Villagrá, Historia de la Nueva México, 1610.* Albuquerque: University of New Mexico Press, 1992.

Esquibel, José Antonio. "The Jewish-Converso Ancestry of Doña Beatriz de Estrada." *Genealogical Society of Hispanic America Journal* 9 (Winter 1997): 134–43.

———. "Juan Chamiso, Albañil Maestro: Research and Summary Notes Prepared for the Palace of the Governors, 2005." Unpublished manuscript used by permission of the author.

———. "New Light on the Jewish-Converso Ancestry of Don Juan de Oñate: A Research Note." *Colonial Latin American Historical Review* 7 (1998): 182–83.

———. "The Palace of the Governors in the Seventeenth Century." El Palacio 111, no. 3 (Fall 2006): 24–29.

———. "Parientes: Founders of the Villa of Santa Fe #10." *La Herencia: Journal of the Hispanic Genealogical Research Center of New Mexico* (Winter 2009): 30–33.

———. "The People of the Camino Real: A Genealogical Approach." In *The Royal Road: El Camino Real from Mexico City to Santa Fe,* by Douglas Preston and José Antonio Esquibel, 145–76. Albuquerque: University of New Mexico Press, 1998.

———. "The Romero Family of Seventeenth Century New Mexico, Part 2." *La Herencia: Journal of the Hispanic Genealogical Research Center of New Mexico* 11, no. 3 (July 2003).

———. "Thirty-eight Adobe Houses—The Villa de Santa Fe in the 17th Century." In *All Trails Lead to Santa Fe,* 109–28. Santa Fe: Sunstone Press, 2010.

Favata, Martin A., and José B. Fernández. *The Account: Álvar Núñez Cabeza de Vaca's Relación.* Houston: Arte Público Press, 1993.

Fedewa, Marilyn. *María of Ágreda: Mystical Lady in Blue.* Albuquerque: University of New Mexico Press, 2009.

Ferry, Barbara, and Debbie Nathan. "Mistaken Identity? The Case of New Mexico's Hidden Jews." *Atlantic Monthly* 283, no. 6 (December 2000): 85–96.

Few, Martha. "Chocolate, Sex, and Disorderly Women in Late-Seventeenth and Early-Eighteenth-Century Guatemala." *Ethnohistory* 52, no. 4 (Fall 2005): 673–88.

Flint, Richard, and Shirley Cushing Flint. "Diego Dionisio de Peñalosa Briceño y Berdugo." Santa Fe: Office of the State Historian. http://newmexicohistory.org/people/diego-dionisio-de-penalosa-briceno-y-berdugo.

———. *Documents of the Coronado Expedition, 1539–1541.* Dallas: Southern Methodist University Press, 2005.

———. *Great Cruelties Have Been Reported: The 1544 Investigation of the Coronado*

Expedition. Dallas: Southern Methodist University Press, 2002.

———. *The Latest Word from 1540: People, Places, and Portrayals of the Coronado Expedition*. Albuquerque: University of New Mexico Press, 2011.

"1492 / Granada: Unifying the Body Politic." *Lapham's Quarterly* 5, no. 4 (Fall 2012): 109–10. www.laphamsquarterly.org/politics/purifying-body-politic. Reprinted from University of Pennsylvania Press, 1997.

Garate, Donald T. "Juan de Oñate's *Prueba de Caballero*, 1625: A Look at His Ancestral Heritage." *Colonial Latin American Historical Review* 7 (1998): 132–33, 144.

Gavin, Robin Farwell. "La Sala de Estrado: Women's Place in the Palace." *El Palacio* 115, no. 4 (Winter 2010): 49–55.

Gavin, Robin Farwell, Donna Pierce, and Alfonso Pleguezuelo. *Cerámica y Cultura: The Story of Spanish and Mexican Majolica*. Albuquerque: University of New Mexico Press, 2003.

Gerber, Jane S. *The Jews of Spain: A History of the Sephardic Experience*. New York: Free Press, 1992.

Giles, Mary E., ed. *Women in the Inquisition: Spain and the New World*. Baltimore, Md.: Johns Hopkins Press, 1999.

Gitlitz, David M. *Secrecy and Deceit: The Religion of the Crypto-Jews*. Philadelphia: Jewish Publication Society of America, 1996. Reprint, Albuquerque: University of New Mexico Press, 2002.

González, Gerald, and Frances Levine. "In Her Own Voice: Doña Teresa Aguilera y Roche and Intrigue in the Palace of the Governors, 1659–1662." Santa Fe: Sunstone Press, 2010.

Green, Jesse. *Cushing at Zuni: The Correspondence and Journals of Frank Hamilton Cushing, 1879–1884*. Albuquerque: University of New Mexico Press, 1990.

———. *Selected Writings of Frank Hamilton Cushing*. Lincoln: University of Nebraska Press, 1979.

Greenfield, Amy Butler. *A Perfect Red: Empire, Espionage, and the Quest for the Color of Desire*. New York: Harper Perennial, 2006. First published 2005.

Griffen, Nigel, ed. and trans. *A Short Account of the Destruction of the Indies*, by Bartolomé de Las Casas. London: Penguin Classics, 1992.

Gutiérrez, Ramón A. *When Jesus Came, the Corn Mothers Went Away: Marriage, Sexuality, and Power in New Mexico, 1500–1846*. Stanford: Stanford University Press, 1991.

Guy, John. "'One Thing Leads to Another': Indian Textiles and the Early Globalization of Style." In *Interwoven Globe: The Worldwide Textile Trade, 1500–1800*, edited by Amelia Peck, 12–27. New York: Metropolitan Museum of Art, 2013.

Hackett, Charles Wilson. *Historical Documents Relating to New Mexico, Nueva Vizcaya, and Approaches Thereto, to 1773*. Vol. 3. Washington, D.C.: Carnegie Institution of Washington, 1937.

Hallenbeck, Cleve. *The Journey of Fray Marcos*. Dallas: Southern Methodist University Press, 1949.

Hammond George P. "Don Juan de Oñate and the Founding of New Mexico." *New*

Mexico Historical Review 1, no. 1 (1926): 42–77. Reprint, Santa Fe: El Palacio Press, 1927.

Hammond, George P., and Agapito Rey. *Don Juan de Oñate, Colonizer of New Mexico, 1595–1628*. Albuquerque: University of New Mexico Press, 1953.

———. *The Rediscovery of New Mexico, 1580–1594*. Albuquerque: University of New Mexico Press, 1966.

Head, Genevieve N., and Janet D. Orcutt. *From Folsom to Fogelson: The Cultural Resources Inventory Survey of Pecos National Historical Park*. 2 vols. Intermountain Cultural Resources Report, no. 66. Santa Fe: National Park Service, 2002.

Herz, Cary. *New Mexico's Crypto-Jews: Image and Memory*. Albuquerque: University of New Mexico Press, 2009.

Hickerson, Nancy Parrott. Jumano Indians. *The Handbook of Texas Online*. n.d. www.tshaonline.org/handbook/online.

———. *The Jumanos: Hunters and Traders of the Southern Plains*. Austin: University of Texas Press, 1994.

Hidalgo Strolle, Martha, Jerry R. Craddock, and John H. R. Polt. *Dossier concerning the abuses of Luis de Rosas, governor of New Mexico (1637–1641), his murder in 1641, and the extrajudicial execution of the alleged conspirators in the murder by Alonso Pacheco de Heredia, governor of New Mexico (1642–1644)*. Berkeley: University of California, Cíbola Transcription and Translation Project, 2010. http://escholarship. org/uc/item/0fr37213.

Hodge, Frederick Webb, George P. Hammond, and Agapito Rey. *Fray Alonso de Benavides' Revised Memorial of 1634, with Numerous Supplementary Documents Elaborately Annotated*. Albuquerque: University of New Mexico Press, 1945.

Hordes, Stanley M. "The Participation of Crypto-Jews in the Settlement of the Far Northern Frontier of New Spain, 1589–1663." *Chronicles of the Trail: Quarterly Journal of El Camino Real de Tierra Adentro Trail Association* 6, no. 1 (Winter 2010): 16–21.

———. *To the End of the Earth: A History of the Crypto-Jews of New Mexico*. New York: Columbia University Press, 2005.

Jacobs, Janet Liebman. *Hidden Heritage: The Legacy of the Crypto-Jews*. Berkeley: University of California Press, 2002.

Kamen, Henry. *The Spanish Inquisition: A Historical Revision*. New Haven, Conn.: Yale University Press, 1997.

Kessell, John L. *Kiva, Cross, and Crown: The Pecos Indians and New Mexico, 1540–1840*. Washington, D.C.: National Park Service, 1979.

———. *Pueblos, Spaniards, and the Kingdom of New Mexico*. Norman: University of Oklahoma Press, 2008.

———. *Spain in the Southwest: A Narrative History of Colonial New Mexico, Arizona, Texas, and California*. Norman: University of Oklahoma Press, 2002.

Kritzler, Edward. *Jewish Pirates of the Caribbean*. New York: Doubleday, 2008.

Kunin, Seth D. *Juggling Identities: Identity and Authenticity among the Crypto-Jews*. New York: Columbia University Press, 2009.

Lavrin, Asunción. Foreword to *The Inquisition in New Spain, 1536–1820: A Documentary History*, edited by John F. Chuchiak, xv–xvi. Baltimore, Md.: Johns Hopkins Press, 2012.

Levine, Frances. "So Dreadful a Crime." *El Palacio* 117, no. 4 (Winter 2012): 52–59.

Levine, Frances, and Gerald González. "Doña Teresa in the Palace." *El Palacio* 116, no. 3 (Fall 2011): 40–47.

Liebman, Seymour B., *Los judíos en México y América Central: Fe, llamas e Inquisición*. Mexico City: Siglo Veintiuno Editores, 1971.

López Pérez, María del Pilar. "La vida en casa en Santa Fe en los siglos XVII y XVIII." In *Historia de la vida privada en Colombia*. Vol. 1, *Las fronteras difusas del siglo XVI a 1880*, edited by Jaime Borja Gómez and Pablo Rodríguez Jiménez, 80–107. Bogota, Colombia: Aguilar, Altea, Taurus, Alfaguara, 2011. Reprint, 2013.

Martinez-Davila, Roger L., Ron Duncan-Hart, and Josef Díaz, eds. *Fractured Faiths: Spanish Judaism, The Inquisition, and New World Identities*. Albuquerque: Fresco Books / SF Design, 2016.

Martín Rodríguez, Manuel M. *Gaspar de Villagrá: Legista, soldado y poeta*. León: Universidad de León, 2009.

———, ed. *Gaspar de Villagrá, Historia de la Nueva Mexico*. Alcalá de Henares: Instituto Franklin, Universidad de Alcalá de Henares, 2010.

McDonald, Margaret Espinosa. Introduction to the compilation of the baptismal records of the Church of Nuestra Señora de la Inmaculada Concepción, Tomé, New Mexico. Albuquerque: New Mexico Genealogical Society, 1998. www.nmgs.org/bksA11-12.php.

Menocal, María Rosa. *The Ornament of the World: How Muslims, Jews and Christians Created a Culture of Tolerance in Medieval Spain*. Boston: Little, Brown, 2002.

Morrow, Baker H. *A Harvest of Reluctant Souls*. Niwot: University Press of Colorado, 1996.

Neulander, Judith. "Crypto-Jews of the Southwest: An Imagined Community." *Jewish Folklore and Ethnology Review* 16 (1994): 64–68.

———. "The New Mexican Crypto-Jewish Canon: Choosing to be 'Chosen' in Millennial Tradition." *Jewish Folklore and Ethnology Review* 18 (1996): 19–58.

New Mexico History Museum. *The Threads of Memory / El hilo de la memoria*. Albuquerque: Fresco Fine Art Publications, 2010.

Peck, Amelia, ed. *Interwoven Globe: The Worldwide Textile Trade, 1500–1800*. New York: Metropolitan Museum of Art, 2013.

Phipps, Elena. "The Iberian Globe: Textile Traditions and Trade in Latin America." In *Interwoven Globe: The Worldwide Textile Trade, 1500–1800*, edited by Amelia Peck, 28–45. New York: Metropolitan Museum of Art, 2013.

"La Pintura de Castas." *Artes de México* (Mexico City), n.s., no. 8 (Summer 1990).

Post, Stephen S. "Excavations for the New Mexico History Museum (LA 111322): 350 Years of Occupation and Changing Land Use behind the Palace of the Governors, Santa Fe, New Mexico." Manuscript in author's possession. Office of Archaeological Studies, Santa Fe, New Mexico, in preparation.

Riley, Carroll L. "Bernardo López de Mendizábal: Could He Have Prevented the Pueblo Revolt?" *El Palacio* 112, no. 3 (2007): 38–46.

———. *The Kachina and the Cross: Indians and Spaniards in the Early Southwest*. Salt Lake City: University of Utah Press, 1999.

Rivas Pérez, Jorge F. "Domestic Display in the Spanish Overseas Territories." In *Behind Closed Doors: Art in the Spanish American Home, 1492–1898*, edited by Richard Aste, 49–104. New York: Monacelli Press and Brooklyn Museum, 2013.

Rose, William Stewart. *The Orlando Furioso: Translation in English Verse from the Italian of Ludovico Ariosto, with Notes*. London: John Murray, Albermarle Street, 1823.

Sánchez, Joseph P. "The Peralta-Ordóñez Affair and the Founding of Santa Fe." In *Santa Fe, History of an Ancient City*, edited by David Grant Noble, 15–23. Santa Fe: School for Advanced Research Press, 2008.

———. *The Río Abajo Frontier, 1540–1692*. Albuquerque: Albuquerque Museum, 1996.

Scholes, France V. *Troublous Times in New Mexico*. Publications in History 11. Albuquerque: University of New Mexico Press, 1942.

———. "Troublous Times in New Mexico, 1659–1670." Chapters 1–2. *New Mexico Historical Review* 12, no. 2 (1937): 134–74.

———. "Troublous Times in New Mexico, 1659–1670." Chapters 3–4. *New Mexico Historical Review* 12, no. 4 (1937): 380–452.

———. "Troublous Times in New Mexico, 1659–1670." Chapter 5. *New Mexico Historical Review* 13, no. 1 (1939): 63–84.

———. "Troublous Times in New Mexico, 1659–1670." Chapter 6. *New Mexico Historical Review* 15, no. 3 (1940): 249–68.

———. "Troublous Times in New Mexico, 1659–1670." Chapters 7–8. *New Mexico Historical Review* 15, no. 4 (1940): 369–417.

———. "Troublous Times in New Mexico, 1659–1670." Chapter 9. *New Mexico Historical Review* 16, no. 1 (1941): 15–40.

Scholes, France V., Marc Simmons, and José Antonio Esquibel, eds. *Juan Domínguez de Mendoza: Soldier and Frontiersman of the Spanish Southwest, 1627–1693*. Albuquerque: University of New Mexico Press, 2012.

Schroeder, Albert H. "Pueblos Abandoned in Historic Times." In *Handbook of North American Indians*. Vol. 10, *Southwest*, edited by Alfonso Ortiz, 236–54. Washington, D.C: Smithsonian Institution, 1983.

Schroeder, Albert H., and Dan S. Matson. *A Colony on the Move: Gaspar Castaño de Sosa's Journal, 1590–1591*. Santa Fe: School of American Research Press, 1965.

Segovia, Rodolfo. *Las fortificaciones de Cartagena de Indias: Estrategia e historia*. Bogota, Colombia: El Áncora Editores, 2009.

Simmons, Marc. *The Last Conquistador: Juan de Oñate and the Settling of the Far Southwest*. Norman: University of Oklahoma Press, 1991.

———. *Witchcraft in the Southwest: Spanish and Indian Supernaturalism on the Rio Grande*. Lincoln: University of Nebraska Press, 1974.

Snow, Cordelia Thomas. "A Brief History of the Palace of the Governors and a Preliminary Report on the 1974 Excavation." *El Palacio* 80, no. 3 (1974): 6–21.

Temkin, Samuel. *Luis de Carvajal: The Origins of Nuevo Reino de León*. Santa Fe: Sunstone Press, 2011.

Trigg, Heather B. *From Household to Empire: Society and Economy in Early Colonial New Mexico*. Tucson: University of Arizona Press, 2005.

Villagrá, Gaspar Pérez de. *A History of New Mexico*, translated by Gilberto Espinosa. Los Angeles: Quivira Society, 1933.

Waldman, Guido, trans. *Orlando Furioso*, by Ludovico Ariosto. New York: Oxford University Press, 1983. Reprinted 2008.

Weber, David J. Introduction to *The Journey of Fray Marcos*, by Cleve Hallenbeck. Dallas: Southern Methodist University Press, 1987. Reprint.

———. *Myth and the History of the Hispanic Southwest*. Albuquerque: University of New Mexico Press, 1988.

———. *The Spanish Frontier in North America*. New Haven, Conn.: Yale University Press, 1992.

Wheelwright, Jeff. *The Wandering Gene and the Indian Princess: Race, Religion and DNA*. New York: Norton, 2012.

Wroth, Will H. "Adolph Bandelier: A Biography." Santa Fe: Office of the State Historian, n.d. http://newmexicohistory.org/people/adolf-bandelier-a-biography-by-william-h-wroth.

Index